EUL VERLAG

Thomas Bernhardt

The European Alternative Investment Fund Managers Directive (AIFMD)

An Appropriate Approach to the Global Financial Crisis?

EUL VERLAG

Bibliografische Information der Deutschen Nationalbibliothek

Die Deutsche Nationalbibliothek verzeichnet diese Publikation in der Deutschen Nationalbibliografie; detaillierte bibliografische Daten sind im Internet über <http://dnb.d-nb.de> abrufbar.

ISBN 978-3-8441-0285-7
1. Auflage Oktober 2013

JOSEF EUL VERLAG GmbH
Brandsberg 6
53797 Lohmar
Tel.: 0 22 05 / 90 10 6-6
Fax: 0 22 05 / 90 10 6-88
E-Mail: info@eul-verlag.de
http://www.eul-verlag.de

Bei der Herstellung unserer Bücher möchten wir die Umwelt schonen. Dieses Buch ist daher auf säurefreiem, 100% chlorfrei gebleichtem, alterungsbeständigem Papier nach DIN 6738 gedruckt.

Meinen Eltern
Waltraud und Helmut Bernhardt

Preface

This thesis has been written in fulfilment of the requirements of the Master of Laws by Research degree of the University of Glasgow, Scotland, which I was awarded in September 2013.

The research project has been started in 2010 under the impression of increasing public and political debates and actions to respond to the global financial crisis through legislative measures.

My long-term affinity to the Private Equity industry and my keen interest in matters of the European Integration made the critical study of the European Alternative Investment Fund Mangers Directive (AIFMD) an obvious choice for my LL.M.

I am most grateful to my Supervisor Prof. Dr. George A. Walker, Queen Mary University of London, for his support, guidance and mentorship during my research project.

At the University of Glasgow I would like to thank Prof. Dr. Fiona Leverick, Dr. Kay Munro and Susan Holmes for all their assistance during my three years of part-time study at the School of Law.

Singapore, October 2013 Thomas Bernhardt

Abstract

The European Alternative Investment Fund Managers Directive (AIFMD) has been formulated as a response to the global financial crisis, which climaxed in the collapse of Lehman Brothers on 15 September 2008. Although many financial analysts expected such a crisis in the US for some time before that incident, its transnational dimension has exceeded the expectations of many market participants and stakeholders. The securitisation of real estate risks that came about by the launching financial innovations such as asset-backed securities (ABS), mortgage-backed securities (MBS), collateralised debt obligations (CDO) or structured investment vehicles (SIV) contributed to the fast worldwide circulation of 'poisoned' papers.

It is questionable whether any legal response to the recent financial crisis should single out the abovementioned or other related financial innovations. Until the outbreak of the financial crisis of 2008/2009, the alternative investment segment and the private equity segment in particular, was not regulated in the European Union (EU) in a targeted and specific way. The UNCITS Directive is primarily addressed to small (portfolio) investors and captures, not institutional strategic or financial investors. Thus, the European Commission as the European legislator does not avail itself of real, resilient experience that could contribute to a proportional, sustainable and path-breaking response to the financial crisis of 2008/2009. A strong private equity segment seems almost indispensable for the steady credit supply of an increasing part of the real economy and the consolidation of young, growth or strategically repositioned corporations that need a well-functioning access to capital.

Assuming that the financial crisis of 2008/2009 was the consequence of wrongfully set incentives that primarily concerned the fund managers' remuneration, the European Commission followed the ideas of Jacques de Larosière, Klaus-Heiner Lehne and Poul Nyrup Rasmussen and set the legal focus on the fund managers, as these entities launch and distribute financial products such as those mentioned above and also decide on the investment strategy that might bear systemic risks. Due to their financial market potential and in view of the design of financial products, these entities admittedly have a strong impact on the financial market development and may jointly be responsible for the realisation of systemic risks of transnational dimensions. In particular, in the view of a steady credit supply of the real economy, the enormous transnational mobility of capital and the global competition of financial market regulations, it seems doubtful whether one can identify the fund managers as those responsible for the financial market crisis of 2008/2009. This thesis highlights the history, symptoms and supposed core reasons of the financial crisis of 2008/2009 and critically assesses whether the AIFMD can reach its objective to effectively contain systemic risks in the context of a globalised financial system.

Table of Contents

Table of Abbreviations

ABCP	Asset-Backed-Commercial-Paper-Program
ABS	Asset-backed Security/Asset-backed Securities
AG	Aktiengesellschaft
AIF	Alternative Investment Fund
AIFM	Alternative Investment Fund Manager
AIFMD	Alternative Investment Fund Managers Directive
AIFMD-IRR	Supplementing Directive 2011/61/EU of the European Parliament and of the Council with regard to exemptions, general operating conditions, depositaries, leverage, transparency and supervision (AIFMD-implementing rules and regulations
AIG	American International Group
ARM	Adjustable-rate mortgages
AuM	Assets under Management
BaFin	German Federal Agency for Financial Market Supervision
BAI	Federal Association of Alternative Investment Funds (Bundesverband Alternativer Investments)
BJR	Business Judgment Rule
BKR	Zeitschrift für Bank- und Kapitalmarktrecht (Journal, year and pages)
BOA	Bank of America
BRIC	Brazil, Russia, India and China
BVCA	British Venture Capital Association
BVerfG	Bundesverfassungsgericht (Federal Constitutional Court of Germany)
CCP	Central Counterparty
CDO	Collateralised Debt Obligation (s)

CDS	Credit Default Swaps
CEO	Chief Executive Officer
CRA	Credit Rating agency
CRA 1977	Community Reinvestment Act 1977
CESR	Committee of European Securities Regulators
dAktG	German Aktiengesetz
DB	Deutsche Bank
dInvG	(German) Investmentgesetz
dUBGG	German Gesetz über Unternehmens-beteiligungsgesellschaften
dWpHG	German Security Trading Act (Wertpapierhandelsgesetz)
EBIT	Earnings before Interest and Tax
EBITDA	Earnings before Interest, Tax, Depression and Amortisation
EBOR	European Business Organisation Review (Journal, year and pages)
ECB	European Central Bank
ECJ	European Court of Justice
EESA	Emergency Economic Stabilization Act
e.g.	exempli gratia (for example)
EMH	Efficient Market Hypothesis
ESC	European Securities Committee
ESM	European Stability Mechanism
ESMA	European Securities and Markets Authority
ESRB	European Systemic Risk Board
ETF	Exchange Traded Funds
EVCA	European Venture Capital Association
EWS	Europäisches Wirtschafts- und Steuerrecht (Journal, year and pages)

Fannie Mae	Federal National Mortgage Association
Fed	Federal Reserve
FCIC	Financial Crisis Inquiry Commission
FDI	financial derivative instruments
Freddie Mac	Federal Home Loan Mortgage Corporation
FSA	Financial Service Authority
FSB	Financial Stability Board
FTT	Financial transaction tax
G20	Group of Twenty (Association of the twenty most important industrial and emerging countries)
GDP	Gross Domestic Product
GesKR	Zeitschrift für Gesellschafts- und Kapitalmarktrecht (Journal, year and pages)
GG	Grundgesetz (German Constitution)
GSE	Government sponsored entities
HFT	High-Frequency Trading/High-Frequency Trade
HRE	Hypo Real Estate
HSH	Hamburg and Schleswig-Holstein Nordbank
Ibid.	ibidem
IFRS	International Financial Reporting Standards
IKB	Deutsche Industriebank AG
IMF	International Monetary Fund
IPO	Initial Public Offering
IRR	Internal Rate of Return
JuS	Juristische Schulung (Journal, year andpages)

KfW	Reconstruction Loan Corporation (Kreditanstalt für Wiederaufbau)
LBO	Leveraged Buy-out
LLR	Lender of last ressort
LoI	Letter of Intent
M&A	Mergers and Acquisitions
MBS	Mortgage-backed Security
MBO	Management Buy-out
MiFiD	European Financial Market Directive
Mio	Million (s)
ML	Merrill Lynch
MMF	Money Market fund
NAFTA	North American Free Trade Agreement
NAV	Net Asset Value
NINJA	"No income, no job, no assets"-loan
NPV	Net Present Value
NYSE	New York Stock Exchange
OECD	Organisation for Economic Co-operation and Development
OGAW	Organismen für gemeinsame Anlagen in Wertpapieren
OTC	Over-the-Counter Market
OTD	Originate-to-distribute
OTH	Originate-to-hold
PII	Professional indemnity insurance
PIMCO	Pacific Investment Management Company

RIW	Recht der Internationalen Wirtschaft (Journal, year and pages)
RTA	Regulatory technical standards
RTS	Draft regulatory technical standards
SEC	Securities and Exchange Commission
SIV	Structured Investment Vehicle (s)/Special Investment Vehicle
SoFFin	Sonderfonds für Finanzmarktstabilisierung (special fund for the stabilisation of the financial market)
SPV	Special purpose vehicle
TARP	Troubled Asset Relief Program
TEU	Consolidated version of the Treaty on European Union
TFEU	Consolidated version of the treaty on the functioning of the European Union
TSE	True-Sales-Initiative
UBS	Union de Banques Suisse
UCITS	Undertakings for Collective Investment in Transferable Securities
UCITSD	European Directive on Undertakings for Collective Investment in Transferable Securities
U.S.	United States (of America)
USD	US Dollar
VaR	Value at Risk
VGF	German Association of Closed Funds
WM	Wertpapiermitteilungen (Journal, year and pages)
WTO	World Trade Organisation

ZBB	Zeitschrift für Bank- und Betriebswirtschaft (Journal, year and pages)
ZBB/JBB	Zeitschrift für Bankrecht und Bankwirtschaft/JBB (Journal, year and pages)
ZGR	Zeitschrift für Unternehmens- und Gesellschaftsrecht (Journal, year and pages)
ZRP	Zeitschrift für Rechtspolitik (Journal, year and pages)

Introduction

Due to the recent financial crisis of 2008/2009, the European Commission recently made a proposal for the future regulation of private equity[1] and other alternative investments, which is based on the reflections of the former French secretary of finance, Jacques De Larosière. In his report[2] dated 25 February 2009, Monsieur Larosière pointed out that *"any appropriate regulation of alternative investments must be extended, in a proportional manner, to all firms or entities conducting financial activities which may have a systemic impact (...) even if they have no direct links with the public at large."* This proposal is aimed at the containment of similar systemic risks as those that can be seen as the initial cause of the financial crisis of 2008/2009[3] , doing so by focusing not on the financial firms themselves but on the business attitudes of its managers. This focus is based on the belief that the portfolio managers had false extrinsic incentives that led them to run a too short-term portfolio strategy with too strong speculative elements, which finally led to a deepening of moral hazard scenarios.[4] In general, alternative investments cover a broad category of investments, other than stocks and bonds, including venture capital, private equity, real estate, precious metals, collectibles and hedge funds.[5]

---

1 On the economic need and the legal requirements of private equity cf. *Kiebeck/Jesch,* Corporate Finance law No. 6/2010, pp. 372-378; *Leible/Lehmann,* Hedgefonds (2009).

2 Report of the high-level group on financial supervision in the EU, dated February/25th/2009, p. 23; published in the Internet under http://ec.europa.eu/internal_market/finances/docs/de_larosiere_report_en.pdf, requested August/25th/2011.

3 As it is not otherwise explained above, the terms "financial crisis", "financial market crisis" or "recent financial crisis" refer to the financial crisis of 2008/2009 that was strengthened with the collapse of *Lehman Brothers* on September/15th/2008 as the initial point of a global economic depression.

4 The moral hazard phenomena results from the conflict of interest that typically exists between the directors, respectively the staff and the investors.

5 Cf. *Grabaravicius Dierick,* ECB-Occasional Paper No. 34 (August 2005), p. 69.

The Financial Crisis Inquiry Commission (FCIC[6]) came to the final conclusion that too many financial institutions acted recklessly and dared short-term financial engagements, extending too much trust while bearing non-acceptable risks.[7] In the context of a market economy such as that of the United States and most Member States of the EU, it is the first objective of every corporation to obtain a suitable return of investment that normally conveys the basis of a sustainable economic development. To reach this first objective, the managers of a corporation should be given a suitable freedom of action which enables them to employ the most profitable business strategy and to react to sudden market developments. This freedom of action is called the business judgment rule (BJR). The abovementioned extrinsic incentives fulfil the function of conducting the portfolio strategy of the managers. Thus, it is doubtful whether the assumption of the European Commission that the recent financial crisis was caused by the involved portfolio managers is a suitable approach to prevent a similar financial crisis in the future. Nevertheless, one has to consider that those extrinsic incentives that entail the managers' portfolio strategies and that set the framework for their economic freedom of action are extrinsic incentives that are set by their corporations. If the portfolio manager does not follow the economic philosophy of her or his corporation, she or he may be fired. In light of this, it shall be discussed here whether the Alternative Investment Fund Managers Directive (Directive 2011/61/EU, AIFMD[8]) of the European Commission that was set into action

6 As an independent Commission, the *Financial Crisis Inquiry Commission* (FCIC) was implemented by the US-Government in May of 2009 and recruited of ten members (former US-American politicians, CEOs and economists). Under its chairman *Phil Angelides*, former treasury of California (1999-2007), it was the central objective of the FCIC to identify and to discuss the main causes of the financial crisis of 2008/2009. The widespread competence of the FCIC reaches from the enforcement of evidence, the inspection of confidential documents and the hearing of witnesses. Its final Report was published in January of 2011 and set the closing point of the Commission´s investigation. It follows a descriptive and analytical method consisting of the publishing of facts, the identification of responsible persons and the understanding of the crisis.

7 Cf. *Nationale Kommission zur Untersuchung der Finanz- und Wirtschaftskrise,* Schlussfolgerungen (2009), p. 8.

8 Directive of the European Parliament and the European Council on Alternative Investment Fund Managers and for the amendment of the directives 2003/41/EG and 2009/65/EU Nr. 1095/2010 – AIFMD, published under http://eur-lex.europa.eu/LexUriServ/LexUriServ.do?uri=OJ:L:2011:174:0001:0073:EN:PDF.

in November 2010 is really a suitable and a sustainable regulatory approach to preventing a similar crisis in the future.

Before the contents of the Alternative Fund Managers Directive[9] (Proposal for a Directive of the European Parliament and of the Council on Alternative Investment Fund Managers and amending drafts 2003/41/EC and 2009/65/EC[10]) – AIFMD – are introduced in detail, a brief overview on the history will be given, including the symptoms and the supposed core reasons of the recent financial crisis. The objectives of this thesis are to focus critically on the contents of the AIFMD and to discuss possible alternative approaches of Walker.[11] This discussion will not only offer a legal analysis but also the economic and monetary issues of a sustainable European solution for the financial architecture of the 21st century.

9 For further information on the AIFMD see *Jaskolski/Grüber,* Corporate Finance Law (2010), pp. 188, 191-196; *Kramer/Recknagel,* DB No. 37/2011, p. 2077 ff.; *Tollmann,* Hertz-Eichenrode/Illenberger/Jesch/Keller/Klebeck/Rocholl, Private Equity-Lexikon (2011), p. 4 ff.; For information on the discussed alternative solutions see *Thomsen,* EBOR 10:1/2009, pp. 97-114; about the transformation into German law: *Haisch/Helios,* BB (No. 1/2013), p. 23 ff.; *Krause/Klebeck,* BB (No. 34/2012), p. 2063 ff.; *Loff/Klebeck,* BKR (No. 9/2012), p. 353 ff.; *Schwaldt,* DIE WELT (2011/01/15), p. 21.

10 Published in the Internet under http://ec.europa.eu/internal_market/investment/ alternative_investments_de.htm (requested March/21st/2011).

11 See the following contributions edited by *George Walker*: *Walker,* JBR (09/2010), Editorial 1-5; *Walker,* BJIBF (11/2007), pp. 567 ff.; *Walker,* European Banking Law (2007), pp. 1 ff.; *Walker,* Financial Regulation International (12/2008), pp. 1 ff. *Walker,* in: The Future of financial regulation (2010), pp. 179 ff.

First Chapter:

Origins of the Recent Financial Crisis

1. History

1.1. The rise of the "originate-to-distribute" model

Normally, it should be compulsory for each merchant to restore an adequate relationship between her or his equity position and her or his loan capital (its risks).[12] According to the opinions of economic experts, an equity position of 4% should be compulsory for each corporation.[13] An adequate relationship between the equity position and loan capital is one essential condition to preserve the steady solvency[14] of an enterprise and to build a shield against the consequences of an economic crisis. Although the financial crisis of 2008/2009 actually resulted more from an initial lack of liquidity than from an insufficient solvency, the steady solvency of a corporation cannot be underestimated because it is the condition for the "breath" of a corporation: When the solvency of a corporation comes to an end, the economic viability stops immediately. Because the financial crisis of 2008/2009[15] concerned the lower-income brackets, one can also call it a subprime crisis.[16,17]

Obviously, the protagonists of the recent financial crisis did not realise the requirement of a proportional relationship between equity position and risks. Instead of setting the focus on real economic development, they overrated the op-

12 *Dam* in Straus, Subprime Crisis (2009), pp. 95, 102.

13 *Sinn,* Kasino Kapitalismus (2009), p. 243 ff.

14 The solvency is the ability of a corporation to fulfil its contemporary payment obligations.

15 Background information and further facts on the financial crisis 2008/2009: *Bermudez/ Vidal* in O'Neill, Global Financial Crisis (2009). pp. 13-27; *Bruno* in O'Neill, Global Financial Crisis (2009), pp. 7-11; *Dam,* Subprime Crisis (2009), pp. 95-106; *Herzog,* Finanzmarktkrise (2008), pp. 9 ff.; *Sinn,* Kasino Kapitalismus (2009), p. 1 ff.

16 On the situation in the subprime market at the eve at the recent financial crisis cf. *Walker,* BJIBF (11/2007), p. 567 (568).

17 For the issue "Subprime Crisis and Financial Regulation" see *Dam* in Straus, Subprime Crisis (2009), pp. 95-106.

portunities of their businesses and ignored the risks of the securitisation of real estate risks for a long time. In lending with homes as security, what the American banks often do is make (or buy) a large number of such mortgage loans and then package them together in securities, using the underlying packaged mortgages as collateral (mortgage-backed securities, or MBS).[18] Normally, the process of mortgage securitisation helps financial institutions to manage their asset portfolios, interest rate exposure, capital requirement and deposit insurance premiums.[19] According to Saunders and Cornett, asset securitisation provides a mechanism for financial institutions to hedge the interest rate risk, to enhance the liquidity of the asset portfolio of financial institutions and to provide an important source of fee income.[20] In September 2008, however, this mechanism seemed to fail dramatically.[21]

Traditionally, there was an on-going relationship between the bank which lent the money and the customer who borrowed the money, which led to a direct financial interest on the part of the money lending Institutions to make sure that customers were likely to be able to repay the money.[22] This traditional model, which can be described as "originate to hold" (OTH), changed into another model, "originate to distribute" (OTD). The OTD was also practiced by government-backed social mortgage lenders, such as Fannie Mae (the Federal National Mortgage Association) and Freddie Mac (the Federal Home Loan Mortgage Corporation).[23]

Many large credit institutions such as these began to create loans on generous terms for people who otherwise could not have afforded a mortgage. But instead of holding these mortgage loans, the institutions gave them to commercial finan-

---

18 *Dam,* Subprime Crisis (2009), pp. 95, 99.
19 *Lee/Lee,* Finance (2006), p. 518, 519.
20 Ibid.
21 *Sinn,* Kasino Kapitalismus (2009), p. 167-175 (Die Verbriefungskaskade).
22 *McIlroy* in Straus, Future of Banking (2009), pp. 119, 121.
23 *McIlroy* in Straus, future of banking (2009), pp. 119, 121; For further information on the rise and fall of Fannie Mae and Freddy Mac see *Bermudez/Vidal* in *O'Neill,* Global Financial Crisis (2009), pp. 13-27.

cial institutions that found it attractive to purchase these loans: If the borrowers were unable to repay the loans, the repayment was guaranteed by the U.S. government.[24] The originating bank had no direct interest in making sure that the borrower could repay the loan because in the case that the borrower was unable to repay, another bank would suffer the loss.

Nevertheless, the FCIC emphasizes that Fannie Mae and Freddy Mac did not set a primary condition for the financial crisis of 2008/2009.[25] Indeed, the FCIC qualifies Fannie Mae and Freddie Mac as the two „kings of leverage[26]“ because their common debt ratio inclusively credits amounted to 75:1 by the end of the year 2007. They turned out to be a wrongfully public promoted business model and contributed significantly to the outbreak of the financial crisis. However, they did not cause it. According to the FCIC, it was important that the mortgage security instruments of these two companies significantly kept their value during the crisis and did not contribute to the heavy losses of those corporations that stood in the middle of the crisis.[27]

The OTD of banking created a serious problem of moral hazard.[28] Moral hazard refers to the phenomenon that the separation of ownership and control within a modern organisation makes it difficult and costly to monitor and evaluate the efficiency of management effectively.[29] Thus, the originating bank often does not have a substantial incentive to be careful to whom it loans money and to which amount.[30] The OTD encourages reckless lending that leads to serious consequences, not only in the United States but also all over the world.[31] Many lenders

---

24 *McIlroy* in Straus, Future of Banking (2009), pp. 119, 121.

25 Cf. *FCIC,* Financial Crisis Inquiry Report (2011), p. 309 ff.

26 Whereas economic leverage is associated with increased assets under management, financial (investment) leverage refers to making investments on margin, where the cost of investment is less than the exposure it generates (e.g. through the use of financial derivates), cf. *Grabaravicius/Dierick,* ECB-Occasional Paper No. 34 (August 2005), p. 59.

27 Cf. *Nationale Kommission zur Untersuchung der Finanz- und Wirtschaftskrise,* Schlussfolgerungen (2009), p. 17.

28 *McIlroy* in Straus, Future of Banking (2009), pp. 119, 122.

29 *Lee/Lee,* Finance (2006), p. 544.

30 *McIlroy* in Straus, Future of Banking (2009), pp. 119, 122.

31 Ibid.

seemed to have ignored the warnings of several financial experts who propose to retain 20% of the risk in relation to the original loan, so that the originating banks had a sufficient incentive to taking proper precautions to see if the borrowers could afford to make the repayments.[32] It is necessary to clarify that the crisis of Fannie Mae and Freddie Mac was actually not a bank run because these entities were "securitisators" rather than deposit-takers.

1.2. The fall of the originate-to-distribute model

Finally, these firms neglected to build a (sufficient) shield on the basis of an adequate equity position for the case where too many creditors asked for the repayment of their money at the same time. On 15 September 2008, many creditors wanted to return their securities and asked for their money simultaneously. Big American credit institutions could not react to this (almost) unexpected development and became insolvent immediately.

The consequences of this incident are well-known. Also, many European creditors and well-known credit institutes and insurances could not realise their claims for the repayment of their investments. Because indemnity insurance did not exist, the insolvency of the abovementioned American institutions caused liquidity problems for their creditors all over the world. The spread of the subprime crisis from the United States to Germany and to other European Member States is a good illustration of a "domino effect," through which financial stability can spread not just from one bank to another but from one country to another.[33]

32 *McIlroy* in Straus, Future of Banking (2009), pp. 119, 123.
33 *Dam,* Subprime Crisis (2009), pp. 95, 98.

2. Symptoms

2.1. Significant market failure

A significant market failure can be claimed as one essential financial crisis symptom. In the centre of any market economy stands the equilibrium of supply and demand. Normally, these two powers keep the price mechanism, which can be identified as the core mechanism of a market economy,[34] in shape. The price of a product stands for its valuation, specifically its appreciation by the market participants. As a very simple formula, it expresses the relation between its available amount and its demand. Thus, the price of a product can be identified as the central tool of the market communication. Under regular circumstances, it makes the communication among the market participants easy, rapid and transparent.

At the very beginning of the recent financial crisis, the price mechanism failed dramatically. One could see that the prices of loans and other credits did not convey a realistic notion of their real worth. In the first place, many investors decided on the briefed loans and mortgages because they were convinced that the price of those products also expressed their real worth. At the very beginning of the worldwide financial crisis, their real worth was successively revealed, and the affected investors started worrying about their money. They rapidly recalled their investments from the credit institutes, which were unable to repay the requested volume of money all at once. As a consequence, many of those credit institutes, such as Lehman Brothers,[35] became directly insolvent. Moreover, it should be considered that any national regulation of private equity neglects the necessity of a preferably coherent solution and contributes to a regulatory arbitrage:[36] Whereas the holders of capital could seek out the laxest rules, the national gov-

[34] Cf. *Horn,* Marktwirtschaft (2010), pp. 87-102.

[35] Basically on the bankruptcy of Lehman Brothers cf. *U.S. House of Representatives* (April/20th/2010), p. 1 ff.; for further information on Lehman certificates see *Maerker,* BKR (2011), pp. 147-150.

[36] For further information on the global tax competition and tax corporations see *Soltysinski,* Competition (2009), pp. 83-88.

ernments that were eager to attract financial flows allowed regulators to fall asleep on their watch.[37]

2.2. Inability of consumers to short-term redemption of loans

Another major symptom of the recent financial crisis was that many consumers who received their mortgage loans at prices that did not convey a realistic impression of the real estate's real worth were unable ten to repay these loans immediately. Therefore, they were asked by their creditors to leave their homes and became homeless.

2.3. Dramatic drop in prices in the real estate business

As a consequence, there was an enormous surplus of demand that directly led to a dramatic drop in real estate prices that continued into 2010. On the one hand, this drop in prices conveyed for many people the unique opportunity to realise their wishes for a home at an unrivalled price. On the other hand, many credit institutes suffered a loss in a dimension that caused the necessity for a monetary state intervention. That dramatic drop in prices was revealed in the burst of the so-called credit bubble.

2.4. Crisis of liquidity and trust

At the eve of the financial crisis of 2008/2009 there was a widespread assumption that everyone within the distribution system could rapidly transfer the overrated mortgage papers to another owner – this assumption also did not work.[38] As a consequence of the abovementioned development, a serious crisis of liquidity and trust resulted. The willingness of many seriously affected credit institutes to borrow and to grant credits that were essential for the functioning of the real economy[39] dropped dramatically. Among bankers and (other) financial

---

37 Cf. *N.N.*, rulebook, Auszüge aus Presseartikeln No. 37/2010, pp. 8 (8).

38 Cf. *Nationale Kommission zur Untersuchung der Finanz- und Wirtschaftskrise,* Schlussfolgerungen (2009), p. 14.

39 The often-used but legally not determined expression "real economy" stands for that segment of the national economy that is opposed to the financial segment. It stands for all (pri-

experts there was the repeated tone of a credit crunch ("Kreditklemme"): The affected enterprises in the real economy could not achieve the requested credits any longer – credits that were indispensable for an on-going operative business.

As another consequence, the real economy in most European countries suffered a loss that was the biggest in history since the world-wide Depression of 1929/1930. Although that financial crisis, which began in 1929, might have been more severe, the financial crisis of 2008/2009 affected many different countries in a serious and simultaneous manner, and its economic impact was felt throughout the world as a result of the increased interconnectedness of the global economy.[40] In most European countries, the gross domestic product (GDP) decreased from 5% to 10% in the year 2009. The development of the worldwide financial crisis pointed out the very close interdependencies between credit institutes, financial markets and the real economy, which underlines the fact that any regulation of private equity can also affect the real economy. Therefore, the G20 and the Bale Committee[41] voted to wait for a new regulation until the end of the financial crisis.[42]

A lack of trust such as in the recent financial crisis undermines the current fiscal stimulation, and correspondingly higher financial costs make any consolidation more difficult. Thus, trust in the soundness of public finances is a major prerequisite for both the stability of financial markets and the anchoring of moderate inflation expectations.[43]

---

vate) corporations that produce goods and services that are of direct practical use for the consumer and that have to be determined from the question of financing these goods; Cf. also *Wieland,* BB (2012), p. 917 ff.

40 Cf. *FSA,* The Turner Report (2009), p. 5.

41 Referring to the requirements of the Bale 3 Agreement this also seems noteworthy: *Schmidt,* BB (2011), pp. 105-109.

42 *N.N.,* G20-Agenda, Auszüge aus Presseartikeln No. 5/2010, pp.3 (4).

43 Cf. *N.N.,* Lessons, Auszüge aus Presseartikeln No. 5/2010, pp.5 (5).

2.5. Breakdown of inter-bank markets

As a consequence of the wide-spread securitisation of risks and the insufficient transparency of financial products, those credit institutes that were seriously affected by the financial crisis lost the trust in each other that is indispensable for well-functioning business in the financial sector. The capital costs increased, and, as already mentioned, many companies suffered a dramatic squeeze of liquidity that encouraged strong intervention by the governments of the affected countries.

Until 15 September 2008, Lehman Brothers was one of the oldest, biggest and most profitable investment banks[44] worldwide: In 2006 it had a balance volume of US$504,000 million, a market capitalisation of US$54,000 million and equity profitability of 33%.[45] Due to its tradition and profitability, however, the American public retained its faith that the American government would save Lehman Brothers. On 10 September 2008, however, the former US Treasury Secretary, Hank Paulson, who was also the president of the worldwide biggest investment bank, Goldman Sachs, declared that the US-American government had decided not to save Lehman Brothers.[46]

Soon the media reported on long lines of customers waiting at the doors of the Lehman Brothers offices demanding their money immediately. Their fear was justified because on 15 September 2008 Lehman Brothers was unable to fulfil its payment obligations. Moreover, the inconsistency of the political reaction of the Bush administration to save Bear Stearns (the investment bank), the American International Group (AIG) (the insurance company), and Fannie Mae and Freddy Mac but not to save Lehman Brothers caused a widespread insecurity and panic among the financial market participants.[47] The insolvency of Lehman Brothers is

---

44 On investment banking: *Hockmann/Thießen,* Investmentbanking (2009), p. 1 ff.
45 *Sinn,* Kasino-Kapitalismus (2009), p. 88.
46 *Hank Paulson* and *Timothy Geithner* wanted banks to save *Lehman Brothers* themselves without Government assistance.
47 Cf. *N.N.,* Finanzkrise, Auszüge aus Presseartikeln No. 5/2011, pp.5 (5).

quickly affected the entire United States and the global financial system, which then was reflected in the U.S. money markets.[48]

The widespread insecurity and panic among the financial market participants was particularly highlighted by the contradictory response of the US Government that revealed in the different treatment of Lehman Brothers and Merrill Lynch (ML[49]). Due to the financial crisis of 2008/2009, the Bank of America (BoA[50]) decided to purchase ML as the former third biggest investment bank of the United States at a price of 50.000 Mio. US$, which corresponds to some 29 US$/shares.[51] As a consequence of heavy losses that covered several thousand million US$, ML had come under pressure: Within only a few months, the shares of ML declined from some 80 US$/Share to 17.05 US$ by 13 September 2008. Due primarily to the intervention of the US Government, Merrill Lynch was rescued in the end. In contrast, BoA refused to purchase Lehman Brothers.[52] Lehman Brothers spent trusts to be overtaken by the British bank Barclays – in the end, Barclays rejected to purchase Lehman Brothers. John Thain, the former chairman and CEO of ML, had achieved the acquisition during the rescue discussions about the competitor Lehman Brothers.[53] ML announced its sale on 15 September 2008. On 1 January 2009, the closing date of the acquisition, a single share of ML was traded at a market value of 0.8595 shares of BoA.

---

48 The money market covers a segment of the financial market where financial instruments with high liquid maturities are traded. It is used by participants as a means for borrowing and lending in the short term, from several days to just under one year. Money market securities consist of negotiable certificates of deposit (CDs), bankers acceptance, U.S. treasury bills, commercial papers, municipal notes, federal funds and repurchase agreements (Repos), cf. http://www.investopedia.com/terms/m/moneymarket.asp.

49 http://www.ml.com/index.asp?id=7695_15125_17454, last time requested February/18th/2013; Since 1 January 2009 ML is a complete affiliate of BoA and signs responsible for the business with prosperous private clients, the investment banking branch and the capital market business.

50 https://www.bankofamerica.com/, last time requested February/18th/2013; since July of 2006 BoA is the biggest credit institute in the United States with a top line of 94.000 Mio. US$ and a total balance sheet of 2.130.000 Mio. US$ in the year 2011.

51 http://newsroom.bankofamerica.com/?s=43, last time requested February/18th/2013.

52 Cf. New York Times (September/14th/2008): "Lehman Files for Bankruptcy - Merrill is Sold".

53 http://www.time.com/time/business/article/0,8599,1873835,00.html, last time requested February/18th/2013.

In Germany, between the 39th and the 43rd calendar weeks of 2008, the balance between the deposits and the disbursements differed enormously in comparison to 2007: There was an increased demand for cash and temporarily changed behaviour having to do with the daily deposits and disbursements that did not normalise before 24 October 2008 when the volume of disbursements fell below that previous year.[54] In October 2008, the daily disbursements mostly moved at a level that can be compared with the level at Christmas time.[55] In particular, it was significant that the enormous increase of disbursements was not compensated by higher deposits: Thus, 10 October 2008was the day with the biggest volume of disbursements, whereas in the financial crisis (€4,200 million) the volume of deposits only covered €1,500 million.[56]

As was underlined by Douglas Diamond and Philip Runs, the so-called "bank run", which can be seen in the disequilibrium of deposits and disbursements, is a typical symptom of each financial crisis.[57] In that situation, the capital resources underlie a dramatic change, which causes the necessity for the government to save the affected credit institutes.[58] Those credit institutes that can still fulfil the respective capital requirements can take further risks to raise their profitability: They bet that they will be saved by the government – a typical moral hazard problem.[59] As a consequence, the refuted assumption by the American public and among financial experts that the Bush administration would save Lehman Brothers resulted in a widespread distrust towards the financial authorities, towards financial analysts and, in particular, towards any credit rating agency (CRA). This distrust caused liquidity supply shortfalls among private corporations.[60]

54 Cf. *Deutsche Bundesbank,* Monatsbericht No. 6/2009, pp. 56 (56).
55 Ibid.
56 Ibid.
57 Cf. *Balling,* Refinanzierung, Auszüge aus Presseartikeln No. 37/2010, pp. 7 (7).
58 Cf. *Balling,* Refinanzierung, Auszüge aus Presseartikeln No. 37/2010, pp. 7 (8).
59 Ibid.
60 On the necessity of a steady liquidity support as one essential requirement of well-functioning markets cf. *Walker,* BJIBF (11/2007), p. 567 (569).

Moreover, the *Lehman Brothers* incident revealed the extraordinary macroeconomic significance of the term "transformation".[61] Transformation, specifically maturity transformation, is one of the most important devices of the profitability of private banking: Whereas the private investors tend to make short-term deposits, the corporations normally ask for long-term credits.[62] Holding longer term assets than liabilities and thus enabling the non-bank sector to hold shorter term assets than liabilities, maturity transformation is probably one of the key functions of the banking system.[63]

By using maturity transformation, the credit institutes combine the requirements of the opposed market participants as they borrow money at the lowest conditions and lend that money at the highest interest rate possible. For the national economy, maturity transformation has an important function because long-term investments in the real economy depend on the willingness of the depositors to lend their money short-dated.[64] As the Turner Report emphasises, on the eve of the financial crisis of 2008/2009, changes in pattern of maturity transformation created huge and inadequately appreciated risks.[65] After the insolvency of Lehman Brothers, that essential macroeconomic function was eliminated because its breakdown directly resulted in the collapse of interbank commerce: Whereas those credit institutes that possessed money could not dispose of it, the other ones that were in need of money to lend were cut off from the credit supply.[66]

2.6. Nationalisation of losses

The burdens of the abovementioned[67] governmental measures ran up to several thousand million Euros, covered by anyone who pays taxes. If one considers that these burdens go beyond the productivity of the present generation – the big-

61 On the increasing importance of maturity transformation cf. *FSA,* The Turner Report (2009), pp. 21 f.

62 Cf. *Balling,* Refinanzierung, Auszüge aus Presseartikeln No. 37/2010, pp. 7 (7).

63 Cf. *FSA,* The Turner Report (2009), pp. 21 f.

64 *Sinn,* Kasino-Kapitalismus (2009), p. 90.

65 Cf. *FSA,* The Turner Report (2009), pp. 21 f.

66 Ibid.

67 Cf. first chapter, 3.

gest part of the abovementioned programs is debt-financed – they also concern the next generation. Referring to the inquiries of Reuters, Fitch Ratings, Morgan Stanley and Bloomberg, the public debt of the United States was raised from approximately $US57.000.5 million at the beginning of the financial crisis to approximately US$100,000 million at the end of 2010; in the worldwide economic depression of the earlier part of the century, it only went up from approximately $US17.5 billion in 1929 to approximately $US40 billion in the middle of the 1930s.[68] Against the abovementioned background is a nationalisation of losses. If one considers that the present generation should not spend more money than it can afford or is able to repay, the nationalisation of losses is one severe violation of the principle of sustainability.

3. Immediate governmental measures

The recent inquiry of the Federal Reserve (Fed) resulted in the conclusion that the worldwide financial crisis was the consequence of human behaviour, omissions and misjudgements.[69] Also, the FCIC points out that within the context of individual responsibility, one cannot explain the financial crisis by the typical human failures as avidity and arrogance – nevertheless, one must consider that typical human failures were ignored anyway: Thus, the FCIC understands the crisis as the result of human failures, false estimations and misdeeds that directly resulted in a systemic failure. The human failure concerns the lack of understanding of the financial market risks – for instance, many financial corporations were convinced of risk diversity although there indeed was a risk convergence. In view of this awareness, the FCIC regards it as the biggest imaginable tragedy if one shares the opinion that the Crisis was unforeseeable and inevitable: If one shares this opinion, a comparable would happen again.[70] It was the „product" of human

[68] Cf. *N.N.*, DIE WELT (July/1st/2011), p. 15.
[69] *N.N.*, Finanzkrise, Auszüge aus Presseartikeln No. 5/2011, pp. 12.
[70] Cf. *FCIC,* Financial Crisis Inquiry Report (2011), p. 28.

actions, foreseeable and evitable! Thus, the FCIC points out that *„there is still much to learn, much to investigate, and much to fix“.*[71]

As was underlined by Ben Bernanke, president of the Federal Reserve and the chief of the investigative commission, it was said to have been possible that another 12 of the most important American financial institutions on Wall Street could have collapsed within a short time period – among them Goldman Sachs.[72] In that situation, there was almost no other possibility but a strong monetary intervention by the government and the other financial authorities. Nevertheless, to avoid the insolvency of the abovementioned creditors, the governments of their home countries were urged to take immediate steps to back up the companies that were concerned.

Among the immediate administrative and legislative actions that were taken by the US Government, there are in particular the Troubled Asset Relief Program (TARP[73]), the Federal Reserve Emergency Support Programs[74] and the Dodd-Frank Wall Street and Consumer Protection Act[75].[76] By name, the Dodd-Frank Wall Street Reform and Consumer Protection Act enhances the powers of the SEC and adds a number of requirements for the Nationally Recognized Statistical Rating Organizations (NRSRO,) which became effective immediately.[77] Also, in many European countries the government decided on immediate stimulus programs. For instance, the German government set up an extraordinary fund called

---

71 Cf. *FCIC,* Financial Crisis Inquiry Report (2011), p. 24.

72 Ibid.

73 TARP was implemented on the legal basis of the US Emergency Economic Stabilization Act (EESA) that granted the Secretary of the Treasury widespread authority to either purchase or insure up to $700 billion in troubled assets owned by financial institutions. In particular, the definitions of both “troubled asset” and “financial institution” allowed the Secretary wide leeway in deciding what assets might be purchased or guaranteed and what might qualify as a financial firm, cf. *Webel,* TARP (2012) p. 1 ff.

74 For any further information see http://www.federalreserve.gov/faqs/why-did-the-Federal-Reserve-lend-to-banks-and-other-financial-institutions-during-the-financial-crisis.htm, requested on February/19th/2013.

75 For any further information see http://www.sec.gov/about/laws/wallstreetreform-cpa.pdf, requested on February/19th/2013.

76 Cf. Levin-Report, p. 43 f.

77 Cf. http://www.sec.gov/spotlight/dodd-frank/creditratingagencies.shtml, requested on February/19th/2013.

SoFFin.[78] SoFFin is the German abbreviation for Sonderfond zur Finanzmarktstabilisierung.[79]

Many of the abovementioned measures succeeded. Nevertheless, one should consider that each taxpayer still has to pay for these extraordinary measures, which is one reason for the delay of the expected economic recovery. Not only did financial experts talk about the "nationalisation of losses":[80] Each taxpayer, including those in the following generation, bears the costs of a systemic failure.

Moreover, the abovementioned programs can be qualified as extraordinary subsidies. On the one hand, they aimed at stabilising the financial situation of the affected companies and overcoming their liquidity squeeze. On the other hand, it was the objective of these programs to invest in the creation of future infrastructures, such as motorways that were urgently needed for the development of new industrial areas. The realisation of these infrastructural measures set one essential condition for a fast recovery of the real economy and built a "bridge" over the credit squeeze.

All in all, the infrastructural measures laid an important foundation for the future competitiveness of each national economy. Nevertheless, many financial experts criticised the function of these programs, claiming that they would be exhausted by building a bridge over the crisis. Many consumers advanced their expenses for bigger purchases. As one example, the governments of France and Germany granted a financial subsidy to consumers if they sold their used cars und purchased new ones. Retrospectively, these fears really did not come true. Although European law generally forbids any monetary subsidy, the measures that were taken by the governments in Paris and Berlin set one essential condition to fulfil the requirements of the Kyoto Agreement[81] , which aim at

---

[78] *Koberstein-Windpassinger* in Theewen, Bank- und Kapitalmarktrecht (2010), p. 827.

[79] For further information on the governmental rescue packages in Germany see *Ungeheuer* in *O'Neill,* Global Financial Crisis (2009), pp. 97-101; see also *Horn,* BB 2009, pp. 450-454.

[80] For further information on the "nationalisation of losses" see *N. N.,* F.A.S. (2009/03/15), p. 40-41.

[81] The Kyoto Agreement that is almost synonymous for the principle of sustainability binds the industrial nations to reduce its CO^2-emissions by 5.2% until 2010 (Article 3 paragraph 1 of the Kyoto-Protocol), cf. *Gärditz,* JuS (2008), pp. 324-329.

the reduction of the global emission of CO^2. The European Charter of Basic Rights[82] and the German Grundgesetz (dGG[83]) contain a compulsory constitutional obligation for the state to undertake suitable measures to protect the environment.

The report of the FCIC draws the conclusion that the US government had been prepared to the crisis very badly and, moreover, inconsistent governmental responses caused uncertainty and panic in the financial markets.[84] In particular, it appeared contradictory that the US-government decided to rescue Bear Stearns and AIG, but not to rescue Fannie Mae and Freddie Mac – another response that amplified the insecurity and panic at the financial markets.[85] That insecurity and panic was additionally driven by the extraordinary public debt, the obscurity of independencies between the „too big to fail"-institutes[86] and, finally, invisible and unknown derivate contracts.[87]

82 Europäische Charta of Basic Rights (Charta), Official Journal of the European Communities 2007 C 303, p. 1.

83 Grundgesetz für die Bundesrepublik Deutschland (dGG) as amended on the Federal Law Gazette Chapter III, Division No. 100-1, last time amended by the law dated July/11st/2012 (Federal Law Gazette I 2012, p. 1478).

84 Cf. *FCIC,* Financial Crisis Inquiry Report (2011), pp. 21 ff.

85 Cf. *FCIC,* Financial Crisis Inquiry Report (2011), pp. 280 ff.

86 Cf. *FCIC,* Financial Crisis Inquiry Report (2011), pp. 16 f.; 65 ff., 380, 414.

87 Cf. *Nationale Kommission zur Untersuchung der Finanz- und Wirtschaftskrise,* Schlussfolgerungen (2009), p. 10.

Second Chapter:
Core Causes of the Recent Financial Crisis

1. Core causes

1.1. Overview

Notably hedge funds were already subject to legal regulation at the eve of the financial crisis 2008/2009. Nevertheless, that crisis revealed the possible need for a harmonized legal approach at European level.[88] To create a new regulatory framework for the activities of hedge funds,[89] private equity funds and other alternative investments that face the challenging requirements of the 21st century, it is necessary to take a broad look at the supposed core causes[90] that directly led to the global financial crisis. In accordance with Walker, as core cause of the recent financial crisis, one can identify the massive accumulation of credit and debt stock, the increasing product complexity and the lack of transparency, credit rating errors and mispricing of risks, risk separation and risk mixing (co-mingling of financial items with a higher credit standing with those of a subprime standing) that means infection and the lack of effective market support[91] In spite of the existing disclosure requirements, the capital markets[92] did not reach their objec-

---

88 Cf. *FSA,* Discussion Paper 05/4, pp. 1 ff.

89 On the issue on hedge funds in Corporate Governance and Corporate Control cf. *Grabaravicius/Dierick,* ECB-Occasional Paper No. 34 (August 2005), pp. 1 ff.; *Kahan/Rock,* Law Review (May 2007), pp. 1021 ff.

90 Discussion on the (supposed) core reasons of the financial crisis: *Avgouleas,* ECFR (2009), pp. 440 ff.; *Dam,* Subprime Crisis (2009), p. 95 ff.; *Kindler,* NJW (2010), pp. 2465 ff.; *Kübler,* in: Festschrift für Schwark (2009) p. 499 ff.; *Litten/Bell,* WM (2011), pp. 1109 ff.; *N.N.,* Lessons, Auszüge aus Presseartikeln No. 5/2010, pp.5 ff.; *Oehlrich/Baltes,* ZRP (2011), pp. 40 ff.; *Pacces,* ECFR (2010), pp. 479 ff.; *Rudolph,* ZGR (2010), pp. 1 ff.; *Sinn,* Kasino-Kapitalismus (2009), p. 1 ff.; *Walker,* in: The Future of financial regulation (2010), pp. 179, 195 ff.

91 Cf. *Walker,* in: The Future of financial regulation (2010), pp. 179 (195 ff.).

92 The capital markets can be defined as those financial markets for a long-term debt with a maturity at over one year and for equity shares and that are used by corporations to raise additional funds, cf. *Lee/Lee,* Encyclopedia of Finance (2006), p. 46.

tive because of the often enormous product complexity of financially advanced products.[93]

The massive accumulation of credit is underlined by the development of the financial segment in the United States: During the period from 1960 to 2007, the relative size of the financial sector increased from 4% to 8% of the GDP, while the profits rose from 16% in the 1973 to 41% at that point in time immediately before the outbreak of the financial crisis.[94] Lord Turner should have caused an outcry in the financial sector when he stated that "the financial sector had grown beyond a socially reasonable size".[95] According to his point of view, the growth of the relative size of the financial sector and, in particular, of securitised credit activities, increased the potential impact of financial system instability on the real economy.[96] As is pointed out by Wymeersch,[97] the expansion of the financial sector in recent years has been promoted by the overextension of credit due to very low interest rates for a long periods of time (the "Expansionary monetary policy"). Furthermore, Wymeersch[98] identifies the overleveraging of many financial institutions directly or through derivative techniques.[99] Consequently, the existence of several asset bubbles[100] in the real estate sector, in commodities and in the equity markets, leading to over-optimism and a relaxing of risk management as outstanding core reasons of the recent financial crisis.

---

93 Cf. *Avgouleas,* ECFR (2009), pp. 440, 440.

94 Cf. *Wymeersch,* ECFR (2010), pp. 240, 240.

95 Ibid.

96 Cf. FSA, The Turner Review (2009), p. 18.

97 Ibid.

98 Ibid.

99 For the latest information on the disclosure requirements of credit derivates see *Litten/Bell,* WM (2011), pp. 1109 ff.

100 The term "bubble" refers to the so-called "bubble theory" and to security prices that move wildly above their true values and eventually burst after the prices eventually fall back to their original level, causing great losses for investors. The crashes of the stock markets of 1929, 1987, 2000 and finally 2008 can be seen as proof of the bubble theory, cf. *Lee/Lee,* Encyclopaedia of Finance (2006), p. 40.

1.2. Lack of equity position/excessive leverage position

1.2.1. Definition of the equity position

Probably the main reason for the recent financial crisis is the widespread lack of equity position respective to capital adequacy, which can be defined as a residual that remains if one subtracts the operational debts of a company from its assets.[101] Subsequently, one has to add those capital resources that are placed by the investors at the disposal of the corporation, which cannot be terminated as a credit and which cannot be considered as an insolvency claim.[102] Beside the sales profitability and the return on assets that are very significant to the outside creditors, the equity profitability belongs to the most significant business ratios of a corporation. One can easily calculate the equity profitability by dividing the net income of a business segment by the average equity position.[103]

1.2.2. Systemic risks of insufficient equity

The systemic risk is the risk that a default of one financial institution will lead to defaults of other financial institutions.[104] Generally, a credit institute is systemically significant if the minimum level of its balance sheet total covers no less than €30,000 to €40,000 million.[105] However, even with the integration of the corporation into general monetary transactions, the intensity of its deposit business and its market position with certain products are significant signals of the systemic importance of a corporation.[106] Nevertheless, the systemic impact of a financial instrument not only refers to its business volume but also to its cross-linking, its substitutability and to the general condition of the affected markets.[107]

---

101 *Igel,* Wirtschaftswissen (2004), p 320.

102 *Aleth/Reichel,* in: Eilers/Rödding/Schmalenbach, Unternehmensfinanzierung (2008), p. 77 f.

103 *Reinhart,* Auswirkungen (1998), p. 321; overview of the equity profitability of American banks in the year 2006: *Sinn,* Kasino-Kapitalismus (2009), p. 87.

104 *Hull,* Risk Management (2010), p. 529.

105 *Hank/Siedenbiedel/Von Petersdorff,* F.A.S. (March/15th/2009), p. 41.

106 Ibid.

107 Cf. *N.N.,* G20-Agenda, Auszüge aus Presseartikeln No. 5/2010, pp.3 (4).

In particular, those systemic risks that resulted from mortgages based on flexible interests (e.g., option ARMs[108]) grow up within the financial system because transparency was neither held as necessary nor had it been requested. From 2001 until 2007, the debts resulting from mortgages almost doubled. The high risky loans based on mortgages increased. Massive, short-term borrowing and commitments that were not visible for other market participants boosted the probability that the whole financial system could dissolve rapidly.[109] Against the abovementioned background, the FCIC speaks of „Contagion[110]" as one of the systemic failures.[111] If any financial firm is a large counterparty to other firms, the sudden and disorderly bankruptcy might weaken the finances of those other firms and cause them to fail.[112] The FCIC calls this risk contagion, when, due to a direct financial link between firms, the failure of one causes the failure of another: The one financial firm was „too big to fail" if policymakers fear contagion so much that they are unwilling to allow it to go bankrupt in a sudden and disorderly fashion.[113] Policymakers make this judgment in large part based on how much counterparty risk other firms have to the failing firm, along with judgments about the likelihood and possible damage of contagion.[114] Thus, the FCIC con-

[108] Cf. *FCIC, Financial Crisis Inquiry Report (2011), pp.* 134 ff.

[109] Cf. *Nationale Kommission zur Untersuchung der Finanz- und Wirtschaftskrise,* Schlussfolgerungen (2009), p. 10; „Option ARMs" can be defined as another common high risk loan that has been offered to both prime brokers and subprime brokers during the years leading up to the financial crisis were even known as „Pick-A-Payment". They were primarily adressed to to financially sophisticated borrowers but ultimately became more widespread. According to federal banking regulators and a range of industry participants, as home prices inclined rapidly in some areas of the country, lenders started marketing payment-option ARMs as affordability products and made them available to less-creditworthy and lower-income borrowers, cf. Levin-Report (2011), p. 29 (referring to the GAO report).

[110] On hedge fund contagion and liquidity shocks cf. *Boyson/Stahel/Stulz,* Journal of Finance (January 2010), pp. 1789 ff.

[111] Cf. *FCIC,* Financial Crisis Inquiry Report (2011), pp. 459 f.

[112] Cf. *FCIC,* Financial Crisis Inquiry Report (2011), pp. 459.

[113] Cf. *FCIC,* Financial Crisis Inquiry Report (2011), pp. 459.

[114] Cf. *FCIC,* Financial Crisis Inquiry Report (2011), pp. 459.

cludes that the break-down of the financial markets resulted as a combination of excessive debt, risky investments and a lack of transparency.[115]

In particular, an adequate equity position creates a risk buffer that contributes to the protection of the creditors and the protection of the general public.[116] In contrast, an insufficient equity can cause a real systemic risk. Before the outbreak of the recent financial crisis, many financial firms had chosen an extremely small equity position to realise the biggest short-term rate of return. In many cases, the available equity position was less than 5%.[117] Specifically, the five big investment banks (Bear Stearns, Goldman Sachs, Lehman Brothers, Merrill Lynch and Morgan Stanley) run their business with an extraordinary thin equity – their leverage amounted to 40:1, that means 40 US$ investment value corresponded to 1 $US equity to cover possibly losses.[118] As the Turner Report underlines, that increase of leverage played an important role in driving the boom and in creating vulnerabilities that have increased the severity of the crisis.[119] Any small decline of those investments could wipe out a whole company. So far, the FCIC identifies a too strong leverage, too many short-term lendings and an insufficient risk management as key factors of the crisis.[120] Among the reasons behind the recent financial crisis, one can identify the lack of equity position in the affected companies.[121] The risk of a total loss was intensified by an insufficient equity, in many cases amounting to less than 5%.[122]

On the one hand, the limitation of equity enables the fund manager the use of leverage and can be seen as one of the key factors of the success of alternative

115 Cf. *FCIC,* Financial Crisis Inquiry Report (2011), pp. 16, 19 ff., 269, 380, 414, 438; *Nationale Kommission zur Untersuchung der Finanz- und Wirtschaftskrise,* Schlussfolgerungen (2009), p. 9.

116 Cf. *Hank/Siedenbiedel/Von Petersdorff,* F.A.S. (March/15th/2009), p. 41.

117 Cf. *Sinn,* Kasino-Kapitalismus (2009), p. 155 ff.

118 Cf. *FCIC,* Financial Crisis Inquiry Report (2011), pp. 19 ff.

119 Cf. *FSA,* The Turner Review (2009), pp. 19 f.

120 Cf. *FCIC,* Financial Crisis Inquiry Report (2011), pp. 58 ff.; 141 ff.; 162 ff.; 235 ff.; Cf. *Nationale Kommission zur Untersuchung der Finanz- und Wirtschaftskrise,* Schlussfolgerungen (2009), p. 9.

121 *Sinn,* Kasino Kapitalismus (2009), pp. 18, 202-206, 208.

122 *Sinn,* Kasino Kapitalismus (2009), pp. 202-206.

investment funds (AIF).[123] The limitation of equity can help to overcome periods of reduced liquidity.[124] Thin capitalisation, combined with a "borrow short/lend long" strategy, is necessary for a bank's profitability.[125]

On the other hand, a lack of equity position can cause the risk that the capital of the corporation is not sufficient to cover bigger losses.[126] It reduces the immunity of a corporation against the rapid development of the globalised financial markets and, in dependence of its business volume, can consequently cause a systemic risk. Thus, a serious lack of equity position leads to capital costs increase and leads to a higher risk that the target corporation becomes insolvent.[127] In the financial branch, capital has to be adequate to assure that a bank can pay off its creditors at all times.[128] Moreover, the use of private equity reduces the credit rating of the target corporation, runs the risk that long-term investments are neglected and leads to a negative impact on the relation towards clients and creditors.[129] Financial instability involves the collapse or weakness of other banks – in a rapid and systemic failure of the banking system.[130] Finally, it can directly lead to a nationalisation of losses.

To face these systemic risks in the future, the central banks have undertaken certain measures that consist of having most credit default swaps (CDS[131]) processed through a central entity that acts as the buyer of all CDS sold and the seller of the CDS bought, thereby eliminating counterparty risk and setting off the positions on a multilateral technique that will significantly reduce the nominal

123 *Jaskolski/Grüber,* Corporate Finance Law (2010), pp. 188-189.
124 *Jaskolski/Grüber,* Corporate Finance Law (2010), pp. 189.
125 *Dam,* Subprime Crisis (2009), pp. 95, 98.
126 *Jaskolski/Grüber,* Corporate Finance Law (2010), pp. 189.
127 Ibid.
128 *Dam,* Subprime Crisis (2009), pp. 95, 98.
129 *Jaskolski/Grüber,* Corporate Finance Law (2010), pp. 189.
130 *Dam,* Subprime Crisis (2009), pp. 95, 98.
131 The CDS market has become the indicator of the creditworthiness of numerous firms or states and – theoretically - may even take over the function of the credit ratings, cf. *Wymeersch,* ECFR (2010), pp. 240, 241; in general on the Credit Default Swaps cf. *B. Müller* in Saenger/Aderhold/Lenkaitis/Speckmann, Gesellschaftsrecht (2011), § 16, Marginal no. 105 ff.

amount of outstanding liabilities on a continuous basis, thereby reducing exposures.[132]

1.2.3. Hedge funds as an occurrence of low equity

Although they did not ask for governmental support during the recent financial crisis, hedge funds typically avail themselves of an extreme low equity position that can be identified as a key factor of their business strategy. Hedge funds can be described as special monetary accumulations that are subject to less restrictions and less regulation than mutual funds – they can take short positions and use derivatives, but they cannot publicly offer their securities.[133] They can be identified as very sensitive to any credit gap because they are typically working with a strong leverage and their liability to margin[134] calls in the case that the markets turn.[135] This sensitivity has been proven during the recent financial crisis: Although the hedge funds have shown a relative strong immunity against the realisation of systemic risks, they are generally considered to have contributed to their deepening, mainly as a consequence of their action in the markets.[136] As a result, hedge funds create a form of "regulatory omission" because they are only regulated through the authorised institutions through which they operate or whom they are dealing with.[137] In addition, further difficulties and even systemic risks consequently result from their generally insufficient transparency, their typical complex investment strategies, high levels of leverage, aggressive market

132 Cf. *Wymeersch,* ECFR (2010), pp. 240, 243.

133 To obtain further information on the implementation, organisation and the regulation of hedge funds: *Berger/Steck,* ZBB (2003), pp. 192-202; *Fischer,* NZG (2009), p. 703; *Leible/Lehmann,* Hedgefonds (2009); *Nietsch/Graef,* ZBB (2010), pp. 12-20; *Pütz/Schmies,* BKR (2004), pp. 51-60; Cf. *Ricke,* BKR (2004), pp. 60-65; *Rosowski,* Hedgefonds (2009); *Spindler/Bednarz,* WM (2006), p. 553-600; *Spindler/Bednarz,* WM (2006), p. 601-607; *Wentrup,* Hedgefonds (2009); *Zetsche,* NZG (2009), p. 692-697.

134 The margin defines that cash or traded securities that are required from a trader to reduce potential losses in the event that the trader defaults cf. *Hull,* Risk Management (2011), p. 523.

135 As it has shown at the background of the financial crisis 2008/2009.

136 *Wymeersch,* ECFR (2010), pp. 240, 244.

137 Cf. *Shadab,* Hedge Fund Regulation (2007), pp. 1 ff.

positions, high liquidity concentration and possible market distortion, market herding and "crowded trade" settlement.[138]

By choosing a very small equity position, the hedge funds managers try to neutralise the normally high volatility of financial markets to build a shield against the cyclical ups and downs. Therefore, their financial strategy can be qualified as extremely counter-cyclical. To implement this counter-cyclical strategy and to build a strong shield against the "moods" of the markets, the hedge fund managers normally work with an excessive leverage position combined with one highly speculative portfolio strategy. If the real economic events correspond to the assumptions of the hedge fund managers, this portfolio strategy is highly profitable. In the recent financial crisis, the speculative assumptions of hedge fund managers and other financial protagonists did not come true. Thus, hedge funds and other concerned companies were unable to correspond to the unexpected reclaim of saving deposits. Although they did not ask for governmental or other public support, even this "fund run" can be identified as another initial point of the already-mentioned nationalisation of losses. Moreover, another reason that contributed to the financial crisis of 2008/2009 consisted in the fact that all of the main broker-dealers, such as Lehman Brothers, acted as prime brokers with all of the assets of the hedge funds subsequently "frozen" until bankruptcy was complete.

1.3. Short-term incentives

1.3.1. Corporate conducting by incentives

Another significant circumstance that can be identified as a core reason of the recent financial crisis is the false structure of incentives.[139] Although these incentives are often set by the corporation, it is its proprietors who finally define its

[138] In particular, such features result from the hedge funds as an specific appearance of shadow banking as one segment that notably does not underlay the respective equity and supervisory requirements.

[139] That notably distorted incentives can be identified as one major cause of the here discussed financial crisis was commonly examined under „behavioural economics".

business strategy, which is then executed by the agents. Therefore, the recent financial crisis can also be seen as a result of wrongfully set incentives.

In general, incentives do result from extrinsic circumstances that motivate someone to do something to contribute with her or his actions to the realisation of a common superior objective. They are set to conduct the behaviour of a person and can consist of financial or economic advantages for the person.

That mechanism can be described as behaviour control by incentives; it also works in the financial segment and "conducts" the relation between the corporation, its managers, its investors and the general public. Previous to the recent financial crisis, numerous managers set too-strong a focus on short-term capital gains. Under normal circumstances, the shareholders expect the fund manager to realise a maximum short-term profit. If the fund manager corresponds to the investor's expectation, she or he gains a maximum remuneration. Thus, the fund manager realises a strong material incentive for a short-term profit. However, a short-term business strategy also increases the volume of systemic risks that can be defined as risks that affect not only a single enterprise or a single branch, but also the national economy as a system. A short-term business strategy increases the risk of a total loss for the corporation.

1.3.2. Consequences of the business judgment rule

With the business judgment rule (BJR) the directors of a corporation have widespread freedom of action concerning their economic decisions. They are free to make the economic decision which is best with regard to the objectives of the corporation. If they do respect the limits of this freedom of action, the managers of the corporation do not bear any personal liability – also in the case that their assumptions do not come true and directly lead to the realisation of a risk that consequently results in the insolvency of the corporation.

1.3.3. The yield as an investment parameter

The yield of a corporation is one essential parameter for the decision of internationally operating investors. Under the conditions of the economic globalisation, its information value can be compared with that of the tax rate. Under the conditions of the increasing digitalisation of financial information, which forces internationally operating investors to reach their investment decisions rapidly if they want to be competitive, the yield of a corporation conveys a brief, consolidated and significant parameter of effective investment decisions. In many cases it helps to avoid a detailed and therefore time-consuming analysis of the target corporation. Moreover, with the regime of the International Financial Reporting Standards (IFRS), which advises the concerned corporation to be truthful and fairin terms of their net operating results, the yield of a corporation is a very serious and reliable parameter. Because the IFRS are respected as one international compulsory standard of financial information, the managers of a corporation are authorised to trust it without committing a breach of their legal or contractual obligations.

However, the direct relation between yield, risks and the manager's extraordinary remuneration results in an increase of systemic risks and, in particular, a negative correlation of personal liability that is essential to a well-functioning and sustainable market economy. Up to the outbreak of the recent financial crisis the validity of the BJR resulted in the widespread practice that managers profited from hazarding higher risk by contracting highly speculative transactions if their economic assumptions were realised. However, they did not have to pay for it if their assumptions were not realised.

1.3.4. Widespread use of highly speculative business models

In many cases those fund managers who run a highly speculative portfolio strategy obtained a comparatively more comfortable remuneration than those who preferred a sustainable portfolio strategy, which is defined by a reasonable, cautious composition of risks (low risks, middle risks and high risks). In particular, the German Sparkassen[140] were by far less concerned with the recent financial crisis than the investment banks.

To reach the ambitious targets of equity profitability, there was a widespread custom among fund managers and other financial protagonists to run highly speculative business models, short sales[141] and derivatives. Despite the portfolio strategies, they had one very significant character: Opportunities and risks of a financial transaction are not in the hands of the same person any longer – from the perspective of (independent) financials one of the most significant reasons for the global financial crisis of 2008/2009.

1.3.5. Asymmetric structure of incentives

One can call this structure of incentives an asymmetric structure of incentives because those managers did not have any incentive to avoid an economic loss that consequently resulted in the corporation's insolvency, a realisation of systemic risks and a nationalisation of the corporation's losses as a consequence of the public deposit guarantee. In the case of the banks, the disclosure-based market discipline mainly failed because of the implicit government guarantee.[142] In many financial corporations, this asymmetric structure of incentives created a very frivolous exposure to other people's money. Numerous managers obtained an extraordinary (financial) settlement (a "golden handshake"), also when their portfolio strategy generated an extraordinary loss and the corporation's public reputation forced the supervisory board to dismiss that operating director. This happened in the case of the Hypo Real Estate (HRE), the Hamburg and Schleswig-Holstein Nordbank (HSH) and Acandor.

---

140 On the "3-column structure" of the banking sector in Germany and the dominating role of the Sparkassen under the impact of economic globalisation and the recent financial crisis: *Kirchner,* in: Festschrift für Schwark (2009) pp. 475 ff.

141 The term "short sales" stands for a portfolio strategy where shares are sold into the market, which have been borrowed from another investor, Cf. *Hull,* Risk Management (2011), p. 528.

142 Cf. *Avgouleas,* ECFR (2009), pp. 440.

1.4. False structure of remuneration

Furthermore, the remuneration design of the directors and officers is acknowledged as one of the major reasons of the recent financial crisis. In the case that the remuneration contains a too-big variable share, this can lead to a misalignment of incentives for the management. Before the outbreak of the recent financial crisis, the managers of the corporation could earn an extraordinary remuneration if their economic assumptions came true and directly resulted in an extraordinary short-term yield of the corporation. This structure of incentives may be non-hazardous if the business volume of a corporation does not reach a systemic significance. However, this structure of incentives is also very common among systemically significant corporations such as HRE,[143] Deutsche Bank (DB) or HSH Nordbank (HSH) – corporations that are positioned in the investment bank segment – where their systemic risk is realised. Nevertheless, this structure of incentives may be essential for a corporation to maintain its global competitiveness. In particular, the report of the FCIC points out that mortgage brokers paid the real estate brokers a margin award in that case where they successfully mediate loans at a higher interest level to reach higher broker fees without informing their clients.[144]

1.5. Conflicts of interest at the rating agencies

1.5.1. Assessment of creditworthiness as the principal function

Conflicts of interest not only existed between financial managers and investors but also at the rating agencies because they issue ratings to issuers and investment banks who bring them business.[145] It is the essential function of the rating agencies to assess the creditworthiness of financial products, countries and

---

143 After the insolvency of *Lehman Brothers* the *Hypo Real Estate Bank,* (HRE) had to gather state guarantees of some €100 billion. Up to now, the HRE received more than €6,000 million in new capital from the German government. With regard to its systemic significance, the HRE was totally nationalised in 2009, cf. *N. N.,* WELT KOMPAKT (22.01.2010), p. 19.

144 Cf. *Nationale Kommission zur Untersuchung der Finanz- und Wirtschaftskrise,* Schlussfolgerungen (2009), p. 12

145 Cf. *FSA,* The Turner Report (2009), p. 78; Levin-Report (2011), pp. 31.

corporations. In general, the rating of credits is a procedure to measure the creditworthiness of a bond.[146,147] The Levin Report defines a credit rating as an assessment of likelihood that a particular financial instrument, such as a corporate bond or mortgage backed security, may default or incur losses.[148] It aims at containing information deficits of the purchasers.[149]

In contrast to the principal function of rating agencies, at the eve of the financial crisis of 2008/2009, many depositors blindly trusted them. In many cases, they were committed to use their assistance. As the FCIC points out, the failure of the rating agencies was an essential „cogs in the wheel" of the financial destruction.[150] Those mortgage securitised instruments that stood in the epicentrum of the financial crisis never could have distributed and sold without the assistance of the rating agencies. Thus, according to the FCIC´s point of view, the financial crisis never would have taken place without the rating agencies. Their assessments led to the financial market rise, and those downgrades of the years 2007 and 2008 heavily damaged markets and corporations.[151] All in all, the rating agencies were involved in a severe conflict of interests.

That conflict of interest that became a core reason for the recent financial crisis resulted from the concentration of assessing the risks of financial products and the purchasing of financial products in the same entity. Up to the recent financial crisis, it was a widespread practice that rating agencies not only assessed the financial risks of financial products, but also the probability of default[152] to enhance the investor protection. Normally, the assessment of a financial product

146 A bond is defined as a long-term debt of a firm, often refers to both secured and unsecured debt and is almost always the same as the face value, cf. *Lee/Lee,* Encyclopedia of Finance (2006), p. 36.

147 *Hull,* Risk Management (2011), p. 516.

148 Cf. Levin-Report (2011), pp. 26 f.

149 Cf. *Kübler,* in: Festschrift für Schwark (2009) p. 499, 499.

150 Cf. *FCIC,* Financial Crisis Inquiry Report (2011), p. 25.

151 Cf. *Nationale Kommission zur Untersuchung der Finanz- und Wirtschaftskrise,* Schlussfolgerungen (2009), p. 16.

152 The term "probability of default" refers to the failure to make obligated interest and principal payments on a loan. It describes the likelihood that an obligor or counterparty will encounter credit distress within a given time period, cf. *Lee/Lee,* Encyclopedia of Finance (2006), p. 83.

as the result of its default probability analysis of the rating agencies represents the essential basis for the investment decision. Under well-functioning market conditions a bad rating is directly reflected in the price of a financial product that informs the investors on the trustworthiness of a certain financial product. Under the conditions of the fast-moving financial markets, the price conveys to the financial investors perhaps the most significant signal of the credit standing of corporations. To realise the financial objectives of their corporation and to restore the trust of investors, the portfolio managers must react rapidly to the development of the financial markets.

1.5.2. Interference of assessing and disposing financial products

Up to the recent financial crisis, the abovementioned mechanism was set in force because the rating agencies not only accessed the creditworthiness of financial products but also disposed of these products. It is easy to understand that the interference of these two functions that normally should be clearly separated can directly cause an interruption of a well-functioning market economy.

It is usually the main task of a rating agency to access the creditworthiness of people, corporations and countries by giving marks that are called "scores". In recent financial practice, it happened that the rating agency that distributed the financial product also had to access this product. Thus, credit institutes were enabled to devise securitised products that enjoyed an "AAA" rating, which represents the best available credit standing – even though the underlying securities were of a far lower grade.[153]

The conflict of interest that resulted from the interference of those two functions not only concerned the access but also the risk weighting of financial products.[154] Many rating agencies did not focus on the protection of investors but pursued the objective to increase the sales volume of those financial products with a high probability of default. The interference at the rating agencies caused a wide-

153 *McIlroy* in Straus, future of banking (2009), pp. 119, 120.
154 *Dam* in Straus, Subprime Crisis (2009), pp. 95, 103.

spread overestimation of financial products. The initial ratings were too high.[155] The risks of AAA-rated tranches of ABS and collateralised debt obligations (CDOs[156]) were higher than either investors or rating agencies realised.[157]

To underline these heavy failures of the rating agencies, the FCIC hints at the fact that, between 2000 and 2007, Moody´s assessed 45.000 mortgage securitised instruments as AAA.[158] In contrast, in the first half of 2010 there were only six US-American corporations that received the AAA-assessment.[159] In 2006 alone, Moody´s assessed mortgage securitised instruments as AAA thirty times each day – with disastrous consequences: 83% of the mortgage securitised instruments were downgraded in the end.[160] Thus, it can be seen as an actual cause of the recent financial crisis that the rating companies mispriced structured debt.[161] Moreover, it was also an apparent failure of risk management theory.[162] Moreover, as the FCIC highlights, without the rating agencies assessment failures, the market for mortgage securitised instruments never would have collapsed.[163]

The responsible managers at the rating agencies, meanwhile, admitted to themselves that their institutions made significant assessment faults.[164] These assessment faults sustainably damaged the reputation and the credibility of the whole rating agencies segment.[165] The insufficient performance of the rating agencies in the sector of structured products[166] – a structured financial product is a derivative designed by a financial institution to meet the need of clients (e.g.,

---

155 Cf. *FCIC,* Financial Crisis Inquiry Report (2011), p. 426.
156 Security created from tranches of different ABSs; cf. Levin-Report (2011), p. 28 f.
157 *Hull,* Risk Management (2010), p. 341.
158 Cf. *FCIC,* Financial Crisis Inquiry Report (2011), p. 25.
159 Cf. *FCIC,* Financial Crisis Inquiry Report (2011), p. 25.
160 Cf. *FCIC,* Financial Crisis Inquiry Report (2011), p. 25.
161 Cf. *Volpin/Pagano,* Credit Ratings Failures (2009), pp. 1 ff.
162 Ibid.
163 Cf. *Nationale Kommission zur Untersuchung der Finanz- und Wirtschaftskrise,* Schlussfolgerungen (2009), p. 16.
164 Cf. *New York Times* (January/28th/2008), C 13: Moody´s Official concedes failure in some ratings.
165 Cf. *Kübler,* in: Festschrift für Schwark (2009) p. 499, 503.
166 For further information on structured finance cf. *De Vries Robbé,* Structured Finance (2010), pp. 1 ff.

CDOs)[167] – consequently led to the necessity of an extraordinary regulatory intervention in almost all industrial countries.[168]

Rating agencies will be subject to some form of supervision in the future, mainly dealing with their organisation and governance, their internal processes, the absence of conflicts of interest and an effective disclosure.[169] Moreover, there will be the necessity for an international corporation to avoid separate and different ratings to be issued, depending on the local entity in the rating group that has issued the rating.[170]

Those assessment faults that resulted in the overestimating of the quality of those financial products with a high risk level is probably one of the core causes for the recent financial crisis[171] Many of the financial products that were not properly assessed by the rating agencies are meanwhile possessed by a "bad bank" – a credit institute that was founded because of the recent financial crisis to purchase those financial products that cannot trade on the "first" financial market any longer because their real financial standing is sometimes at the "D" level, which indicates the worst accessed financial products. As an extraordinary phenomenon of the recent financial crisis, the bad bank does not underlie the legal requirements of the lending law. It overtakes risks papers that suffered extraordinary losses and consequently could not be traded on the market any longer and that no longer fit into a bank's portfolio strategy; therefore, the "bad bank" is allowed to run a smaller equity position than other credit institutes.[172]

---

[167] *Hull,* Risk Management (2011), p. 529.

[168] Cf. *Wymeersch,* ECFR (2010), pp. 240, 241.

[169] Cf. *Wymeersch,* ECFR (2010), pp. 240, 243; on the future European financial supervision see *Heun*, JZ (No. 5/2012), p. 235 ff.

[170] *Wymeersch,* ECFR (2010), pp. 240, 243.

[171] Cf. *IMF,* Initial lessons of the crisis (2009), published under http://www.imf.org/external/np/pp/eng/2009/020609.pdf (requested July/17th/2013).

[172] Cf. *N. N.,* WELT KOMPAKT (22.01.2010), p. 19.

1.5.3. Interference by securitisation

The securitisation of risk[173] is a technique to transform illiquid wealth position/assets as the book claim of a corporation into a transferable wealth position.[174] Probably the most important distinction in relation to structured finance applies to the fact that banks securitize credit instruments such as mortgages, car loans and student loans by selling them to a single special purpose vehicle (SPV) ,which pays for the purchase by issuing new ones, notes or commercial papers. In contrast, structured finance thereupon informs the secondary securitisation or re-securitisation of the securities produced by the first securitisation with large numbers of securitisations that possibly reach a volume of 250 to 350, all being sought by a higher new SPV that would issue those securities in tranches with a number of various risk levels.

Until the financial market crisis of 2008/2009 there was an increasing practical demand for securitisations because credit institutes used this technique to reduce their capital buffers. Moreover, it even became popular because securitisations contribute to minimise counterparty risk and their conception is comparatively easy.[175] Even a future claim can be securitised. All in all, securitisation is a comparatively new technique to finance a corporation. The originating corporation can avail itself of liquid assets before the expiry date. In this context, the corporation as the source of the claim takes the position as the originator.

From a corporation's perspective, securitisation became a very popular technique starting in the mid-1990s to fit its short-term capital demand and to obtain investment capital. Under the regime of the Third Basel Capital Accord (Basel III[176]), from a bank's perspective, it has become a very popular technique to generate cash because the synthetic securitisation enables a credit institute to the iso-

173 For on-going information on the legal framework of the securitisation of risks see *Prüm/ Thomas,* BKR (2011), pp. 133-143.

174 Cf. *Gronewold,* Kapitalanlagegesellschaften, p. 59.

175 Cf. *Decker/Hubli in* Busack/Kaiser, Alternative Investments II, 2006, p. 496 f.

176 On the development towards a harmonised European banking supervision under the Basel III-regime cf. http://www.bis.org/list/bcbs/index.htm, requested October/24th/2012.

lated transfer of risks (investment risk, solvency risk, risk of creditworthiness etc.) at a SPV, respectively an asset-backed securities corporation (ABSC) that takes the position of the distributor and packs the assigned claims from several corporations into a transferable, respectively fungible product with an often blue-chip solvency. In this context, it seems essential to clarify the widespread simplification that the SPV was founded to acquire non-transferable assets from the originator. The respective assets are either legally assigned to the SPV by the originator on a legal basis or the economic risk transfer based on credit derivatives, such as CDS under a synthetic CDO. Synthetic CDOs that were used until the outbreak of the financial crisis of 2008/2009 did not contain actual mortgages or other assets that produce income but simply "referenced" existing assets and thereupon permitted investors to use credit default swaps to place bets on the performance of those referenced assets.[177] The SPV finances the purchase from the originator by editing asset-backed commercial papers (ABCP), and transfers the risk of bad debt to the investors.[178] The SPV refinances itself by the capital market and conducts the interest and amortisation payments by backflows of the purchased assets from depositor credits resulting from the operative business of the originator.[179]

By using credit enhancements, the SPV normally obtains a better credit rating, like the originator. The resulting commercial paper is often an ABS or a MBS. Practically, it takes a specific design to make sure that the ABSC does not belong to the relevant consolidating group of the originator.[180] Because the SPV often combines several traditional financial means into a new financial product one can call this a structured financial product. However, the financial expression of the structured financial products not only stands for a financial product, but also represents an active portfolio strategy that more strongly corresponds with

---

177 Cf. Levin-Report (2011), p. 28.

178 Hertz-Eichenrode/Illenberger/Jesch/Keller/Klebeck/Rocholl, Private Equity-Lexikon (2011), p. 192.

179 Cf. *Volkart,* Corporate Finance (2008), p. 883.

180 Hertz-Eichenrode/Illenberger/Jesch/Keller/Klebeck/Rocholl, Private Equity-Lexikon (2011), p. 192.

the individual demands of the investor/depositor and that can generate protection against the volatility of the (financial) markets.

There is a difference between the true sale securitisation and the synthetic securitisation. On the one hand, true sale securitisation that is based on a real transfer of the original claim that can legally be qualified as a transfer of property with a balance sheet-liberating effect. Generally, in the case of derivatives, the investors share the risk that the put-options are taken under a disadvantageous market trend, and that they are, consequently, committed to accept the repurchase of subprime shares.[181] The (prospective) value of the securitised claim depends on its further development. The true-sale securitisation is preferable if the principal objective of the originator is the rise of its liquidity.[182]

On the other hand, under the synthetic securitisation, only the relevant risks, the risk of bad debt, are transferred to the SPV. The relevant assets and the original claim remain in the balance sheet of the originator. Because Basel III requires the involved credit institutes to highlight any risk with an equity position, the synthetic securitisation contributes to a bank's interest to generate cash flow. Until the outbreak of the financial crisis of 2008/2009, a very popular technique of the investment banks was to achieve an above-average performance. In the case that the relevant risks are realised, the SPV is committed to perform an equalisation payment to the originator.

Among those corporations that systematically use the technique of securitisation are General Motors (GM) and Ford, who finance their debtors by these financial means, and big commercial banks that outsource and securitize mortgage loans.

[181] Cf. *Volkart,* Corporate Finance (2008), p. 488.
[182] Vgl. *Gronewold,* Kapitalanlagegesellschaften, p. 64.

1.5.4. Interference by Structured Finance

Structured financial products aim at the individual requirements and demands of the depositor. They represent a combination of several traditional financial products. Typically, several conventional financial products are combined into an unusual innovative financial item to fit the specific needs of the issuers and the depositors/investors.[183] Essentially, structured financial products follow three objectives. On the one hand, they aim at credit institutes and other financial market participants to discharge them from different types of risks and to enhance their cash flow. On the other hand, they protect them against the volatility of the cash market and keep the requested interest level. In addition, whereas the so-called interest caps generate a protection against the transgression of a certain interest level under the conditions of variable interest rates, the so-called interest floors generate the provision to build a protection against the undercut of a certain interest level (a financial means to hedge the price level).[184] Finally, structured financial products, such as futures, forwards and swaps[185] contribute to generate a scope for the calculation of market prices by fixing certain market prices at a certain point of time.[186]

In comparison with other types of investment funds, the customer of a structured financial product bears a counterparty risk because these products can be legally qualified as claims that are secured with a credit risk towards the bank.[187]

183 Cf. *B. Müller,* in: Saenger/Aderhold/Lenkaitis/Speckmann, Gesellschaftsrecht (2011), § 16, Marginal no. 105; *Lenenbach* in: Assies/Rösler, FAHdB Bank- und Kapitalmarktrecht (2012), § 36, Marginal no. 353.

184 Cf. *B. Müller,* in: Saenger/Aderhold/Lenkaitis/Speckmann, Gesellschaftsrecht (2011), § 16, Marginal no. 109.

185 On the one hand, a swap can be defined as a contract that commits the involved persons to exchange payment streams at a certain point of time in the future. On the other hand, it is a combination of a purchased call (long) and a sold put (short) with the same tick size and the same strike. They help to protect assets against the volatility of the market, cf. *Heidorn/ Trautmann* in: Busack/Kaiser, Alternative Investments II, 2006, p. 536 f.

186 Cf. *B. Müller* in Saenger/Aderhold/Lenkaitis/Speckmann, Gesellschaftsrecht (2011), § 16, Marginal no. 110.

187 Cf. *Kaiser,* Konstruktion, p. 84.

In general, one can distinguish structured financial products by the three main criteria of capital protection, profit potential and coupon payments.[188]

In view of the abovementioned functions, structured finance can be defined as the coordinated use of credit financing to optimise the relevant financing conditions, even under the tax and company-law perspective.[189] The depositor/investor purchases a product that combines the bond of an often blue-chip issuer with certain payments of interests and amortisation whose volume depends on the development of a specific reference value.[190] Very often those bonds that are issued by the SPVs get a better rating at the capital market than the originator because the outsourced assets normally are of a premium quality, and the intelligent structuring of the refinancing into several tranches with different seniorities conveys another advantage.[191] As a result, the payment flows economically represent a combination of bond, reference value and the relevant put/call-options on this reference value.[192]

1.5.5. Further analysis and conclusions

Although it is still unknown whether the rating agencies made those fatal assessment faults, financial analysts assume that the rating agencies were not properly informed by the issuers and their investment banks; it is still not clear why those information deficits were not discovered by the rating agencies and whether they did not sanction this behaviour.[193] Moreover, one assumes that also the increasing regulatory use of ratings and several abovementioned conflicts of interests contributed to several assessment faults.[194] Finally, one has to consider that the rating of financial products is completely different from the rating of corporations; whereas the rating of corporations refers to their financial stability

188 Ibid.

189 Cf. Hertz-Eichenrode/Illenberger/Jesch/Keller/Klebeck/Rocholl, Private Equity-Lexikon (2011), p. 191 f.; Levin-Report (2011), pp. 26 ff.

190 Cf. *Volkart,* Corporate Finance (2008), p. 488.

191 Cf. *Volkart,* Corporate Finance (2008), p. 883.

192 Cf. *Volkart,* Corporate Finance (2008), p. 488.

193 Cf. *Kübler* in Festschrift für Schwark (2009) p. 499 (505).

194 Cf. *Kübler* in Festschrift für Schwark (2009) p. 499 (505).

and their prospective cash flow, the rating of financial products sets the focus on a "pool" of claims that are directed towards a couple of debtors whose individual financial status cannot be identified – in one case, it happens as an empirical analysis and assessment, and in the other case, the assessment is based on quantifying methods.[195] Below the line, there are various factors that reduce the reliability and accuracy of the assessment of structured financial products that become even more serious by the "pooling" of MBS, the issuing and distribution of new titles (CDOs, SACs) and the impossibility to assess the risk of the untimely debt retirement of a mortgage.[196]

Furthermore, the main problem with the CRAs was that they were primarily involved with the assessment of single instruments, such as bonds and, moreover, that they did not avail of the necessary expertise to launch financial products with a higher complexity such as CDOs. Thus, there was an inherent conflict of interest with the rating being paid for the originating bank. The CRAs also would have used the originating investment firms' own models and were compelled under substantial pressure to provide triple A ratings if they did not want to lose the investment firm to another CRA – consequently there were substantial conflicts of interest. In retrospective, the initial ratings were too high, beginning with the first downgrades which became even more serious with subsequent down grades.

The CRAs evidently misplaced the relevant risk. All in all, one can identify two major faults within all of the financial models that were used before the financial crisis of 2008/2009. Firstly, they did not incorporate any data on a decline in housing prices. This assessment fault is particularly due to US property prices, which alwayshad influence, apart from the development in the 1930s. Secondly, the financial models used by the CRAs did not incorporate correlation data, including market prices that were moving together rather than against each other.

---

[195] Cf. *Kübler* in Festschrift für Schwark (2009) p. 499 (506).

[196] Ibid.

If one can draw any lesson from the interference at the rating agencies, the future regulatory framework should embrace a mandatory financial supervision that should be located at the European level and that should grant an independent assessment of financial products, corporations and countries. Following Walker, one way to avoid a similar crisis in the future is that all debts are rated properly in very case[197] because this had not been the case up to September 2008. A bigger transparency of the rating agency's creditworthiness statements could have contributed to a more critical public opinion of the role of the rating agencies.

The recent financial crisis demonstrated the signification of an independent rating for a well-functioning financial market and a well-functioning economy as a whole. A realistic assessment of financial products contributes to an adequate balance of interests between all market participants. It is one essential condition of a more sustainable regulatory framework. One first step towards the realisation of this objective has been undertaken with the implementation of the European Systemic Risk Board (ESRB[198]).

1.6. International separation and securitisation of risks

1.6.1. The originate-to-hold model as the initial point

Another core reason of the recent financial crisis is the international separation, specifically the securitisation of risks that was already mentioned in the context of the OTD. Traditionally, under the OTH, the risks of mortgage loans and other comparatively complex financial products remain in the hands of the same credit institute that issued the mortgage loan. If one concentrates the expectation of profits and the risk of losses in the hand of the same credit institution, the respective financial vehicle is comparatively easy to handle because its editor can monitor the growth of the product at any time. Also under the conditions of eco-

---

197 Cf. *Walker,* in: The Future of financial regulation (2010), pp. 179 (195 ff.).

198 For further information on the new European supervisory architecture see *Bauer/Boegl,* BKR (2011), pp. 177 ff.; *N.N.,* Larosière-Gruppe, Auszüge aus Presseartikeln No. 37/2010, pp. 7-8; *Nietsch/Graef,* ZBB (2010), pp. 12 ff.; *Zülch/Hoffmann/Detzen,* EWS (2011), pp. 167 ff.

nomic globalisation the editor of the financial product retains the impact on the financial product all the time. Its growth is comparatively easy to monitor and thus transparent.

1.6.2. The originate-to-distribute model

Under the OTD that was based on the separation of chances and risks came a dramatic change. The OTD can be described as the practice where a bank originates loans and credit card receivables and securitises them, so that the credit risks are distributed to other investors.[199] Credit risk exists because the cash flows to be received by the bond markets investors are not certain.[200] The securitisation of financial products stood for an important and useful tool in financial markets for many years and finally contributed to the housing bubble based on the idea to sell portfolios of mortgages to companies that created products for investors from them.[201] In comparison to structured finance that tends to a particular type of more traditional financial instruments – such as bonds, loans and notes –[202] the technique of securitisation is based on a general asset pool.[203]

On the one hand, the securitisation of risks leads to a suppression of the portfolio manager's personal liability. In particular, the model of transnational risk separation consequently led to a separation of the underlying risk management from the rating and trading of financial instruments involved.[204] The portfolio managers speculatively set on a continuous growth of those financial products they edited themselves and concurrently lost the impact on that growth because their risks were distributed all over the world. In particular, the allocation or distribution of risk across the market probably became obscure with the over-the-

199 *Hull,* Risk Management (2011), p. 525.
200 Cf. *Lee/Lee,* Encyclopedia of Finance (2006), p. 75.
201 Cf. *Hull,* Risk Management (2010), p. 336.
202 The term "note" stands for an unsecured debt with maturity of usually less than 15 years, cf. *Lee/Lee,* Encyclopedia of Finance (2006), p. 192.
203 Cf. *Basel Commitee on Banking Supervision,* Revisions (2013), pp. 4 ff.
204 Cf. *N.N.,* Growth Strategies, pp. 19 (30 ff., 42 ff.).

counter (OTC[205]) character of securitisation and the increasing use of off-balance sheet holding instruments, SIVs and bank conduits.[206] In particular, the OTC business became very successful after the terminating of the convertibility of gold in 1971. Up to that year, the Breton Woods Agreement, which was based on David Ricardo's idea of the comparative advantages of costs[207] , defined a fixed (mutual) currency exchange system on a gold standard, which consequently led to the expansion of currency swaps such as the OTC; the OTC transactions are executed by the banks in their currency commerce centres for their customers.[208]

Finally, the FCIC draws the conclusion that OTC-derivates significantly contributed to the outbreak of the crisis. Namely, the taking effect of the law on the prohibition of the regulation of OTC-transactions in the year 2000 could be seen as a turning point on the road towards the financial crisis of 2008/2009.[209] Without underlying any supervision, the OTC-derivates became rapidly out of control while increasing to a total transaction volume of 673 trillion US$.[210] The existence of millions of derivate contracts of many different kinds, from the most important and systemically relevant financial institutions led to insecurity and panic and contributed additionally to the acceleration of governmental support for the affected companies.[211]

---

205 The so-called over-the-counter market is a market where traders deal by phone and usually represent financial institutions, corporations and fund managers, cf. *Hull,* Risk Management (2010), p. 526; in other words, it stands for a telecommunications network of dealers who provide liquidity to investors by their willingness to "make markets" in particular securities, cf. *Lee/Lee,* Encyclopedia of Finance (2006), p. 199.

206 By name, financial corporations such as Citigroup, UBS and Goldman Sachs restricted into difficulties with their use of conduits that can be defined as specific-purpose highly geared investment vehicles (conduits, SIVs) established off-balance sheet. As subsidiaries or funds, conduits invest in assets with a comparatively high return and long duration. They finance themselves by the release of ABCPs. Famous conduits are the government-sponsored entities *Fannie Mae* and *Freddie Mac.*

207 On the theory of comparative advantages of costs cf. *Tietje,* in: Tietje, Internationales Wirtschaftsrecht (2009), § 3, Bullet No. 8.

208 Cf. *Bloss/Ernst/Häcker/Sörensen,* Financial Engineering (2011), p. 273.

209 Cf. *Nationale Kommission zur Untersuchung der Finanz- und Wirtschaftskrise,* Schlussfolgerungen (2009), p. 15.

210 Cf. *FCIC,* Financial Crisis Inquiry Report (2011), p. 24.

211 Cf. *FCIC,* Financial Crisis Inquiry Report (2011), p. 411; *Nationale Kommission zur Untersuchung der Finanz- und Wirtschaftskrise,* Schlussfolgerungen (2009), p. 15.

One can illustrate this development with the metaphor of a person who only views the world with only one eye open. By doing this, the portfolio managers lost their control on the distribution and the further development of the edited financial products. It became a big speculation bubble that had to burst sooner or later and which could have been prevented if the securitisation of risks had competed with an advanced monitoring system, enabling the portfolio managers to obtain the essential information on the growth of the financial products – including in the case of an intercontinental securitisation of risks. It is necessary to establish a monitoring system that sets the focus on the price inflation and limits asset price bubbles and coordinates relevant interest rates, exchange rates economic policies and fiscal politics.[212] Finally, the rise of the OTD consequently caused increasingly high levels on stress on the more traditional money markets and on the liquidity management devices of central banks in many countries.[213] Because liquidity of financial institutions interacts with their solvency, the frontier between liquidity and insolvency became blurred and, at the eve of the financial crisis of 2008/2009, the central banks primarily acted as the lenders of last resort (LLR).[214]

1.7. Shadow banking as a cause of the financial crisis 2008/2009?

1.7.1. Introduction, overview and background

Probably the most important function of the financial markets is to support the activities of the real economy[215] by financing the respective activities and – moreover – to transform, access and to monitor terms and production batches.[216] To achieve any sustainable and satisfactory economic growth of the real economy and to promote new business models like start up-companies that depend on

---

212 Cf. *Walker*, in: The Future of financial regulation (2010), pp. 179 (196).

213 As Walker emphasizes moreover, the financial crisis 2008/2009 was (therefore) a liquidity crisis rather than capital crisis, cf. *Walker*, in: The Future of financial regulation (2010), pp. 179 (196).

214 Cf. *Le Maux/Scialom*, Cambridge Journal of Economics Vol. 37 (2013), pp. 1 f.

215 Definition cf. Annotation No. 39.

216 Cf. *Walter*, in: Bechtold/Jickeli/Joachim/Rohe, FS Möschel (2011), pp. 969, 970.

a steady and satisfactory supply of venture capital, it takes the legal framework that secures those economic requirements. There is little doubt that the financial crisis of 2008/2009 was a crisis of insufficient liquidity. The steady availability of adequate liquidity is one essential condition of the autonomous value-added process of the banking segment.[217]

The before-mentioned need of corporations and consumers significantly contributed to the rise of a business model that is well known as shadow banking[218]. Notably, the Basel Capital Accord, the global economic disequilibrium between the industrial countries and the emerging countries[219] and the rapid growth of the transnational capital flows after the introduction of the Euro on 1 January 1999 enormously contributed to the rise of shadow banking since the overcapacities in the European banking segment increased the predominant margin pressure – those overcapacities led to the decline of the credit standards and resulted in risky investments on the US-American real estate market.[220] Huertas points out that, with the benefit of hindsight, shadow banking was probably the most severe aspect of finance during the pre-crisis boom.[221]

According to the inquiry results of the FSB, the total transaction volume of the shadow banking segment almost doubled from the beginning of the 20th century until the beginning of the financial crisis of 2008/2009 to some 60 billion US$, whereas that of the regulated banking segment covered little over 100 billion US$.[222] Nevertheless, it seems important to realize that the total transaction volume of the shadow banking segment nationally defers, as it turns out by a

217 Cf. *Walter,* in: Bechtold/Jickeli/Joachim/Rohe, FS Möschel (2011), pp. 969, 970.

218 On the system of shadow banking cf. *Adrian/Ashcraft,* Shadow banking (2012), pp. 1 ff.; *Bengtsson,* Shadow banking (2009), pp. 1 ff.; *Gennaioli/Shleifer/Vishny,* shadow banking (2011), pp. 1 ff.; *Moe,* Shadow banking (2012), pp. 1 ff.; *Ordonez,* Sustainable shadow banking (2013), pp. 1 ff.; *Rudolph,* ZfbF (12/2012), pp. 846 ff.; *Rudolph,* Kreditwesen (13/2012), pp. 650 ff.; *Rudolph,* in: Bortenlänger, Aktie und Kapitalmarkt (2013), pp. 19 ff.; *Schalast,* BB (Die erste Seite 2012); *Schrooten,* ZfBW (1/2012), p. 4 ff.; *Utzig,* Die Bank (10/2012), pp. 80 ff.

219 Notably Brasil, Russia, India, Chine, Vietnam, South Africa, Indonesia and Turkey.

220 Cf. *Zimmermann,* ZfBW (2/2012), pp. 105, 106.

221 Cp. *Huertas,* Crisis (2010), p. 18.

222 Cf. *FSB,* Shadow Banking: Strengthening Oversight and Regulation (2011), published under http://www.financialstabilityboard.org/publications/r_111027a.pdf.

comparison between Europe and the United States where the shadow banking segment dramatically decreased from 20 billion US$ down to 15 billion US$ at the end of 2011, whereas that of the Euro zone still increased from 8.5 billion Euro in 2007 to 11 billion Euro at the end of the first half of 2011.[223] In the November of 2012, the shadow banking segment already covered a total transaction volume by some 67 Billion US$ in the United States.

The enormous growth of the shadow banking segment can be seen as one consequence of the massive (economic) disequilibrium between the demand for safe investments, which means bonds, and the factual offer for safe investments reflecting the global disequilibrium that occurs in the balances on capital accounts and the balance of current accounts between Asia and the United States: The enormous savings of the emerging countries were particularly channeled into the high liquid US-treasury markets.[224] As the US-treasury market has been revealed to be too small to correspond with the enormous demand for safe investments, US-American credit-institutes began to release additional – putatively safe – AAA-rated assets in the subprime segment of the US-American real estate market – a problem that even has not been solved after the burst of the subprime-bubble.[225]

According to the FSB, the national-economic meaning of the shadow banking segment is underlined by the real development between 2002 and 2010: In this time period, the global sales of shadow banking segment doubled up to 46 Billion Euro, which corresponds to 25 percent of the global financial market.[226]

---

223 Cf.. *ECB,* shadow banking in the Euro area - an overview, Occasional Paper No. 133 (2012), published under http://www.ecb.europa.eu/pub/pdf/scpops/ecbocp133.pdf

224 Cf. *Zimmermann,* ZfBW (2/2012), pp. 105, 105.

225 Cf. *Zimmermann,* ZfBW (2/2012), pp. 105, 105; on the origins of the sub-primie crisis in resume cf. *Lewis,* Accounting Forum Vol. 33 (2009), pp. 114 ff.

226 Cf. http://www.handelsblatt.com/unternehmen/banken/schattenbanken-die-67-billionen-dollar-branche/7407732.html

According to the results of the European Commission, the quote of the shadow banking covers some 5 percent, in the United Kingdom remarkably 13 percent.[227]

In Europe, already under Basel II, there were strong incentives to outsource assets from the balance-sheets of the regular banks to SPVs to safe equity.[228] The widespread trend towards shadow banking is obviously driven by Basel III and primarily results from the legal obligation of (traditional) banks to generally underlay each credit risk with a sufficient equity position that gives them a reason to outsource the respective risks at a SPV that is able to circumvent the financial supervision – a business model that significantly contributed to the crisis of financial corporations like HRE or Deutsche Industriebank AG (IKB).[229]

1.7.2. Definition of shadow banking

In view of the before-mentioned development, the term shadow banking is a politically charged buzzword.[230] It is often used in the context of other buzzwords as one drift of the financial crisis of 2008/2009. The expression shadow banking is not legally defined. Neither the international financial law nor the European financial provides any legal definition. Officially, the expression shadow banking was used by Paul McCulley, US-American economist and former managing director of the Pacific Investment Management Company (PIMCO[231]), at the Economic Symposium of the Federal Reserve Bank of Kansas City in Jackson Hyde (USA) in September of 2007. McCulley explained the expression shadow banking as

227 Cf. http://www.handelsblatt.com/unternehmen/banken/schattenbanken-die-67-billionen-dollar-branche/7407732.html

228 Cf. *Zimmermann,* ZfBW (2/2012), pp. 105, 106.

229 Cf. http://www.handelsblatt.com/unternehmen/banken/schattenbanken-die-67-billionen-dollar-branche/7407732.html.

230 Cf. *European Commission,* Green Paper Shadow Banking (2012), p. 3.

231 Presence in the internet: http://www.pimco.com/Pages/default.aspx.

"the whole alphabet soup of leveraged up non-banking investment conduits, vehicles and structures.[232]*"*

This very first definition already hinted at the small equity level as one decisive feature of shadow banking by taking using expression "leveraged" and, moreover, defining conduits as one typical financial mean of shadow banking. Three years later, it was followed by (another) definition that was used by the Federal Reserve Bank of New York:

"Financial intermediaries that conduct maturity, credit and liquidity transformation without access to central bank liquidity or public sector credit guarantees[233]*".*

On the one hand, the before-mentioned definition of the New York Fed also embraced financial corporations, hedge funds, investment funds, Government Sponsored entities as Fannie Mae and Freddy Mac and investment banks – on the other hand, it was even restricted to these entities.[234] Yet the FSB widened the before-mentioned definition by the typical financial operations and activities of shadow banking by comprising the shadow banking phenomena as

"the system of credit intermediation that involves entities and activities outside the regular banking system[235]*".*

According to this definition, shadow banking is notably characterized by three significant features: Primarily, shadow banks fulfill one function that is very similar to that of the regular banks by offering credit intermediation; secondly, the credit intermediation is fulfilled by several actors that closely cooperate at the financial market; thirdly, the actors of the shadow bank market are neither subject to the legal bank supervision nor do they have access to central bank

---

232 Cf. *McCulley,* Teton reflections (2007), published under http://www.pimco.com/EN/Insights/Pages/GCBF%20August-%20September%202007.aspx.

233 Cf. *Pozsar/Adrian/Ashcraft/Boesky,* Shadow Banking, Federal Reserve Bank of New York Staff Report No. 458 (July 2010).

234 Cf. *Utzig,* Die Bank (10/2012), pp. 80, 80.

235 *FSB,* Shadow Banking - Strengthening Oversight and Regulation (2011).

liquidity ("parallelism of credit intermediation[236]"). Nevertheless, the credit intermediation of shadow banks does not involve single retail customers but a complex counter bearing of (private) institutional investors directed to the money market. All in all, shadow banks share a certain financial business model that runs almost the same business transactions like the regulated banking segment.[237]

Following the Green Paper of the European Commission (EC-Green per[238]), which was based on the recommendations of the FSB (FSB Global Shadow Banking Monitoring Report[239]), shadow banking activities typically consist of securitisations, security loan and pension transactions ("Repos"[240]).[241] Furthermore, they cover different kinds of SPVs; money market funds (MMF[242]) and other kinds of investment funds or investment products with features similar to deposits; they serve investment funds that place credits, invest in credit products, operate highly leveraged, and invest in funds that are placed outside of the stock exchange (exchange traded funds, ETF), such as hedge funds.[243] Finally, shadow banks hold financing corporations and securities trading houses that place credits or credit guarantees or that accomplish liquidity- and term-transformations without underlying bank regulation; they invest in assurance and re-assurance companies that launch or secure credit products.

According to the definition of the FSB, shadow banking covers a system of credit intermediation including entities and activities outside the regular banking

---

236 Cf. *Utzig,* Die Bank (10/2012), pp. 80, 81.

237 Cf. *Fischer,* Kreditwesen (10/2012), pp. 485, 485.

238 *European Commission,* Green Paper Shadow Banking, dated 19 March 2012, published under http://ec.europa.eu/internal_market/bank/docs/shadow/green-paper_en.pdf.

239 Cf. *FSB,* Shadow Banking: Strengthening Oversight and Regulation (2011), published under http://www.financialstabilityboard.org/publications/r_111027a.pdf.; *FSB,* Global Shadow Banking Monitoring Report (2012), dated 18 November 2012, published under http://www.financialstabilityboard.org/publications/r_121118c.pdf.

240 On the Repo-market cf. *Hördahl/King,* BIS Quarterly Review (12/2008): pp. 37 ff.

241 Cf. *Fischer,* Kreditwesen (10/2012), pp. 485, 485.

242 So far there has been no harmonization or regulation at the European level on what features constitute a MMF. Typically, a MMF is set up as an UCITS, cf. *Bengtsson,* Shadow banking (2009), European Money Market funds - Backgrounds.

243 On the current discussion of risk and regulatory engagement concerning hedge funds cf. *FSA,* Discussion Paper 05/4, pp. 1 ff.

system.[244] In particular, they cover money market funds, exchange traded index-funds, certain hedge-funds, and security structures offer financial affairs economically similar to the deposit and credit affairs of the (regulated) banks.[245]

Although the before-mentioned definitions demonstrate a broad congruency of the shadow bank activities with those of the regular banks, one cannot deny another significant feature of shadow banks which distinguishes them from regular banks: Shadow banks do not avail of the legal status of a bank. For example, they are SPVs that run transformations of liquidity and terms, such as corporations offering securitisations – conduits (ABCP), other SPVs, MMFs and other kinds of investment funds that offer products with typical features – making them vulnerable for sudden and unexpected calls for the investor deposits (bank-runs) or investment funds that place credits or operating highly leveraged or ETFs.[246]

1.7.3. Conception of shadow banking

The second decisive feature of shadow banking is the close link with the originating bank. Due to the "operating definition" of the FSB, the operating of shadow banks leads to financial disintermediation (legal arbitration) or sets on a close link (network) with the established banking system that defines one essential feature for financial regulation, the setting of systemic risks.[247] Due to the close link between originating bank and shadow bank, numerous banks generate enormous profits resulting from "their" shadow bank activities and hold direct and indirect credit exposures towards the shadow banks.[248]

Shadow banking happens if the regulated credit institute outsources certain components of its balance sheet to a SPV that is not subject to the legal require-

244 Cf. http://wirtschaftslexikon.gabler.de/Definition/verbriefung-von-kreditportfolios.html.
245 Cf. *Fischer,* Kreditwesen (10/2012), pp. 485, 485.
246 Cf. *European Commission,* Green Paper Shadow Banking (2012), p. 4.
247 Cf. *Rudolph,* in: Bortenlänger, Aktie und Kapitalmarkt (2013), pp. 19, 27.
248 Cf. Pozsar/Adrian/Ashcraft/Boesky, Shadow Banking, Federal Reserve Bank of New York Staff Report No. 458 (July 2010), pp. 11-20.

ments.[249] In particular, the SPV must not run a minimum equity position – as one consequence, it can achieve an over-averaged yield which avails of an over-averaged attractiveness towards (international) investors. Namely, it is not subject to the requirements of Basel III. The shadow banking system enables the originating bank to get rid of significant balance risks enhancing solvency and minimizing the respective refinancing costs[250]. In view of the awareness that the financial crisis 2008/2009 was (primarily) a crisis of liquidity, a solid and diversified refinancing, including an adequate number of stable sources, seems essential.[251]

As the traditional banking system, the typical shadow banking concept is based on three actors: The depositor, the debtor and – instead of the regular bank – the shadow bank, the finance corporation with non-banking character. In contrast to the traditional banking system, the depositors do not allocate their financial means at deposit accounts but in money market funds that the respective bank deposits in debts of the shadow banks – the credit intermediation is not accomplished under the same "roof" but within a very large and often non-transparent chain of entities that – as already mentioned – do not avail of the (legal) bank status.[252]

Probably, the most significant difference between the regular bank segment and the shadow bank segment is that the shadow bank system transforms long-term invested savings into short-term money market vehicles to enable refinancing day-by-day.[253] The operative point is that the depositors of the money market

249 On the impact of off-balance-sheet activities on banks returns cf. *Calmès/Théoret,* Journal of Banking & Finance Vol. 34 (July 2010), pp. 1719 ff.

250 The refinancing costs cover that amount of money any borrower is obliged to pay upfront to refinance a mortgage. The Refinancing costs are typically similar to the closing costs a borrower has to invest that point of time he firstly pays for a real estate object, cf. http://www.investorglossary.com/refinancing-cost.htm.

251 Cf. *Walter,* in: Bechtold/Jickeli/Joachim/Rohe, FS Möschel (2011), pp. 969, 974.

252 Cf. Pozsar/Adrian/Ashcraft/Boesky, Shadow Banking, Federal Reserve Bank of New York Staff Report No. 458 (July 2010), p. 11 f.

253 Cf. Pozsar/Singh, The Nonbank Nexus and the Shadow Banking System, IMF Working Paper WP No. 11/289, p. 7.

funds are high volatile actors that are subject to a herd instinct[254] and therefore can easily create a bank-run and – simultaneously – a couple of false incentives by the actors resulting from the complex chain of credit intermediation.[255] In particular, as one consequence of the increasing margin pressure resulting from the deregulation of the banking segment and the introduction of the Euro, many banks could no longer afford to keep credits in their balance sheets instead of selling these credits to institutional investors to finance their credit business: The shadow banking system is particularly based on selling money market vehicles[256] to money market funds.[257]

1.7.4. ABCP-conduits in particular

ABCP-conduits is another type of credit intermediation and probably the prototype of shadow banking[258]. They represent one typical instrument that is used in the shadow banking system. They can be defined as SPVs that are sponsored by commercial banks to purchase long term assets issuing short term commercial paper and, moreover, due to their legal character as SPVs, do not underlay any (legal) capital requirement.[259] Against the background that ABCPs became the most important mechanism used by banks to legal arbitrage[260], from January 2004 to July 2007 the ABCP-segment rose from US$ 650 billion to US$ 1.3 trillion.[261] On the eve of the beginning of the financial crisis of 2008/2009, ABCP was the largest money market instrument in the United States – treasury bills

---

254 Herding can be defined as a situation in which traders emulate or follow the actions of other traders, cf. *Garbaravicius Dierick,* ECB-Occasional Paper No. 34 (August 2005), p. 59.

255 Cf. Zimmermann, ZfBW (2/2012), pp. 105, 107.

256 Definition Money market cf. Annotation No. 49.

257 Cf. *G. Gorton,* Slapped in the face by the Invisible hand. Banking and the panic of 2007, prepared for the Federal Reserve Bank of Atlanta´s 2009 Financial Markets Conference: Financial Innovation and Crisis, 11.-13.05.2009, Version of May/5th/2009, pp. 23 ff.

258 Cf. *Rudolph,* in: Bortenlänger, Aktie und Kapitalmarkt (2013), pp. 19, 27.

259 Vgl. *Bengtsson,* Shadow banking (2009), introduction.

260 As *Garbaravicius/Dierick* points out, arbitrage strategies do not eliminate all risks and do entail some risk of loss or uncertainty about total profits. In theory, a transaction that produces risk-free profit by exploiting mispriced securities or any other assets while hedging all risk, cf. *Garbaravicius/Dierick,* ECB-Occasional Paper No. 34 (August 2005), p. 1 ff.

261 Vgl. *Bengtsson,* Shadow banking (2009), introduction.

only covered a business volume of about $940 billion outstanding.[262] Typical ABCP-conduit-activities consist of activities such as originating, sponsoring and deposing. Another significant feature of shadow banks is the OTC-supply with equity that is typically offered by hedge funds and private equity corporations.

Thus, although shadow banks are neither integrated into the system of state deposit guarantee nor into the liquidity support of the central bank, they cover fundamental functions of a credit institute and the respective risks.[263] As hedge funds or private equity-funds the shadow banking system is not illegal.[264] The outsourcing of typical banking activities at a SPV is evidently one widespread technique of the grey capital market[265]. Nevertheless, shadow banks do not operate within a legal grey area. They operate on a clearly defined legal basis and typically represent high specialized entities that overtake certain activities outsourced by regulated banks.[266]

1.7.5. Effects of shadow banking

One serious economic effect resulting from the shadow bank segment can be seen in the systemic danger by the conduit model. Already the Austrian economist August von Hayek, Nobel laureate and important forerunner of the neo-liberalism, hinted at those risks resulting from off-balanced activities by the his explanation

"The characteristic peculiarity of these forms of credit is that they spring up without being subject to any central control but once they have come into exist-

---

262 Vgl. *Bengtsson,* Shadow banking (2009), introduction.

263 Cf. *Rudolph,* in: Bortenlänger, Aktie und Kapitalmarkt (2013), pp. 19, 27.

264 Cf. *Rudolph,* in: Bortenlänger, Aktie und Kapitalmarkt (2013), pp. 19, 31.

265 The grey capital market either covers a market where a product is bought and sold outside of the manufacturers authorized channels or the unofficial trading of a company´s shares, usually before they are issued in an initial public offering (IPO), cf. http://www.investopedia.com/terms/g/greymarket.asp.

266 Cf. *Zimmermann,* ZfBW (2/2012), pp. 105, 106.

ence their convertibility into other forms of money must be possible if any collapse of credit is to be avoided.[267]"

Not seldom, all securitisation activities of a credit institute are ascribed to the shadow bank as the hidden entity, whereby even the basic securitisation model can cause a systemic risk, if the sponsoring bank additionally overtakes a market-maker-function or the investors run a higher leveraged strategy that makes them themselves systemically significant.[268] Namely, the conduit-model[269] – a widespread financial mean at the eve of the financial crisis 2008/2009 – can cause additional risks up to a bank-run on single or several credit institutes, if the sponsoring bank has (typically) given one promise of liquidity.[270] The danger of systemic risk do often result from shadow banks that offer the processes of the credit-, term- and liquidity-transformation by using the support of a network of bilateral contracts directly over the financial markets.[271]

Within the securitization, the regulated credit institutes give up some of their traditional credit intermediation functions and act as originators of the credit claims. Moreover, they sponsor and consult the SPVs and take the role of investment bankers that place the ABS and the CLOs at the market. By doing this, they transfer their liability for the quality of the pooled credit placements at the SPV that even transfer the generated risk premiums to the holders of the ABS to offer them an incentive to invest in the structured securities. Notably, advanced techniques like the before-mentioned ABCP contributed to the rise of shadow banking by outsourcing not only the respective risks and liquidity but by transferring the cash flow within the pool to a highly specialized management.[272]

Among the (economic) advantages resulting from the use of shadow banks, one can identify typical advantages of specialization and, moreover, regulatory

267 Cf. *Hayek,* Prices and production (1935), pp. 1 ff.
268 Cf. *Rudolph,* in: Bortenlänger, Aktie und Kapitalmarkt (2013), pp. 19, 27.
269 Cf. Annotation No. 206.
270 Cf. *Rudolph,* in: Bortenlänger, Aktie und Kapitalmarkt (2013), pp. 19, 27.
271 Cf. *BVB* (July 2012).
272 Cf. *Rudolph,* in: Bortenlänger, Aktie und Kapitalmarkt (2013), pp. 19, 23.

privileges: Those external effects must not be internalized, which causes competitive advantages.[273] Rudolph holds therefore the view that, to keep a satisfactory level of financial stability[274] and to create a "level playing field", it seems inevitable to subject shadow banks to a possible "run-effect" and a more effective and efficient regulation.[275] Probably the most significant disadvantage of shadow banking consists of the less transparency towards investors, creditors and state supervision.[276]

Another disadvantage that is closely linked to the less transparency is the close relation of the SPV to the credit institute that is subject to the respective regulation. As one consequence, the before-mentioned bank runs can cause fatal chain reactions and a non-controlled insolvency that can easily spill over to other credit institutes even in foreign countries,[277] just as it happened after the collapse of the Government sponsored entities (GSE) Fannie Mae and Freddy Mac. Referring to the before-mentioned FSB-research, this systemic risk is particularly current in times of short liquidity, Notably, the FSB hints at the risk that a non-controlled insolvency could cause systemic risks resulting from the close link towards the originating bank and, moreover, the regulatory omission of shadow banking, which could cause significant regulatory arbitrage.[278]

As one consequence of the 2008/2009 bank run, the business model of the unlimited transformation of risks, terms and liquidity was suddenly destroyed and the affected credit institutes were forced to take those securities collected in the conduits into their own balance sheets and to organize the refinancing on their own – in those cases in which this did not succeed, they were forced to ac-

---

273 Cf. *Rudolph,* in: Bortenlänger, Aktie und Kapitalmarkt (2013), pp. 19, 27.

274 On hedge funds and ist impact to financial stability cf. *Garbaravicius/Dierick,* ECB-Occasional Paper No. 34 (August 2005), pp. 1 ff.

275 Cf. *Rudolph,* in: Bortenlänger, Aktie und Kapitalmarkt (2013), pp. 19, 27.

276 On the question whether the European financial market supervision sets a too strong focus on the speed of regulation cf. *Paul,* ZfBW (1/2013), p. 2 ff.

277 Cf. *Rudolph,* in: Bortenlänger, Aktie und Kapitalmarkt (2013), pp. 19, 27; annotations on the effiency and stability of financial markets cf. *Lux,* ZfBW „Verdient der Markt noch unser Vertrauen" (2013), p. 16 ff.; *Lewis,* Accounting Forum Vol. 33 (2009), pp. 114

278 Cf. *European Commission,* Green Paper Shadow Banking (2012), p. 1.

cept the (direct) support of another credit institute or the state.[279] As Perotti points out, it became clear that Safe harbor not only undermines unsecured claims like deposit insurance and tax claims, but it possibly create external effects on markets.[280]

1.7.6. Regulation of shadow banking

In principal, one could set the regulatory focus on the legal entities, the fund managers, as preferred by the European Commission ("direct approach"), the interfaces between the shadow banks and the sponsoring banks ("indirect approach"), the respective shadow banking activities or consider an approach that is integrated into a macro-prudential regulation, which could be preferable due to the practical challenge to assigning the respective risks to one single financial entity or institution.[281] A direct regulation like the AIFMD does not consider the legal form of the entity which causes a stronger "compliance pressure" on many financial institutions and enhance the compliance costs[282] of these entities.[283]

As already mentioned, due to increasing economic significance of shadow banking even after the financial crisis of 2008/2009, the European Commission produced the Green Paper. It is based on a market survey among market participants and capital market institutions and reflects the research results of the FSB. As one regulatory objective, the Green Paper aims at the containment of regulatory arbitrage into the grey-market to secure an adequate supervision of this market and to identify potential systemic risks on time.[284] As the AIFMD, the Green Paper of the European Commission prefers a direct approach that considers the special assets instead of the financial product, specifically the investment strategy or the business interfaces towards other corporations. Thus, it exclusively defines

279 Cf. *Rudolph,* in: Bortenlänger, Aktie und Kapitalmarkt (2013), pp. 19, 25.
280 Cf. *Perotti,* Shadow Banking (2012), p. 3.
281 Cf. *Rudolph,* in: Bortenlänger, Aktie und Kapitalmarkt (2013), pp. 19, 31.
282 Compliance costs cover those payments that result by those measures that have to be taken by a corporation to secure the steady fulfillment of all respective legal requirements.
283 On the compliance requirements subject to the AIFMD cf. *Klebeck/Zollinger,* BB (9/2013), p. 459 ff.
284 Cf. *Fischer,* Kreditwesen (10/2012), pp. 485, 485.

the special assets that shall underlie a European regulation of the shadow banking segment.

Referring to its legal objective, the Green Paper shall enhance the resistivity of the EU-financial system, secure that any financial operation contributes to economic growth. This objective shall be realized by monitoring the current situation at the financial markets, submitting recommendations on this topic and, through this, enabling a broad consultation of the different stakeholders.[285] Macro-prudentially, it takes one comprehensive identification, valuation and conjunction of systemically relevant information.[286] To effectively face future systemic risks, there is obviously the need for careful monitoring and regulation of the shadow banking system, as the FSB points out.[287]

Instead of the direct regulation of shadow banking, which is the preferable option of the European Commission, the FSB prefers an indirect regulation, focusing on the interfaces between originating banks and shadow banks. Under the conduct of Lord Adair Turner, chief of the British supervisory body Financial Service Authority (FSA[288]) and based on the recommendations of the "High-level-task-force", the FSB recommends an indirect regulation basing on a three-step-concept:[289]

Primarily, the nature and the total transaction volume of the shadow banking activities shall be monitored ("Micro-Mapping"); secondly, the most significant risk factors for financial stability shall be focused, notably those risks resulting from the risk-, term- and stability transformation – besides the last mentioned risks, the FSB regards the regulation arbitrage as another symptom of shadow banking; thirdly, the possible systemic crises that probably result from the before-mentioned risks and the regulatory arbitrage shall be identified. In addition,

285 Cf. *European Commission,* Green Paper Shadow Banking (2012), p. 2.
286 Cf. article 15 statutory order (EU) No. 1092/2010.
287 On the future of shadow banking regulation cf. http://wirtschaftslexikon.gabler.de/Definition/verbriefung-von-kreditportfolios.html.
288 Internet Presence: http://www.fsa.gov.uk/.
289 Cf. *Rudolph,* in: Bortenlänger, Aktie und Kapitalmarkt (2013), pp. 19, 31 f.

the (additional) yield, the respective indicators for the “free lunch”, the relations with the established banking system and the growth of the shadow banking activities shall be disclosed (enhanced disclosure).

According to the regulatory conception of the FSB there are five principles that should be mandatory for any regulation of the shadow banking segment.[290] Primarily, any regulatory measure should carefully designed to target the externalities and risks of the shadow banking system (“Focus”); secondly, any regulatory measure should be proportional to the risks shadow banking poses to the financial system (“Proportionality”); thirdly, any regulatory measure should be forward-looking and adaptable to emerging risks (“forward-looking and adaptable”); fourthly, any regulatory measure should designed and effectively implemented (“effectiveness”); fifthly, the regulators should regularly assess the effectiveness of their regulatory measures after implementation and make adjustments to improve them as necessary in the light of experience (“assessment and review”).

In October 2011, the FSB released recommendations on regulatory measures to be examined by authorities that are meanwhile partially implemented. As indirect approach, these recommendations face the regulation of MMF, other Shadow banking activities and securities- and pension-transactions.

According to the commentary of the True-Sales-Initiative (TSI) that was released in May 2012, ABS do not correspond to those features that are typically associated with the before-defined terminus shadow banking.[291] The already existing regulation was sufficient to subject ABCP-conduit-activities of the regulated institutions (banks, funds, assurance companies) to the supervision of the responsible authorities. In addition, the TSI emphasizes that each direct regula-

290 Cf. *FSB,* Shadow Banking: Strengthening Oversight and Regulation (2011), published under http://www.financialstabilityboard.org/publications/r_111027a.pdf

291 On the legal character of True-Sale-ABS-transactions cf. *Lackhoff,* Kreditwesen (10/2012), pp. 503 ff.;

tion that does not focus CRD II[292]- and CRD IV-activities would bear the risk of further frictions in the financial market regulation. Furthermore, the TSI highlights that notably ABCP-conduits do not accomplish term- and liquidity-transformations since the sponsoring banks place liquidity lines whose risk is already covered by CDR II and CRD IV.

1.7.7. Consequences of a shadow banking regulation

Finally, the before-mentioned regulatory approaches shall be accessed. In comparison, it is obvious that any direct regulation can cause evade reactions and measures of legal arbitration. Thus, the AIFMD that focuses the managers instead of the investment strategy or the financial product can back up the before-mentioned expansion of the shadow banking system. Consequently, any direct regulation could crystallize as totally ineffective should the total business volume of the shadow banking segment, as it already happened in the United States, exceeds the business volume of the regular banking segment.

One proportional legal approach should secure that it covers the majority of financial institutions and must not initialize a "race to the bottom" that negatively affects the public wealth in the European Union. The before-mentioned business volume of the shadow banking segment underlines the systemic meaning of this banking model and the need for a careful and proportional approach: The

---

292 On September/16th/2009 the European Council and the European Parliament officially released the European draft 2009/111/EG which, in combination with the European draft 2009/27/EG and 2009/83/EG, represents the second legal package of measures to secure financial solidity of banks and security firms. This package of measures aims at the steering of large credits, the quality of equity, the steering of liquidity risks and the risk management of securitised products. For internationally operating bank groups, "supervisory colleges" became mandatory. These requirements were part of those measures taken by the European Commission as a response to the financial crisis 2008/2009 and to strengthen the regulatory frame in those segments that are probably responsible for the financial crisis. These amendments must transformed into national law until October/31st/2010. The before-mentioned drafts are available under http://eur-lex.europa.eu/LexUriServ/LexUriServ.do?uri=OJ:L:2009:302:0097:01:DE:HTML; http://eur-lex.europa.eu/Notice.do?val=493338%3Acs&lang=de&list=493338%3Acs%2C&pos=1&page=1&nbl=1&pgs=10&hwords=&checktexte=checkbox&visu=; http://eur-lex.europa.eu/Notice.do?val=498875:cs&lang=en&list=498875:cs,&pos=1&page=1&nbl=1&pgs=10&hwords=.

stronger the European Union controls regular banks, that stronger is their incentive to circumvent the legal supervision and the stronger the risk of another financial crisis in the future – a drying shrinkage of the shadow banking segment by a relentless regulation could accelerate the "vicious circle" of financial market regulation.[293] A superficial effective regulation neglecting the long-term economic effects can easily turn into a boomerang.

In particular, the attempt of the European Commission to define all shadow banking entities exclusively induces the challenge to find clear features of the already regulated banks and financial institutions without shadow banking character, which could finally result in regulatory omissions – this could make another supervision authority ("shadow banking regulatory board") inevitable.[294]

All in all, an indirect approach, as is recommended by the Commission "Neue Finanzarchitektur", seems preferable since it could contribute to keeping the diversity of financial business models and, moreover, to different risk strategies and different group of customers: Diversity can be seen as one essential factor to stabilize a financial system as a whole.[295] If all banks and shadow banks underlie the same regulatory approach and therefore the same legal restrictions, this regulation could easily create a dangerous pro-cyclical crisis-amplifier.[296] Should another shock happen to the financial markets, this could induce the necessity of suitable reactions like "fire sales[297]" – not one for the banks but also for any equally regulated financial institution.[298] Under those circumstances, it could

293 Cf. http://www.handelsblatt.com/unternehmen/banken/schattenbanken-die-67-billionen-dollar-branche/7407732.html.

294 Cf. *Rudolph,* in: Bortenlänger, Aktie und Kapitalmarkt (2013), pp. 19, 35.

295 Cf. *Rudolph,* in: Bortenlänger, Aktie und Kapitalmarkt (2013), pp. 19, 36.

296 Cf. *Rudolph,* in: Bortenlänger, Aktie und Kapitalmarkt (2013), pp. 19, 36.

297 In general, the expression „fire sales“ is a synonym for selling goods at heavily discounted prices. In the context of the financial markets, it refers to securities that are trading well below their intrinsic value, such as during prolonged bear markets, cf. http://www.investopedia.com/terms/f/firesale.asp.

298 Cf. *Rudolph,* in: Bortenlänger, Aktie und Kapitalmarkt (2013), pp. 19, 36.

be advantageous if there still was a "White knight[299]": „As dark as they are often portrayed, shadow banks may now play the role of white knights for lenders trying to offload risky assets to comply with European regulatory capital targets by the middle of 2012."[300]

Notably the securitisation-model as one widespread manifestation of shadow banking could take on increasing importance in the future corporate financing since the strengthened regulation of the financial segment since the financial crisis of 2008/2009 causes increasing costs to many credit institutions that can generally minimized by the outsourcing of credit claims.[301] Nevertheless, Michael Barnier as the reigning responsible EU-Commissioner for the single European Market prefers to aggravate the rules on the outsourcing of financial transactions and announced a regulatory directive on shadow banking for 2013[302].[303]

In contrast, the German commission "Neue Finanzarchitektur[304]" under the patronage of Ottmar Issing, former chairman of the German Bundesbank, prefers a mandatory charge for shadow banks that could minimize the incentive for the outsourcing of risks.[305] "Neue Finanzarchitektur" recommends that the ECB shall monitor and access all the respective risks.[306] Thereby, Issing prefers an indirect approach due to frictions concerning the enforcement of a direct regulation and, moreover, due to the problem that shadow banking will increase in the future because it seems to be able to develop innovative special solutions in the non-

299 In the context of the financial market law, a white knight is corporation that acquires another corporation on the verge of being taken over by forces deemed undesirable by company officials, cf. http://www.investopedia.com/terms/w/whiteknight.asp.

300 Cp. *Halstrick,* Tighter Bank Rules (2011).

301 Cf. *Rudolph,* in: Bortenlänger, Aktie und Kapitalmarkt (2013), pp. 19, 23.

302 Cf. http://ec.europa.eu/internal_market/finances/committees/#maincontentSec2.

303 Cf. http://www.handelsblatt.com/unternehmen/banken/schattenbanken-die-67-billionen-dollar-branche/7407732.html

304 Against the background of the financial crisis of 2008/2009, the „Neue Finanzarchitektur"-Commission was founded in October 2008 under the patronage of reigning German chancellor, Angela Merkel, to submit propositions on defeating that crisis and to prevent similar crisis in the future. The Commission is well known as Issing-Commission.

305 On the new international architecture of finance Cf. *Dombret/Engelen,* Kreditwesen (22/2012), p. 1156 ff.

306 Cf. http://www.handelsblatt.com/unternehmen/banken/schattenbanken-die-67-billionen-dollar-branche/7407732.html.

regulated financial segment, and a regulatory arbitrage can contribute to the public wealth. A modern Europe without any financial innovations that significantly contribute to economic growth and public wealth is hardly imaginable – notably the resulting credit volume, the climatic change and the pension funds would suffer by an interdiction of securitisations.

Whether any of the before-mentioned recommendations succeed, seems very questionable since, on the one hand, dominant financial centers like those in the United States or in the United Kingdom already announced determined resistivity against any shadow bank regulation and, on the other hand, is seems very ambitious to target some shadow banks since these entities transferred their business to tax havens like the Cayman Islands.[307] Notably an exclusive definition of the shadow bank entities as it is driven in the Green Paper of the European Commission would always bear the risk of regulatory omission.

Namely, Article 5 of the European directive 2011/89/EU, released on 16 November 2011, on the amendment of the directives 98/78/EC, 2002/87/EC, 2006/48/EC and 2009/138/EC concerning additional supervision of financial corporations that belong to a conglomerate (financial directive of the European Union) requires the European Commission to weigh up whether the scope of the directive shall expanded to those corporations such as SPVs that, so far, do not underlay any financial market supervision.[308] The responsible European supervisory bodies prefer a wider scope of the before-mentioned directive since SPVs neither underlay any sectoral reporting requirements.[309] Thus, further regulation of shadow banking activities is expected at the European level.

[307] Cf. http://www.handelsblatt.com/unternehmen/banken/schattenbanken-die-67-billionen-dollar-branche/7407732.html.

[308] Cf. http://wirtschaftslexikon.gabler.de/Archiv/16281/verbriefung-von-kreditportfolios-v9.html.

[309] Cf. http://wirtschaftslexikon.gabler.de/Archiv/16281/verbriefung-von-kreditportfolios-v9.html.

1.7.8. Statement and interim result

All in all, it is obviously a too short perspective to only focus on the (possible) negative effects of shadow banking and, in particular, the economic contribution of hedge funds instead of their positive contribution towards market efficiency and public wealth. Primarily, as one consequence of the enormous acceleration resulting from the economic globalization, the global disequilibria of commerce notably between the industrial countries and the emerging countries and the increasing economic pressure resulting from the digitalization of daily life, any legislation of hedge funds should consider that the financial crisis of 2008/2009 was primarily a crisis of liquidity, and that the steady supply is significant for continual economic growth. Thus, any too strong regulation could have the effect that financial innovations become less attractive or nipped in the bud. An entity that does not underlay the respective legal requirements on equity and supervision may cause higher risks than any regulated bank. But these risks could probably be contained more effectively by a legal approach that focuses the interfaces towards other (regulated) credit institutes instead of facing the legal entities itself.

As Walter, the former chief economist of the Deutsche Bank-group (1990-2009) points out, an adequate and satisfactory response to the financial crisis of 2008/2009 should reduce interdependencies and complexity between the financial market participants: Against the background that the (unexpected) insolvency of a big and strongly networked credit institute could easily affect other (economically sane) market players – as it revealed by the phenomena of contagion[310] –, it seems economically reasonable, legally preferable and inevitable to take legal measures to isolate those "candidates" from the other market participants.[311] Under this provision the mere transaction volume of a financial corporation does not have to be a "source of fear" any longer.[312] In view of this aware-

310 On the phenomena of contagion cf. Systemic risks of insufficient equity (1.2.2.) and Annotation No. 110.

311 Cf. *Walter,* in: Bechtold/Jickeli/Joachim/Rohe, FS Möschel (2011), pp. 969, 975.

312 Cf. *Walter,* in: Bechtold/Jickeli/Joachim/Rohe, FS Möschel (2011), pp. 969, 975.

ness, any adequate legal response to the financial crisis of 2008/2009 should neither focus the entity, as the AIFMD (currently) does, or the mere (financial) business volume, but it should try to disentangle the infrastructure of financial market participants.[313] Therefore, any indirect approach that focuses on the interfaces between the financial market participants seems more preferable than the direct approach driven by the AIFMD. Under the provision of a stronger entanglement of the market infrastructure, hedge funds can perform one significant contribution to market efficiency because they do not underline the general equity requirements.[314]

Under the before-mentioned provision of a stronger entanglement, a stronger containment against the realization of systemic risks can be accomplished through a good Corporate Governance that sets on clearly distinguished corporate structures particularly of financial concerns, intervention of the supervisory board in the case of emergency (restructuring, outsourcing of single concern departments, steady survey of the demands and obligations of shareholders), contingent capital arrangements (capital supply even under the conditions of a difficult market situation, transformation of debt securities into adherent equity), stabilizing funds, authorization for early intervention of the supervisory board) and internationally directed insolvency regimes following the Winding Up-directive of the European Commission and the recommendations of the UN-Commission on International Trade Law.[315]

1.8. Policy of low interests

1.8.1. Expansionary monetary policy

Furthermore, the policy of low interest that was run by the Federal Reserve can be identified as another reason for the recent financial crisis. On the one hand, low interest can be seen as a strong stimulus for the private consumer. Low

313 Cf. *Walter,* in: Bechtold/Jickeli/Joachim/Rohe, FS Möschel (2011), pp. 969, 975.

314 Cf. *Grabaravicius Dierick,* ECB-Occasional Paper No. 34 (August 2005), pp. 1 ff.; *Kahan/Rock,* Law Review (May 2007), pp 1 ff.

315 Cf. *Walter,* in: Bechtold/Jickeli/Joachim/Rohe, FS Möschel (2011), pp. 969, 975 f.

interest is essential for a strong domestic demand that is one significant condition of a high and sustainable employment level in the private economy. On the other hand, it led to an increase in the general demand for credit and set the wrong incentives to consumers who forgot their real solvency. As the FCIC points out, the credit lenders allowed credits although they knew that the borrowers could not afford these financial items and that it could cause dramatic losses by the depositors of mortgages.[316]

Policy of low interest represents a business model that can be called the "Expansionary monetary policy". Also the Federal Reserve runs a business model that stands for the advancing of large amounts of credit at very low rates.[317] That Expansionary monetary policy decreases an appreciation for consumer goods and results in the danger of inflation. Inflation is not only a bracket for the general economic development but also an attack on the deposits of lower-income groups that are normally more strongly affected by losses of monetary value than higher income groups. In addition, any inflation has the effect that a person's debts decrease more quickly. However, a rapid decrease in debts can also affect the volume of someone's debts.

The expansionary monetary policy was accompanied by a general undercut of standards. This undercut of standards significantly resulted from the widespread „ratings shopping" by issuers and investment banks, which weakened the rating standards because the CRAs who provided the most favorable ratings got more business.[318] Moreover, the distribution of mortgage loans and mortgage securitised bonds („decline of mortgage-underwriting standards[319]") accelerated

---

316 Cf. *Nationale Kommission zur Untersuchung der Finanz- und Wirtschaftskrise,* Schlussfolgerungen (2009), p. 12.

317 On the policy of low interests cf. Second Chapter, 1.1.

318 Cf. Levin-Report (2011), p. 31.

319 Cf. *FCIC,* Financial Crisis Inquiry Report (2011), pp. 149, 393; Under the federal securities law, particularly the investment banks acted as an underwriter or placement agent liable for any material misrepresentations or omissions of material facts made in connection with a solicitation or sale of a security to an investor. Until the outbreak of the financial crisis of 2008/2009, they sold RMBS securities and CDOs to large institutional investors. cf. Levin-Report (2011), p. 33.

the contagiosity: As the real estate prices declined and the mortgage lenders got into delay of payment, the lights on Wall Street began to shade.[320] The creditors often ignored the solvency of their debtors and many participants of the securitisation system spent too much trust in the rapid risk transfer – as one consequence, it came to enormous losses that affected the whole system as soon as the debtors stopped fulfilling their credit obligations – despite many warnings the *Federal Reserve* also did not take the necessary measures.[321] Many mortgage lenders set the level so low that the lenders gave blind trust to the qualification of the borrower while ignoring his solvency. Namely, the rating agencies let the markets blow up as the risky securitised instruments could not have been distributed without cachet – without the rating agencies the financial crisis would not have taken place.[322]

In particular, concerning the issue as to whether the public housing policy was one major condition of the crisis, the FCIC came to the result that, namely, the former US-presidents Bill Clinton and George W. Bush set ambitious objections to promote houses of one´s own. At the beginning, the Community Reinvestment Act 1977 (CRA 1977[323]) contained the widespread „Redlining" – a practice that rejected credit requests without considering the real solvency of the applicant – and committed the respective financial institutes to loan those municipal bodies, to invest in their municipal development and to offer (public) services, from whom they accepted financial deposits. All of this happened in compliance with the bank´s security and honest business practices.[324]

The FCIC does not consider the CRA 1977 as an essential factor as far as the disposition of second-rate credits is concerned. Many lenders of second-rate

---

320 Cf. *FCIC,* Financial Crisis Inquiry Report (2011), pp. 22 f., 25 f., 39 f., 127 ff., 137 f.

321 Cf. *Nationale Kommission zur Untersuchung der Finanz- und Wirtschaftskrise,* Schlussfolgerungen (2009), p. 13.

322 Cf. *Nationale Kommission zur Untersuchung der Finanz- und Wirtschaftskrise,* Schlussfolgerungen (2009), p. 14.

323 The CRA was passed by the US Congress in 1977 (12 U.S.C. 2901) to encourage banks to make loans in low- and moderate-income neighborhoods, cf. Federal Financial Institutions Examination Council, http://www.ffiec.gov/cra/history.htm, requested February/18th/2013.

324 Cf. *FCIC,* Financial Crisis Inquiry Report (2011), p. 27 f.

credits were not subject to the CRA 1977 and, moreover, investigations have shown that only 6% of the „high-cost-credits" – representative for second-rate credits – had a relationship to the CRA 1977 at all. Among those lenders that granted credits subject to the CRA-legislation, the probability of insolvency was 50% smaller than among those lenders who were not subject to the CRA. As the Report points out, the actual actions undertaken under the CRA-legislation was far beyond the real requirements.[325] Concerning the public housing policy, the FCIC concludes that the US-government failed to grant credits to those families that had no access to the financial markets – in particular, because the Federal Reserve and other financial supervision bodies failed to contain irresponsible credit lending.[326]

1.8.2. Liar loans

Since 2000 the abovementioned Expansionary monetary policy that was run by the Federal Reserve had already begun with the Carter (1977–1981) and Clinton (1993–2001) administrations and was then supported by the Bush administration (2001–2009). It was originally aimed at a widening of the supply of private homes for lower-income groups. In particular, the relaxing of mortgage standards made house purchases also possible for families that had previously been considered to be not sufficiently creditworthy to qualify for a mortgage; that increased the demand for real estate and prices rose.[327] The Expansionary monetary policy aimed at a stronger social integration of those income brackets and provoked the widespread assumption that everyone can afford almost everything. Nevertheless, it is also seen because of a rapidly increasing demand for securitised mortgages that began with the new millennium and which led to many mortgage banks being less-careful with assessments of the borrowers and to the abandon-

---

325 Cf. *Nationale Kommission zur Untersuchung der Finanz- und Wirtschaftskrise,* Schlussfolgerungen (2009), p. 18.

326 Cf. *FCIC,* Financial Crisis Inquiry Report (2011), p. 25, 27 f., 31 ff.

327 *Hull,* Risk Management (2010), p. 333.

ment of careful documentation.[328] Retrospectively, it is assumed that many credits were obtained by fraud; thus these credits are called liar loans.[329,330]

As the FCIC points out, after the refinancing boom, the originators were in need of product innovations that could make expensive homes more affordable to still-eager borrowers: The solution consisted in riskier, more aggressive, mortgage products that brought higher yields for investors but correspondingly greater risks for borrowers.[331] The Center for Responsible Lending[332] warned that holding a subprime loan could become something of a high-stakes wager.[333] Thus, subprime mortgages rose from 8% of mortgage originations in 2003 to 20% in 2005.[334] About 70% of subprime borrowers used hybrid ARMs whose low "teaser" rate lasts for the first two or three years, and then adjusts periodically thereafter.[335] Lenders qualified borrowers at low teaser rates, with little thought to what might happen when rates reset. Primarily because from 2000 to 2007 about 70% of subprime loans were Hybrid ARMs, Hybrid ARMs became the workhorses of the subprime securitisation market.[336]

Apart from the "liar loans", the „teasers" also served as another significant cause for the financial crisis of 2008/2009. „Teasers" can be defined as ARMs with higher re-setting interest rates. As the FCIC points out, after the refinancing boom, the originators were in need for product innovations that could make expensive homes more affordable to still-eager borrowers: The solution consisted of riskier, more aggressive, mortgage products that brought higher yields for investors but correspondingly greater risks for borrowers.[337] Against this back-

328 *Kübler* in Festschrift für Schwark (2009) p. 499, 501.
329 "Liar Loans" can be defined as loans where the borrower lies on the application form, cf. *Hull,* Risk Management (2010), p. 522.
330 *Kübler* in Festschrift für Schwark (2009) p. 499, 501.
331 Cf. *FCIC,* Financial Crisis Inquiry Report (2011), p. 132.
332 http://www.responsiblelending.org/, requested on February/19th/2013.
333 Cf. *FCIC,* Financial Crisis Inquiry Report (2011), p. 132.
334 Cf. *FCIC,* Financial Crisis Inquiry Report (2011), p. 132.
335 Cf. *FCIC,* Financial Crisis Inquiry Report (2011), p. 132.
336 Cf. *FCIC,* Financial Crisis Inquiry Report (2011), p. 134; *Levin/Coburn,* Financial crisis (2011, p. 28.
337 Cf. *FCIC,* Financial Crisis Inquiry Report (2011), p. 132.

ground, the Center for Responsible Lending warned that holding a subprime loan could become something of a high-stakes wager.[338] Thus, subprime mortgages rose from 8% of mortgage originations in 2003 to 20% in 2005.[339] About 70% of subprime borrowers used hybrid ARMs.[340]

Moreover, as the FCIC highlights, the „securitisation machine“ generated mortgage products such as NINJA-loans.[341] Loans of that kind are characterized by negative amortization successively terminating the borrower's equity.[342] Soon there were many different kinds of mortgages available on the market, confounding consumers who did not examine the fine print, baffling conscientious borrowers who tried to puzzle out their implications, and opening the door for those who wanted in on the action.[343]

1.8.3. The asset bubble

The Expansionary monetary policy is directly based on the already-mentioned securitisation of risks.[344] The Expansionary monetary policy ended with the already-mentioned burst of the speculative bubble. In its very beginning, this bubble did not result from the already-mentioned subprime credits but from the flood of savings from rapidly growing international emerging markets that dropped down the level of interest in the United States.[345] Retrospectively, it could have been prevented by a brief look at the structure of real estate credits in France: According to financial experts at the International Monetary Fund (IMF), the structure of French real estate credits is relatively sound because the big French credit institutes, such as Crédit Agricole, predominantly grant these cred-

338 Cf. *FCIC,* Financial Crisis Inquiry Report (2011), p. 132.
339 Cf. *FCIC,* Financial Crisis Inquiry Report (2011), p. 132.
340 Cf. *FCIC,* Financial Crisis Inquiry Report (2011), p. 134.
341 Cf. *FCIC,* Financial Crisis Inquiry Report (2011), p. 34.
342 Cf. *FCIC,* Financial Crisis Inquiry Report (2011), p. 34.
343 Cf. *FCIC,* Financial Crisis Inquiry Report (2011), p. 34.
344 Cf. First Chapter, 2.2.
345 Cf. *Bill Thomas,* Member of the Inquiry Commission of the Federal Reserve, *N.N.,* Finanzkrise, Auszüge aus Presseartikeln No. 5/2011, pp.12 (12).

its at a fixed interest rate instead of granting mortgage loans on the model of Fannie Mae[346] and Freddy Mac.[347, 348]

Concerning the question as to whether an excess of liquidity contributed to the outbreak of the financial crisis, the FCIC points out that low interests, widespread easily available capital and international depositors that preferred an investment in the United States were conditions for the rise of the asset bubble.[349] According to the FCIC´s point of view the US Government ignored that risk for quite a long time and was little prepared for the crisis. The US Government had not developed any strategic plan for the case of the crisis and reacted contradictorily – with the result of a widespread insecurity and panic at the financial markets.[350] As further causes, the FCIC adds the enormous growth of public debt between 1978 and 2007 and, moreover, the incline of the profit quote of the private earnings in the United States. Nevertheless, the FCIC concludes that a possible surplus of liquidity must not necessarily cause a financial crisis. The essential causes of that crisis consisted in the failure to control effectively the excesses at the mortgage and financial markets. Indeed the availability of affordable capital is one essential condition of economic expansion and growth if the respective assets flow into productive channels.[351]

1.9. Financial incentives for an expanding consumption

A low interest rate always conveys a strong incentive to purchase consumer goods one normally cannot afford or pay for immediately. Thus, during the global economic recession, many firms and warehouses offered consumer credits at an interest rate of 0%. This extrinsic incentive has the effect that many consumers do not estimate their future financial solvency carefully enough, not con-

346 Cf. First Chapter, 1.1.
347 Ibid.
348 *Wüpper,* DIE WELT (July/30th/2011), p. 20.
349 Cf. *FCIC,* Financial Crisis Inquiry Report (2011), p. 25.
350 Cf. *FCIC,* Financial Crisis Inquiry Report (2011), p. 21 f., 24 f.
351 Cf. *Nationale Kommission zur Untersuchung der Finanz- und Wirtschaftskrise,* Schlussfolgerungen (2009), p. 17.

sidering an unexpected incident such as the loss of their job. Their insolvency means the loss of their financial freedom for several years and possibly a dependence on public resources.

Against the abovementioned background, wrongfully set incentives that result from low interest rates do not create a welfare surplus for anyone, neither for the firm that sells consumer goods on a credit basis nor for the concerned consumer, the community of tax payers and the general public. It only contributes to the credit institutes that profit from a speedier circulation of money. As is shown by the recent financial crisis, this effect is only a short-term effect that is more than neutralised if the systemic risk realises that the credit granting institute cannot fulfil its obligations towards depositors that result from the abovementioned maturity transformation. As it is demonstrated in the case of Lehman Brothers,[352] the burst of the credit bubble that resulted from the Expansionary monetary policy and the low interest rates in particular can consequently cause the collapse of the concerned credit institute if an adequate CDS does not exist.

1.10. Lack of self-restraint

Among other core reasons, a widespread lack of self-restraint among financial managers and directors refers directly to the already-mentioned[353] falsely set (extrinsic) incentives that result in a false structure of remuneration, and in the widespread faith in an unlimited economic growth and in the already-discussed worldwide separation of risks and the lack of personal liability of managers.

From the author´s perspective individual remuneration at the eve of the financial crisis 2008/2009 was one essential but not the sole crisis cause.[354] This objection cannot be dismissed completely because in many corporations there is indeed a principal pressure that comes from the shareholders as the proprietors of the corporation who decide on the investment and accumulation of their capital,

[352] Cf. First Chapter, 1.2. and 2.2.
[353] Cf. second Chapter, 1.3.
[354] Cf. Second Chapter Annotation 1.4.

often on the basis of the portfolio strategy of the managers. The decision as to whether these managers run a sustainable or speculative portfolio strategy and even the decision as to the kind of extrinsic incentives is predominantly drawn by the association of proprietors, not by the portfolio managers themselves. Thus, one cannot identify the widespread lack of self-restraint as a core reason.

1.11. Insufficient transparency of financial products

Moreover, the recent financial crisis also resulted from the often insufficient transparency of financial products and financial risks. It can be identified as the initial point of the realisation of systemic risks. The transnational securitisation of risks specifically led to a totally insufficient transparency of financial products. If one cannot understand a product, one cannot estimate its risks and cannot take measures to develop safeguarding strategies for the case that these risks are unforeseeably realised. John Moulton, the head of the private equity[355] firm Alchemy Partners, made the observation that many private equity firms "bought all this rubbish themselves, most of which their senior managers did not understand, and they have been left holding the baby with unsalable, overpriced, over-enthusiastic debt." In other words: Many banks allowed a vast amount of money to be gambled on products which their senior managers did not understand.[356] Thus, hardly anyone knew or could calculate the risk profile associated with securitised products such as CDOs.[357]

In particular, the obscurity of CDOs results from the technique of packaging credit risks: Several classes of securities are created from a portfolio of bonds and there are rules for determining how defaults are allocated to classes.[358] The CDOs build, meanwhile, a strong industrial sector of the capital market where selected assets are bundled, which can be compared with the factoring in the in-

355 For a further discussion on the regulation of private equity see *Thomsen,* EBOR 10:1/2009, pp. 97 ff.
356 *McIlroy* in Straus, future of banking (2009), pp. 119, 123.
357 *McIlroy* in Straus, future of banking (2009), pp. 119, 119.
358 *Lee/Lee,* Finance (2006), p. 59.

dividual business: The risk that the creditor cannot repay his loan is transferred to the capital market.[359] On the one hand, a securitisation as it happened in the case of the CDOs can contribute to an efficient (global) contribution of risks and to the stabilisation of a global financial system by diminishing the concentration of risks in the banking sector and distributing those risks more widely.[360] On the other hand, SIVs enable credit institutes to conduct off-balance sheet financing for their securitised debt.[361] It is noteworthy that SIVs were used in the same way as conduits. Finally, the widespread use of these financial innovations minimised the transparency of financial products, which is essential to an effective protection of the financial consumer.

The rise of securitised financial products is also to be seen in view of the First Basel Capital Accord (Basel I)[362] that required banks to hold specified amounts of capital in reserve against loans made in certain broad categories.[363] As one consequence of the Basel I capital requirements, many American banks began to develop a new kind of mortgage loan that follows this principle to originate the loans and then (immediately) sell them to other banks and insurances, all over the world.

Many credit institutes purchased the abovementioned financial products. They failed to implement an adequate risk management in time to identify their risks, and they did not take measures to minimise their consequences before they were realised. As a consequence, the recent financial crisis hit these credit institutes dramatically. In the author´s point of view it was particularly the commingling of higher-rated debt in financial innovations such as CDOs that created a

359 *Volkart,* Corporate Finance (2008), pp. 784, 948.
360 *McIlroy* in Straus, future of banking (2009), pp. 119, 124.
361 Ibid.
362 For further information on the Basel Capital Accord see *Arnold/Boos*, Die Bank 2001, pp. 712-715; *Boos/Schulte-Mattler*, Die Bank 2001, pp. 346-354; *Elsas/Krahnen*, Die Bank 1999, pp. 298-304; *Enrich/Paletta,* The Wall Street Journal (July/27/2010), p. 19; *Osman/Riecke/Afhüppe,* HANDELSBLATT (July/28th/2010), pp. 34-35; *Schmidt,* BB 2011, pp. 105-109.
363 For the latest information on the capital requirements under the regime of "Basel 3" see *Schmidt,* BB 2011, pp. 105-109.

significant risk of infection and distress.[364] Normally, the (national) central banks take the responsibility not only to issue the currency but also to set and to manage the monetary policy.[365] In the event of the financial crisis 2008/2009 they seemed to be unable to immediately give a sufficient answer.[366]

2. Provisional comments

Against the abovementioned background, one has to realise that the effect of a regulatory framework depends on the level of detail. What does this mean for the supposed core reasons of the recent financial crisis? It means that a detailed and careful analysis is also always a retrospective analysis. Those core reasons that were really crucial for a financial crisis in the past must not be that crucial in the future. They convey one general conclusion that the origin of a financial crisis that appeared in the past that does not have to be valid in the future among other global circumstances.[367] As already mentioned, the rapid and long-lasting growth of the Chinese economy can be identified as one fundamental symptom that global circumstances can turn rapidly. In this context, one could add the global disequilibrium of currency and commerce and the unexpected Euro crisis. As a conclusion, one has to consider that the supposed core reasons do not offer any claim for universal validity. To establish a proportional and sustainable regulatory framework, they have to be considered among the presently foreseeable economic and financial circumstances. They also must not neglect the global economic development that one can foresee for the future.

---

364 Cf. First Chapter, 1.4. and Second Chapter, 1.1.; cf. *Walker,* in: The Future of financial regulation (2010), pp. 179 (198).

365 *Lee/Lee,* Encyclopedia of Finance (2006), p. 54.

366 Cf. First Chapter, 3; on the future role of the central banks as the lender of last resort cf. *Walker,* in: The Future of financial regulation (2010), pp. 179 (199 f.).

367 On the consequences of uncertainty for regulation: Cf. *Pacces,* ECFR (2010), pp. 479 ff.

Third Chapter:

Requirements of an Appropriate Response to the Recent Financial Crisis

1. Compulsory international standards on capital, supervision and transparency

1.1. Principle of proportionality

Moreover, the FCIC concludes that the financial crisis resulted from an undercut of standards. It considers the break-down of financial markets stability as the result of a widespread failure of financial regulation and supervision.[368] In view of this awareness, the European Commission made a proposal for a possible future regulation of the AIF segment that covers the activities of hedge funds and private equity – one possible conclusion of the recent financial crisis? This approach does not apply to the funds as such but to the management function. According to the AIFMD, the managers of the funds have to register. Furthermore, it provides a minimum level of capital to contain excessive leverage, requirements to the fund manager's remuneration and further general provisions on risk management, liquidity management, asset valuation, conflicts of interest and other business conduct requirements. Because this directive caused a controversial discussion at the European Council, our focus is on the requirements of an appropriate, sustainable and proportional regulatory framework that respects the various contents of economic freedom that are granted in the Lisbon Contract.[369]

The Lisbon Contract is mandatory among the current 28 European Member States and the EU and came into force on 1 December 2009, representing a new legitimacy basis for this supranational European subject community. With its

[368] Cf. *Nationale Kommission zur Untersuchung der Finanz- und Wirtschaftskrise,* Schlussfolgerungen (2009), p. 7.

[369] For further information on the Lisbon Contract see *Nowak,* Lissabon (2011), p. 73-81.

enforcement, the Treaty on the functioning of the EU (TFEU[370]) was put into force. Moreover, those (economic) guarantees of the European Charter of Fundamental Rights (ECFR[371]) obtained the status of real, basic rights. For instance, in the currently discussed context this has the effect that each market participant can directly refer to the guarantee of free entrepreneurship (Article 16 ECFR) and the guarantee of private property (Article 17 ECFR) if she/he holds the view that she/he is hurt by a legal act of the European Commission, the European Council or even the European Parliament. The respective guarantees convey the status to claim directly.

Any sustainable response that is given for the recent financial crisis should correspond to the principle of proportionality.[372] Why should one choose a legal regulation if a corporate governance regulation has the same effect on the financial market participants but causes less welfare losses?[373] It is the essential objective of a financial market regulation to protect the financial market participants against the realisation of systemic risks. It should not be an objective of a financial market regulation to give the state authorities another occasion to demonstrate their power and impact. If there is no necessity for a state regulation, it is necessary to abstain from a state regulation. This should also be respected by the European Commission, which tries to face the financial crisis by the AIFMD, which was set into effect on 11 November 2010. Legally, the principle of proportionality is one constitutional and economic essential element of the European Contract (Article 5 paragraph 4 of the TFEU) and of the constitution of almost every European Member State. It says that any regulation of an economic behaviour that is always curtailing private freedom must correspond with the basic economic rights. It must be suitable, necessary and adequate to reach the overrid-

370 Consolidated version of the treaty on the functioning of the European Union, Official Journal of the European Union, C 115/47, dated May/9th/2008.

371 European Charter of Fundamental Rights (ECFR), Official Journal of the European Communities 2007 C 303, P. 1.

372 Cf. third chapter, 1.1.

373 On Corporate Governance and the new hedge fund activism cf. *Briggs,* Journal of Corporate Law (2007), pp. 681 ff.

ing aim of the regulation. However, the principle of proportionality is not only a legal requirement.

Following Walker, the financial supervisory authorities must consider that any overreaction to the recent financial crisis could have the effect of unnecessarily limiting future innovation and welfare benefits while possibly overextending the duration and depth of the crisis with unnecessary measures that would only restrict liquidity,[374] credit creation and supply.[375] In view of the perpetual risk of over-regulation, any regulation should align not only regulatory incentives but also economic incentives.[376] To ensure that the "breath" of a corporation as the elementary condition for the "breath" of each national economy is not restricted under severe economic conditions, each regulation must correspond to the principle of proportionality. All in all, the governmental entities should take care to carefully regulate the investment segment and the operational activities of hedge funds since these entities seem indispensible for a satisfactory liquidity of many segments of the real economy.[377]

1.2. Principle of sustainability

The abovementioned principle of proportionality as one legal requirement of a sufficient response to the recent financial crisis is an almost natural requirement and finds its expression in the principle of sustainability.[378] This sophisticated principle goes back to the final Report of the Brundtland-Commission of 1987 (Brundtland-Report[379]) and demands a development corresponding with the requirements of the present generation without neglecting the possibilities of the

374 The liquidity of a corporation that is expressed by its cash flow refers to the ease and quickness of converting money to cash, cf. *Lee/Lee,* Encyclopedia of Finance (2006), p. 167; Walker, BJIBF (11/2007), pp. 567 ff.

375 Cf.*Walker,* in: The Future of financial regulation (2010), pp. 179 (195 ff., 202 ff.).

376 *McIlroy* in Straus, Future of Banking (2009), pp. 119, 120.

377 Definition of the Real Economy cf. Annotation No. 39.

378 On the meaning of the sustainability principle for re-organising economy in the post-financial crisis-age cf. *Faxon/Köhler/Michie/Oughton,* Cambridge Journal of Economics Vol. 37 (2013), pp. 187 ff.

379 Cf. Brundtland-Report (1987), bullets No. 72 ff.

future generation to satisfy its requirements.[380] The economical, ecological, social and cultural development shall correspond with the steady preservation of the conditions of human existence.[381] Nobody shall use anything that is essential for our daily life in a manner which destroys its source. Each legal measure should respect the prohibition of disproportionate measures in order not to destroy something that is steadily necessary for the functionality of a civil society, such as a steady credit supply for the real economy. By defining these requirements, the principle of sustainability primarily aims at the means of livelihood for future generations. Since the taking effect of the Rio Declaration on Environment and Development in 1992 („Rio-Declaration“[382]), it defines a global standard for the actions of any state.[383] It requires that our present behaviour shall respect the requirements of future generations and secure that the future generation must not suffer any disadvantage from our present behaviour.[384]

Legally, the principle of sustainability is defined in Article 3 No. 3 of the Treaty on European Union (TEU[385]). According to this legal requirement, the EU shall work for the sustainable development of Europe based on balanced economic growth and price stability, a highly competitive social market economy, aiming at full employment and social progress (...). The principle of proportionality is furthermore based on Article 5 No. 1 TEU and Article 11 TFEU.

In relation to the regulation of the financial markets and, in particular, alternative investments, the principle of sustainability requires that the trust among financial market participants shall be preserved to secure the most reliable credit supply, also for future generations. The principle of sustainability requires that any legal measure in view of its transaction costs and its complexity should bring

---

380 Cf. *Käller,* in: Schwarze, Europarecht (2012), AEUV, Article 11, bullet No. 14.

381 Cf. *Käller,* in: Schwarze, Europarecht (2012), AEUV, Article 11, bullet No. 14.

382 Published in the internet under http://www.unesco.org/education/nfsunesco/pdf/RIO_E.PDF, requested on February/18th/2013.

383 Cf. *Käller,* in: Schwarze, Europarecht (2012), AEUV, Article 11, bullet No. 14.

384 Cf. *Käller,* in: Schwarze, Europarecht (2012), AEUV, Article 11, bullet No. 14.

385 Consolidated version of the treaty on European Union, Official Journal of the European Communities, C 325/5, dated December/24th/2002.

the best possible effect. One also could call this aspect of the sustainability principle the efficiency criteria. For instance, if one really decides to launch the European-wide discussed financial transaction tax (FTT), one has to be sure that it not only contributes to generate public money, but that it also assists in containing systemic risks, now and in the future. The principle of sustainability that is closely linked to the principle of proportionality has a constitutional dimension because it concretises the defence function of the basic rights of all (national) European countries and even of the (supranational) EU. Referring to the regulation of alternative investments, at the European level it concretises the basic rights of free entrepreneurship (Article 16 ECFR) and of property (Article 17 Abs. 1 ECFR) that are acknowledged as real, basic rights under the regime of the Lisbon Contract.

Admittedly, each legal measure represents a mandatory compromise between the counter-rotating interests that have to be equalised by the state because the state has to enable the peaceful coexistence of different social actors with counter-rotating interests which can be seen as the legitimate basis of the state. A legal measure in compliance with the principle of sustainability is one essential key for the steady fulfilment of the abovementioned state function. As is shown by the FTT, the effective containment of systemic risks is in the public interest. Nevertheless, it is also in the public interest not to endanger the steady private credit supply that can be seriously affected by an overregulation that not only concerns the individual yield interest of financial market corporations but also the public interest of a vital domestic demand if – as a consequence of an overregulation – the credit prices rise, and bigger consumer goods become unaffordable for many consumers.

Any sustainable response to the recent financial crisis should reflect all the different aspects of the crisis. It ought to set the focus not only on the behaviour of bank managers and those incentives that led them to run a to short-term business strategy. It can be seen as one key aspect as to what constrictions on private profit-making are justified to prevent the public costs of a systemic failure in the financial markets:[386] Can that development that directly led to the recent financial crisis be justified ethically? Could anyone have prevented this development? Is it really a financial crisis, or does it possibly express a lack of ethical values among bankers and among consumers? Is it possible to identify one major responsibility of anyone? In any case, the FCIC draws the conclusion that it was a systemic collapse of accountability and ethical principles – for example, the number of borrowers that could not repay their mortgage already a few months after the closing has already doubled between summer of 2006 and the end of 2007.[387] Consequently depositors, corporations and the public lost their trust in the financial system.[388]

At the beginning of the third year after the outbreak of the recent financial crisis, there was a breadth correspondence among financial experts[389] claiming that the recent financial crisis was the consequence of a couple of things and needs a sustainable approach that sets the focus not only on the financial reasons. The principle of sustainability has its origin in environmental law and is based on the idea that the consumption of the present generation must also consider the requirements of the future generation.[390] What is to be done to avoid a similar systemic failure in the future? Whatever this approach consists of, a sufficient answer must also set the focus on other possible reasons.

Any sustainable regulatory framework should focus on the fact that the economic circumstances that can be identified as the fundamental of any economic regulatory framework change very speedily, which can be seen in the enormous

---

386 *McIlroy* in Straus, Future of Banking (2009), pp. 119, 120.

387 Cf. *FCIC,* Financial Crisis Inquiry Report (2011), pp. 22.

388 Cf. *Nationale Kommission zur Untersuchung der Finanz- und Wirtschaftskrise,* Schlussfolgerungen (2009), p. 12.

389 *Sinn* points out that the financial crisis of 2008/2009 results from a couple of different things: *Sinn,* Kasino Kapitalismus (2009), pp. 108-229; *Dam* and *Herzog* hold the opinion that the recent financial crisis is based on different circumstances: *Dam,* Subprime Crisis (2009), pp. 99-106; *Herzog,* Finanzmarktkrise (2008), pp. 9-13.

390 For further information on the principle of sustainability and its significance to the regulation of the financial market see *Kitterer,* Wirtschaftsdienst 2002, pp. 67-73; *Klesse,* Manager-Eid (2009), p. 1; *Polleit,* Wirtschaftsdienst 2008, pp. 720-722; *Raffelhüschen,* Wirtschaftsdienst 2002, pp. 73-76; *Steinbrück,* DIE WELT (2008/06/21), p. 12.

volatility of the equity price. The volatility is an economic measure of the uncertainty of the return realised on an asset.[391] Whereas in risk management, the daily volatility of a market variable is defined as the standard deviation of the percentage of daily change in the market variable, the volatility can generally be defined as the standard deviation of the return provided by the variable per unit of time when the return is expressed using continuous compounding.[392] The volatility is represented by the equity price that can underlie dramatic changes within one single day.

1.3. Economic guarantees of the Lisbon Contract

Under the Lisbon Contract[393] any appropriate response to the recent financial crisis has to respect the contents of the ECFR.[394] The Member State constitutional law, the Lisbon Contract,[395] is based on the priority of private economy and grants a couple of economic basic rights, such as the guarantee of private property (section 17 of the ECFR), the liberty of private enterprise (section 16 ECFR), the liberty of business (section 15 ECFR) and the guarantee of association (Section 12 ECFR).

The constitutional priority of private economy determines the type of regulation (legal regulation or corporate regulation) and the content of the regulation. Private corporations can be seen as the "cluster" of a modern civil society. Also, the private corporations in the financial sector grant employment and convey a real chance for a financial existence independent from the state to many people. Therefore, a regulation should not endanger the liquidity situation of private corporations: The end of private liquidity means the end of an independent existence.

391 *Hull,* Risikomanagement (2011), p. 210.
392 *Hull,* Risk Management (2010), pp. 175, 197.
393 Basically to the amendments of European law by the Lisbon Contract: *Nowak,* Europarecht nach Lissabon (2011), p. 1 ff.; *Suhr,* in: FS Fiedler (2011), p. 715 ff.; *Wittinger,* in: FS Fiedler (2011), p. 739 ff.
394 For this issue see *Congdon* in *O'Neill,* Global Financial Crisis (2009), pp. 29-39.
395 For further information on the Lisbon Contract see *Nowak,* Lissabon (2011), p. 73-81.

1.4. Disclosure as a cornerstone of investor protection

As Walker mentions, in connection with more complex innovative products and techniques, it is essential to maintain adequate levels of transparency and disclosure. Transparency is one key requirement of the sustainable equilibrium of those powers that represent a market economy and its well-functioning (price) mechanism. It saves the trust of market participants – among investors and among consumers – that the product really has the worth that it has in the conditions of a free competition. Moreover, it is a shield against a too-strong intervention – specifically, regulation by the financial authorities that causes welfare losses because any regulation that binds public resources sets one essential reason for the widening of taxes and minimises corporations' liquidity resources. Finally, it creates a substantial competitive disadvantage to the national economy. Thus, Avgouleas[396] emphasises that disclosure is the cornerstone of any investor protection in securities markets. Avgouleas points out that up to the outbreak of the recent financial crisis, it was assumed that on the basis of all available information, market actors would adjust their decisions and positions and strategies for information content with the aid of arbitrage efficient markets and would be perpetuated in accordance with the main assumption of the efficient market hypothesis (EMH), which is a direct application of rational choice theory to market behaviour.[397] The EMH is based on the assumption that asset prices completely reflect relevant (available) information.[398]

Any standardisation or interdiction of securitised products is a too-strict measure of financial market regulation. Nevertheless, to achieve a sufficient level of transparency[399], one should seriously consider restricting the use of securitised or those products whose risk profile is unascertainable or uncertain.[400] Allowing

396 Cf. *Avgouleas,* ECFR 4/2009, p. 441.
397 Ibid.
398 Cf. *Hull,* Risk Management (2010), p. 518; *Lee/Lee,* Encyclopedia of Finance (2006), p. 103.
399 For the future transparency requirements in Germany see *Schwald,* DIE WELT (2011/01/15), p. 21.
400 *McIlroy* in Straus, Future of Banking (2009), pp. 119, 125.

banks to securitise and sell on their loans without bearing any continuing risk of those loans has encouraged insufficient discipline in terms of the loans made.[401] As a consequence of the recent financial crisis, banks ought to continue to bear some (substantial) portion of the risk on the loans they have originated to encourage them to be careful about the loans they make in the first place.[402] In particular, CDOs should be transparent so that the person who bears the risk can easily be identified.[403]

A stronger transparency of risks is one way to achieve a stronger protection of the financial consumer. Among financial analysts a stronger transparency is held as a standard liberal response because better-informed participants are more likely to act rationally in their own interest and thus maximise overall social welfare.[404] A stronger level of transparency, therefore, contributes to a minimum of democracy among the participants of the financial markets. Finally, the editing credit institute profits from a stronger level of transparency because it can reduce its contractual and transaction costs. Transaction costs are those costs that are necessary to execute a transaction.[405] In particular, they cover the costs of information and the costs of communication and coordination between the participants of the transaction.[406]

The level of transparency that is adequate to contain systemic risks cannot be answered generally. Nevertheless, it is important that the level of transparency refers to the specific risk of the traded financial product. The higher its specific risk, the higher are the transparency requirements that have to be granted by the editing institution. All in all, a sustainable regulation of private equity and other alternative investments should set the focus on a stronger transparency of finan-

---

401 *McIlroy* in Straus, Future of Banking (2009), pp. 119, 128.
402 *McIlroy* in Straus, Future of Banking (2009), pp. 119, 129.
403 Ibid.
404 *Thomsen,* EBOR 10:1/2009, pp. 97, 105; on the requirement of steadily well-informed market participants cf. *Walker,* BJIBF (11/2007), pp. 567 ff.
405 *Jost* in Köhler/Küpper/Pfingsten, Betriebswirtschaft (2007), pp. 782, 783.
406 *Dietl* in Köhler/Küpper/Pfingsten, Betriebswirtschaft (2007), pp. 1750, 1751.

cial products to enable every market participant a realistic view of the worth of a financial product.

In this context one has to consider whether a stronger transparency really needs a stronger regulation by the financial authorities, or if a kind of self-regulation is sufficient. The idea of a stronger self-regulation of the mortgage markets was promoted by Alan Greenspan, the former president of the Fed.[407] After the breakout of the financial crisis, representatives of the American Republican Party held the view that a stronger regulation and a reduction of subsidies for privately owned homes and a stronger liability of bank directors would not be the appropriate response to the financial crisis.[408]

In contrast, the FCIC holds the view that the policy of stronger self-regulation led finally to the abandoning of essential protection mechanisms that could have contributed to the effective containment of the financial crisis. The policy of self-regulation led to the decline of the regulatory requirements subject to financial institutes.[409] Moreover, the abandoning of the respective protection mechanisms contributed to serious gaps in the supervision of critical sections in the volume of several billions of dollars – namely, the system of shadow banking and the OTC-segment. The policy of stronger self-regulation that was driven by the US Government until the outbreak of the financial crisis of 2008/2009 permit financial corporations to choose the supervision of their own preference which caused a "race to the bottom"[410] for the most neglectful supervisory body.[411] This

[407] Cf. *N.N.*, Finanzkrise, Auszüge aus Presseartikeln No. 5/2011, pp.12 (12).

[408] Ibid.

[409] Cf. *Nationale Kommission zur Untersuchung der Finanz- und Wirtschaftskrise,* Schlussfolgerungen (2009), p. 19.

[410] Within the international competition of locations for business and industries, it normally prevails that location with the comparatively most liberal legislation. On the one hand, this competition forces the national governments to an efficient use of taxes, other common goods and contributes to their monetary budget discipline - on the other hand, it consequently results in a loss of labour standards and infrastructural standards. Finally, it can also force other governments to reduce their standards, cf. *Hirte,* in: Hirte/Bücker, Gesellschaften (2006), p. 52 (§ 1, Marginal no. 94) and *Bonin,* in: Hirte/Bücker, Gesellschaften (2006), p. 316 (§ 10, Marginal no. 2).

[411] Cf. *Nationale Kommission zur Untersuchung der Finanz- und Wirtschaftskrise,* Schlussfolgerungen (2009), p. 8.

race also revealed in the widespread „ratings shoppings": Issuers and investment banks were engaged finding the CRA that offers the highest ratings.[412] All in all, the almost unlimited trust into the self-regulation of financial corporations resulted in serious supervisory gaps.[413] In particular, those supervisory gaps also revealed in the omission of any statutory basis of the SEC to exercise regulatory authority over the CRAs until the enactment of the US Credit Rating Agency Reform Act in September 2006.[414]

1.5. Coherence of chances and risks

It is essential to establish a regulatory framework that terminates the separation of chances and risks and reconstructs the direct coherence between the manager's personal profit participation and the manager's personal liability.

This is an ethical principle that goes back to the teachings of Adam Smith[415] and which is also an important conclusion of the "Freiburger Schule"[416],which holds that every participant of a market economy should be liable for his own debts. If one considers that the fund managers have a widespread room for manoeuvre that results from the acknowledgement of the BJR[417], it should be their first objective that the fund is not her or his own property but represents the money of other people. This is relevant to the risks of an investment and to the information requirements that should be respected when closing the investment contract. Liability of the fund managers is the key for the realisation of a stronger sustainability and to prevent a nationalisation of losses in the future.

412 Cf. Levin-Report (2011), p. 31.
413 Cf. *Nationale Kommission zur Untersuchung der Finanz- und Wirtschaftskrise,* Schlussfolgerungen (2009), p. 19.
414 Cf. Levin-Report (2011), p. 43 f.
415 *Adam Smith*, The theory of moral sentiments by Adam Smith, cf. *Bonar,* Journal of Philosophical Studies, I (1926), pp. 333-353.
416 For further information on the Freiburger Schule and the German "Ordoliberalismus" see cf. *Horn,* Marktwirtschaft (2010), pp. 20-26.
417 In the German corporation law the BJR, whose origin can be seen in the American corporation law, is integrated in § 93 paragraph 1 S. 2 of the German Aktiengesetz (dAktG); For further information on the BJR see *Göppert,* Business Judgment Rule (2010).

A direct coherence between chances and risks seems essential for that trust that is essential for a well-functioning interbank commerce, for the general public acceptance of credit institutes and for the acceptance of the system of a market economy. It helps to reduce those transaction costs[418] that arise with any financial transaction and contributes to the speed of monetary circulation. Among financial experts, there is a widespread consent that a high level of monetary circulation sets one significant condition for the realisation of higher yields. Based on this assumption, a higher level of monetary circulation creates a welfare surplus and contributes to the wealth of a national economy as a whole. Thus, a direct coherence between the manager's personal profit participation and the manager's personal liability is one essential parameter of a more sustainable regulatory framework.

2. Capital requirements

2.1. Minimum capital levels

The Basel Committee recently released the contents of Basel III that focuses on a strengthening of the available equity position. In view of the enormous losses that happened during the recent financial crisis, the Basel Committee proposes a range of amendments that lead to a general change away from a stronger self-regulation that were granted under the Second Basel Capital Accord (Basel II) and that contain stronger equity requirements, the introduction of a "stress-test" implemented by the financial supervisory bodies, a supervision of OTC derivatives and the implementation of clearing devices for CDS.[419] Thus, the latest edition of the Basel Capital Accord intends to strengthen regulation, supervision and risk management of the banking sector to improve the immunity of credit institutes against the various financial and economic turbulences, to enhance the risk management devices and governance and strengthen their transparency and

418 Transaction costs are those that result from carrying out any trade that means the commissions plus the difference between the price obtained and the midpoint of the bid-offer spread, cf. *Hull,* Risk Management (2011), p. 530.

419 *Hull,* Risikomanagement (2011), p. 289.

disclosures[420] Normally, well-informed investors could make the right decisions or at least would be fully informed that they would be acting on their own risks.[421] In particular, Basel III is based on different tiers that foresee stronger capital requirements by doubling the "Core 1 capital" from 2% to 4.5% and adding one conservation buffer of 2.5% that raises the "core tier 1 ratio" to 7%.[422]

2.2. Adequate liquidity support by the central banks

The credit supply of the real economy can be identified as one indispensable condition for a sustainable economic growth.[423] A healthy financial sector is crucial to the stability and growth of the entire economy of a country.[424] The real economy and the consumer have a vital economic interest in a well-functioning credit supply.[425] The recent economic growth that can be seen in Germany not only results from its strong export trade; it is also based on a revived private consumption. The real economy itself has a vital economic interest in the credit supply of private consumers because it is less restful to put the economic growth on a different basis. Otherwise, a company runs the risk of one-sided dependence.

Walker holds the view that an adequate liquidity support by the central banks should be granted at any time, whereas central banks – this comment of Walker seems to aim at the European Central Bank (ECB[426]) and the corresponding national institutes, such as Deutsche Bundesbank and others – must review the operations of domestic and cross-border inter-bank markets to ensure that they work effectively in all conditions and at all times with necessary funding facilities being made available where appropriate. This point of view seems correct because the recent financial crisis became evident when the interbank market

420 Cf. Basel Commitee on Banking Supervision, Revisions (2013), pp. 4 ff.
421 Cf. *Wymeersch,* ECFR (2010), pp. 240, 240.
422 Cf. *Basel Committee on Banking Supervision,* Basel III (2011, pp. 13 ff.
423 *Strobel,* DIE WELT (2010/11/22), p. 2; on the meaning of the central banks for financial stability cf. *Le Maux/Scialom,* Cambridge Journal of Economics Vol. 37 (2013), pp. 1 ff.
424 *Dam,* Subprime Crisis (2009), pp. 95, 98.
425 *Strobel,* DIE WELT (2010/11/22), p. 2.
426 Short information on the election of the president of the European Central Bank: Cf. *Haede,* EWS (2011), pp. 173-175.

started to collapse:[427] The revitalisation of the well-functioning interbank market required an enormous financial intervention by the central banks.[428] At the beginning of the recent financial crisis, big-sized and very experienced credit institutions had to explain to their shareholders and to the markets that they were unable to sell securitised mortgages they had purchased for several thousand millions of US$[429] – the losses of these institutes run up to more than US$20,000 million.[430]

Nevertheless, the function of the central banks is actually not to compensate the consequences of any insufficient portfolio strategy of the commercial banks[431] and of investment banks. As it was already mentioned, another reason of the recent financial crisis was that the portfolio managers often rely on state assistance when they decided on a high-risk portfolio strategy. Any future regulatory framework should include a legal clarification that there won't be any bail-out: Every credit institute is generally responsible for the consequences of its own portfolio strategy, and it is responsible in the case the assumptions of the portfolio managers do not correspond to the actual developments. The principle of second liability is also applicable between investment banks and the central bank. Nevertheless, during the recent financial crisis, the financial losses of several credit institutes ran up to an extent that they really caused the necessity of several bail-out-packages in the United Kingdom[432]

2.3. Implementation of a systemic risk buffer

To effectively contain one similar financial crisis in the future it seems notably essential to protect (financial) institutions from insolvency where the asset values fall, although these are only ancillary to the referred-to liquidity meas-

---

[427] Cf. First Chapter, 2.5.
[428] Cf. *Kübler,* in: Festschrift für Schwark (2009) p. 499, 500.
[429] Ibid.
[430] Cf. *New York Times* (February/1st/2008), C 6.
[431] A commercial bank is a credit institute that takes deposits and make loans.
[432] Cf. *Walker,* in: The Future of financial regulation (2010), pp. 179 (184 ff.).

ures.[433] Thus, many banks implemented a systemic risk buffer by operating with a higher equity level.[434]

3. Monitoring of credit accumulation

The information basis of the directors can be seen as the initial point of hidden information and hidden transaction if the directors use their freedom of action to pursue their own individual agendas. This phenomenon is well-known as principal-agent conflict or moral hazard, and can be identified as another core reason for the recent financial crisis. To reduce this conflict of interest that can be found in almost every capital corporation, it is discussed whether a compulsory and advanced monitoring system should be established. The monitoring of money and credit growth is essential to contain inflation and to avoid cyclic disruption.[435]

In addition, a compulsory monitoring system contributes to the transparency of the director's portfolio strategy, and it can be seen as one significant parameter of an effective risk management that helps to avoid systemic risks. Financial supervisory bodies must allow (financial) institutions to continue to innovate and expand although minimum levels of disclosure and transparency must be maintained at all times to ensure an effective supervisory and market oversight.[436] It is significant that the monetary authorities monitor and manage any credit accumulation appropriately at all times.[437]

The group of financial experts working with De Larosière proposes ESRB[438] to coordinate the supervision of systemic risks.[439] The ECSR can be described as

433 Cf. *Deloitte,* Global systemic risk (2012), pp. 8 ff., 13 ff.; *Walker,* in: The Future of financial regulation (2010), pp. 179 (197).

434 *Walker,* in: The Future of financial regulation (2010), pp. 179 (196).

435 Cf. *Walker,* in: The Future of financial regulation (2010), pp. 179 (196).

436 Cf. *Walker,* in: The Future of financial regulation (2010), pp. 179 (196).

437 Cf. *Walker,* in: The Future of financial regulation (2010), pp. 179 (196).

438 Introduction and overview on the new European financial supervisory system: Cf. *Bauer/Boegl,* BKR (2011), pp. 177-186; cf. also *Diekmann/Fleischmann,* WM (2011), pp. 1105-1109; *Zülch/Hoffmann/Detzen,* EWS (2011), pp. 167-173.

a parent authority that aims at concentrating the expertise of the European Member State's central banks and all supervisory bodies in the branch of banks, insurances and market supervision, identifying systemic risks and finding solutions to prevent those risks in the future.[440] The ESRB shall ensure overall financial stability, which can be seen as a first step towards a European financial monitoring,[441] bringing together the heads of national central banks, the ECB and the EU officials.[442] By possessing comparative advantages of information and action that results from their oversight of payment systems, their own refinancing operations, their various activities in the financial markets[443] and their presence in international committees, these bodies are able to assess possible domino effects and to identity disequilibria.[444] The ESRB would be an essential element of the future European monetary supervision, which will be able to provide a Europe-wide view of developments in the different EU markets and therefore would be able to address warnings and recommendations to the national supervisors.[445]

As is proposed by walker, The ERSC could also have been an advanced monitoring system that could have contributed to contain the dimension of the recent financial crisis. It can be seen as a part of an advanced risk management, which[446] conveys a suitable early-warning system and is one essential element of an advanced corporate compliance.[447] To maintain suitable working conditions at the international financial markets, the concerned credit institutes take over an

439 About the supervision of hedge funds under the regime of the AIFM cf. *Nietsch/Graef,* ZBB (2010), pp. 12-20.

440 Cf. *N.N.,* G20-Agenda, Auszüge aus Presseartikeln No. 5/2010, pp.3 (4, 5).

441 Monitoring means the long-term identification, collection and evaluation of financial data in the frame of a systematic investigation, respectively an inquiry that is centralised by a superior body or authority.

442 Cf. *N.N.,* rulebook, Auszüge aus Presseartikeln No. 37/2010, pp. 8 (8).

443 About the requirements of a sustainable regulation of the financial markets: *N.N.,* Regulierung, Auszüge aus Presseartikeln No. 8/2011, pp.16-20.

444 Cf. *N.N.,* Lessons, Auszüge aus Presseartikeln No. 5/2010, pp.5 (7).

445 Cf. *Wymeersch,* ECFR (2010), pp. 240, 250.

446 For further information on the requirements of an advanced risk management system see *Bloss/Ernst/Häcker/Sörensen,* Financial Engineering (2011), p. 532 ff.; *Hull,* Risk Management (2011), p. 14 ff.; *Lee/Lee,* Encyclopedia of Finance (2006), p. 491 ff.

447 The term "corporate compliance" stands for those measures that are taken by a firm or corporation to act in accordance with the relevant legal requirements. Corporate Compliance can be seen as a part of the risk management of a corporation.

essential part of the financial supervisory and thereby keep the impact on the volume of compliance costs. It is generally well-known that the financial institutes try to shift their compliance costs onto their customers by increasing the credit costs. Higher credit costs have a negative impact on the domestic demand, on the development of the GDP and finally on the rate of employment. As a conclusion, an advanced monitoring system, as proposed by *Walker,* combines the advantage of an effective risk management with the advantage of a lower credit rate level and several other benefiting economic effects. It creates a win-win-situation for all market participants: for the credit institutes, for their customers and the general public.

4. Well-functioning risk management

Normally, the institutional position and the validity of the abovementioned BJR convey to the directors a comfortable projection of information. However, this projection is significant to a well-functioning board of directors and to enable the ruling of a portfolio strategy that is predominant in the global economic competition. Moreover, it is essential to take the necessary compliance measures and to establish a well-functioning risk management for the case of unexpected risks – in particular, in view of the awareness of the FCIC that the dramatic failure of corporate governance and risk management of systemically relevant financial institutions set another essential reason of the financial crisis of 2008/ 2009.[448]

A well-functioning risk management is important because financial institutes have recently widened their portfolio by using securities and dealing with financial vehicles of an increasing complexity[449] An effective individual bank internal risk management system provides that those areas of underlying high risk activity (e.g., subprime-lending[450]) should be managed directly and immediately, and nei-

[448] Cf. *FCIC,* Financial Crisis Inquiry Report (2011), p. 18 f., 26 f., 183 f., 307 ff.; 319; 336 ff.
[449] Cf. *Walker,* in: The Future of financial regulation (2010), pp. 179 (198).
[450] On the necessity of an advanced risk management cf. First Chapter, 1.1.

ther delegated nor incorporated into larger, more complex products.[451] Therefore, a well-informed board of directors is also in the vital interest of each investor. Walker further states that a well-functioning risk management requires that all areas of underlying high-risk activity, such as the segment of sub-prime lending, should be managed directly and immediately; they should neither be delegated nor incorporated into larger, more complex products with the destabilising effects that they may have on the repackaged debt and the subsequent solvency of the purchasing banks or other institutions concerned.

5. Stronger economic convergence among the European Member States

5.1. Stronger economic convergence by a European transfer union?

Whatever the answer is to the recent financial crisis, the significance of private credit supply and the declining significance of national frontiers[452] should be considered. One must find a sustainable compromise between the interest of the private lending business and the investors to realise a satisfactory yield – otherwise, there is no attraction for private investors – and the general public interest of avoiding systemic risks. The recent financial crisis has shown that the prevention of systemic risks is a public concern. In particular, it endangers employment, public finances, and, finally, national independence, as is shown in the case of Greece. The realisation of systemic risks endangers the supranational "community of values" that is represented by the EU. The community of values finds its direct expression in the European Charter of Basic Rights (the EU Charter)[453] or in the Charter of the United Nations (the UN Charter)[454], which represent two strong sources of transnational law.

---

451 Cf. *Walker,* in: The Future of financial regulation (2010), pp. 179 (198 f.).

452 For further information on the declining meaning of national frontiers see *Renner,* Transnationales Recht (2011).

453 *Borowski* in Meyer, Charta (2011), preliminary remark article 1, bullet No. 1a; *Meyer* in Meyer, Charta (2011), preamble, bullet No. 28.

454 *Neu*, A., UN-Reform (2006), p. 1.

With regard to the enormous mobility of private capital and the fact that the EU is both an economic place without national frontiers and a community with common values, the prevention of systemic risks is not only a national concern but a European concern. Thus, a common European response to the recent financial crisis could be one step to achieving a stronger economic convergence among the Member States of the EU. One essential step would be to achieve a stronger convergence between the northern states that set a stronger financial focus on monetary stability and the many southern states that set their focus on social welfare.

A common European answer to the recent financial crisis is the proposal to implement effective measures against a transfer union in the European Contract and to work towards a stronger financial discipline of each European Member State. The term "transfer union" describes a joint responsibility of the more prosperous European Member States such as Germany, as well as for the less prosperous European Member States such as Ireland.[455] A transfer union stands for the (unlimited) purchase of governmental bonds by the ECB[456] and is an expression that either hints at the rescue of the European currency union or its collapse. The transfer union is a governmentally organised transfer of wealth on a legal basis and, according to an international contract, several states are committed to each other to a regular financial equalisation.[457]

The European Constitution contains the interdiction of "no bail out"; according to the constitutional principle that was implemented by the Maastricht Contract, the EU bears no responsibility to adhere for the debts of any single European Member State. The former president of the Deutsche Bundesbank, Ottmar Issing, stated that a monetary union without a stable Euro could only survive if

455 On the legal development of the EU towards a transfer union cf. *Callies/Schoenfleisch,* JZ (5/2012), p. 477 ff.; *Müller-Franken,* JZ (5/2012), p. 219 ff.; *Sester,* EWS (3/2012), p. 80 ff.; *Weber,* DVBl. 2012, p. 801 ff.

456 On the role of the ECB under the conditions of the European debt crisis: *Sester,* EWS (3/2012), p. 80 ff.

457 Cf. http://www.boerse.de/boersenlexikon/Transferunion, requested October/19th/2012.

central bank independence is respected, which implied that the ECB abstains from fiscal policy actions, such as buying sovereign bonds in secondary markets. However, to change the "no bail-out" clause in the direction of a bail-out regime was not a step towards a democratically-legitimised political union.[458] Even if the ECB is authorised to purchase an unlimited amount of governmental bonds of the European Member States, the TFEU still includes a direct interdiction of bail-out in Article 125 paragraph 1.

5.2. Convergence by the introduction of Eurobonds

For the practical implementation of the transfer union, it is important that the ECB is authorised to purchase government bonds from the financially suffering southern European countries such as Greece. In view of the probability of a Greek state insolvency, there is an on-going political debate on the so-called Euro bonds[459], whose introduction is rejected by those countries such as Germany who have a strict budgetary discipline, and who recently launched a constitutional debt bracket to reduce their budgetary deficit. The federal government of Germany has opted to define a "debt brake"[460] in the German Constitution that will be effective in 2016. A similar solution is also being discussed at the European level. The governments of those countries with a constitutional debt bracket reject Euro bonds because they hold the view that these bonds reduce the pressure on the financially suffering countries to reduce their own budgetary deficit by taking suitable measures to improve their competitiveness.

5.3. Convergence by the implementation of the ESM

The discussion of a European transfer union was recently highlighted by the discussion on the steady Euro rescue fund ESM (European Stability Mechanism)

---

458 Cf. *Issing,* Slittering to the wrong kind of union, Financial Times (2011/08/08).

459 For further information on so-called eurobonds see cf. *Müller-Franken,* JZ (5/2012), p. 219 ff.

460 According to Articles 109, 115 and 143d paragraph 1 dGG, the German federal state is committed to reduce its structural deficit down to 0.35% of its GDP at the beginning of 2016, and each single German state is committed to present debt-free budgets until 2020, cf. *IFSt,* contribution No. 479 (May 2012), p. 32.

that was launched in view of the sovereign debt crisis in Greece, Spain, Italy, Portugal and Ireland.[461] The ESM can legally be qualified as an international contract for the supplementation of the EU's integration program that is beyond the control of the European Parliament.[462]

As it is underlined by the defendant in the recently published decision of the German BVerfG, the legal regulations on the ESM contribute to the security and the stability of the European Currency Union and do not enable the introduction of an extensive union of liabilities and transfers but authorise punctuality within a clearly defined situation to temporarily limited relief actions and stipulate a strict conditionality.[463]

5.4. Further analysis and Conclusion

A proper governmentally well-organised transfer of wealth could contribute to the general public welfare within the EU if it helps to equalise the wealth differences between the more prosperous northern European Member States and the less prosperous southern European Member States. In general, the equalisation of wealth differences can be a suitable measure to defang political and social conflicts and to enhance the identification with the European project. Even the most serious competitors of the EU, such as India, know about a kind of interior financial equalisation. Nevertheless, the legal provisions should be comparatively detailed to contain the risk of general welfare losses and the risk of a "suffocation" of the national performance stimulus.

An adequate pressure on the budgetary discipline of each single European Member State is a mandatory provision for the consolidation of the EU as a whole. Among the conditions of globalisation and the tectonic shift that results

[461] On the European debt crisis and its impact on the national budgets of the European Member States cf. *Kopp,* NVwZ (No. 24/2011), p. 1480 ff.

[462] *BVerfG,* Judgment from September/12th/2012; Rs. 2 BvR 1390/12, 2 BvR 1421/12, 2 BvR 1438/12, 2 BvR 1439/12, 2 BvR 1440/12, 2 BvE 6/12, bullet 257; *Lorz/Sauer,* DÖV (2012), p. 573, 575.

[463] *BVerfG,* Judgment from September/12th/2012; Legal case 2 BvR 1390/12, 2 BvR 1421/12, 2 BvR 1438/12, 2 BvR 1439/12, 2 BvR 1440/12, 2 BvE 6/12, Marginal no. 178.

from the emerging countries such as India can be seen as the initial point of a redefinition of the global powers. It is an essential provision for a sustainable coherence between national chances and risks.[464] Indeed, at the national level, one can see a kind of transfer union, such as the financial equalisation among the 16 German federal states since the late 1960s – in Germany the more prosperous federal states such as Hamburg are constitutionally committed to financially assist the less prosperous federal states such as Berlin.

Nonetheless, one has to consider that the EU is neither a state nor a national common destiny but a supranational legal personality that follows the principle of subsidy. It is important that the EU as a community of values faces the challenges of globalisation. To face the challenges of globalisation, it seems important to implement a stronger synchronicity between the EU as a political community and the EU as an economic community. Thus, there is an on-going political discussion on a fiscal union, and on a bank union it is essential to consider the (mandatory) elements of a sustainable reform of the EU and – following Winston Churchill's vision that he presented in his well-known speech – even the concept of a real political union following the political concept of the United States of America. As long as the constitutional provisions of a real political union are not in force, the concept of a transfer union following the conception of the federal financial equalisation seems constitutionally questionable. As it is shown by the example of financially distressed Greece, probably the most essential condition of real political independence is the national financial consolidation that is based on budgetary discipline, which could get lost under a transfer union beyond a real political union. A European transfer union finally honours those Member States with less discipline and less willingness for a substantial contribution to the EU. If it does not consist of mandatory boundaries, it could endanger the whole European project. Thus, any European fiscal transfer mechanism should not consist of

464 On the coherence between chances and risks as a requirement for a sufficient response to the recent financial crisis and for the future European regulation of alternative investments cf. third chapter, 1.5.

long-lasting contributions similar to the system of federal financial equalisation.[465]

Namely, the propositions of the De Larosière group aim at combating regulatory arbitrage by deciding compulsory minimum EU-wide standards, providing a binding mediation between disagreeing national authorities and coordinating international "colleges of supervisors" without forbidding the national bodies to go beyond the common standards.[466] As was highlighted by Axel A. Weber, the former president of the Deutsche Bundesbank, a (legal) solution is needed that strengthens the financial system and its resistivity as a whole – one superior objective that was underlain by a detailed road map for a reform of the financial market regulation at the various G20 meetings.[467]

---

465 *BVerfG,* Judgment from September/12th/2012; Legal case 2 BvR 1390/12, 2 BvR 1421/12, 2 BvR 1438/12, 2 BvR 1439/12, 2 BvR 1440/12, 2 BvE 6/12, Marginal no. 171.

466 Cf. *N.N.,* rulebook, Auszüge aus Presseartikeln No. 37/2010, pp. 8 (8); cf. also *N.N.,* G20-Agenda, Auszüge aus Presseartikeln No. 5/2010, pp.3 (3).

467 Cf. *N.N.,* G20-Agenda, Auszüge aus Presseartikeln No. 5/2010, pp.3 (3).

Fourth Chapter:

The Alternative Investment Fund Managers Directive (AIFMD) as an Response to the Recent Financial Crisis

1. Introduction of the AIFMD

1.1. Chronology, general concept and overview

1.1.1. Chronology

The European Commission has reacted to the recent financial crisis with AIFMD. In its very first design this financial market regulation is based on the ideas of Klaus-Heiner Lehne[468] and Poul Nyrup Rasmussen,[469] who came to the conclusion that – in view of the global financial crisis[470] – a worldwide regulation and supervision of all participants of the financial market,[471] including the financial products, would be necessary. As most of the other propositions for the future regulation of the financial markets, the AIFMD focuses on an improvement of market discipline and the reduction of information asymmetries,[472] whereas not every initiative aims at a strengthening of financial market regulation.[473] The AIFMD aims at the strengthening of investor protection, market integrity, market

468 The report of Klaus-Heiner Lehne aims at the transparency requirements of institutional investors for further information on Klaus-Heiner Lehne see cf. http://www.kh-lehne.de/ (requested on August/24th/2011).

469 The report of Poul Nyrup Rasmussen aims at the regulation of hedge funds, private equity funds, transparency requirements of institutional investors and the future framework of the rating agencies.

470 Cf. introduction.

471 Whereas the worldwide market for equity transactions increased by 5% to almost €900 billion in the year 2010, the west European market for those transactions decreased by more than half to €150 billion - in opposition to the relevant market in the United States (increase of 40% to €356 billion), Asia (increase of 72% to €272 billion) and South America (increase of 211% to a historic top position of €81 billion), cf. *Theisselmann,* CORPORATE FINANCE law 1/2011, p. 1, 2 (on the basis of *Thomson Reuters Deals BI*); Generally resume the development of the capital market law in 2010, cf. *Weber,* NJW (2011), p. 273 ff.

472 On the regulation of information asymmetries in the investment law: *Schmolke,* WM 2006, p. 1909 ff.

473 *Cf. Müller,* Hedgefonds (2011), pp. 243, 280.

efficiency and the monitoring of capital accumulation[474].[475] As already stated, the monitoring of credit accumulation is one decisive provision for the premature identification of systemic risks as a part of an advanced risk management.

As already mentioned, the latest version of the AIFMD,s based on the ideas of Jacques de Larosière, was released by the European Commission on 30 April 2009. This version was generally accepted by the European Parliament on 10 November 2010[476] and finally released in the official gazette[477] of the EU on 1 July 2011. After this final act of legislation, the AIFMD became effective on 21 July 2011. The precise determination of its legal validity is dccisivc for the calculation of the time corridor that is given to the European Member States to transfer the AIFMD into their own national laws.

1.1.2. Overview

Besides general (Articles 1-3 AIFMD) and particular guidelines on the certification of the alternative investment fund manager (AIFM) (Articles 3a-8 AIFMD), the AIFMD includes on the operative business activities of the AIFM that refer to the good conduct,[478] equity requirements, organisational requirements and the outsourcing of AIFM tasks (Articles 8a-18 AIFM). Chapter 4 states transparency requirements (Articles 19-21). The following chapter refers to AIFM that administrate leveraged funds, those with a dominating influence (Articles 25-30 AIFM).

With the conditions of the new information technologies, private capital is a very mobile factor of production. With regard to the BRIC countries and their enormous economic growth – in 2010 China achieved an economic growth rate of almost 10% – the regulation in non-European countries avails of a similar in-

474 Walker identifies a well-functioning monitoring of credit accumulation as one principal economic requirement of an appropriate response to the recent financial crisis, *Walker,* in: The Future of financial regulation (2010), pp. 179 (196).

475 Cf. *Schmuhl,* Corporate Finance biz (2011), p. 139, 139.

476 http://www.aifm.de/tl_files/pdf/Angenommene%20Texte.pdf (requested August/29th/2011).

477 Official Gazette of the European Union L 174, dated July/1st/2011, pp. 1 ff.

478 On the future of "good conduct" in Europe cf. *Fleischer,* ZGR (2011), pp. 155 ff.

dustrial structure that competes with the European countries for the favour of private investors. In the age of a private capital with a high global mobility and under the conditions of the new information technology, it is important to find an answer to the recent financial crisis that does not prevent private investors from choosing the European market. In view of the increasing transnational mobility of capital and the principal objective to implement a harmonised regulation in the EU, Chapter 6 describes rules of the "European Passport of Fund Managers" (article 34 AIFMD) by defining the right of any AIFM to administrate and distribute AIF in all European Member States (Articles 31-34). Particular rules about third countries are described in Articles 34a-35 AIFM. In particular, in view of the necessity of enhanced financial supervision, Articles 40-48 of the AIFM define the responsibilities of the financial authorities and refer to the nomination, capacities and legal measures, remedies, and to the cooperation between the different responsible authorities (Articles 40-48 AIFM). Chapter 9 stipulates transitional and final clauses.

1.2. Objectives of the AIFMD

1.2.1. Overview

The objective of the AIFMD is to implement an enhanced level of financial market transparency (transparency towards investors, supervisors and the employees of the companies in which they invest), enhanced information of the financial market supervision[479] (European Securities and Markets Authority – ESMA)[480] – and ESRB to implement a monitoring of substantial systemic risks, the introduction of a common and resilient approach to the protection of the relevant investors, the strengthening and deepening of the single market and the increasing of accountability of AIFM holding controlling stakes in companies towards employees and the general public. It shall implement a coherent regulatory

[479] Further information on the future regulation of financial market supervision in the EU cf. *Wymeersch*, ECFR (2010), pp. 240, 250 ff.

[480] For further information on the ESMA see *Zülch/Hoffmann/Detzen*, EWS (2011), pp. 167 ff.

framework at the European level to protect investors, depositors and financial markets.

1.2.2. Realisation of a harmonised regulation in the EU

Because of the transnational mobility of capital, the AIFMD aims at a harmonised regulation of alternative investments in the EU. The expression "harmonisation" that is often used synonymously with the expression "approximation" of laws means the issue-related convergence of national law towards a supranational standard that aims at the abolition of national differences in law and the abolition of any distortion of competition.[481] The effort towards a legal harmonisation in the EU shall contribute to the objective of economic decision neutrality[482] in view of the order of a maximum practical effectiveness (effet utile). Decision neutrality demands that all market participants have the freedom to decide autonomously in terms of investment, financing and legal organisation.[483] It is a central objective of the European Commission and the OECD and aims at the reduction of capital export into third countries.[484]

In particular, the European Passport of Fund Managers (article 34 AIFMD) can be seen as one essential step towards a stronger legal harmonisation: For someone to develop her or his business activities in any European country, it takes only *one* registration in any European Member State. The registration procedure (Article 3a-8 AIFMD) can be seen as an integral part of the preventive control of the AIFM and a superior risk management to identify significant systemic risks. An effective preventive control may cause additional administrative costs, but it is the less-serious burden for the GDP than those resulting from the realisation of systemic risks.

---

481 Cf. *Kahl*, in: Calliess/Ruffert, EUV/EGV (2007), Article 94, bullet 1.

482 Cf. *Brähler,* Umstrukturierungen (2006), p. 3; *Fischer/Kleinedamm/Warneke,* Steuerlehre (2005), p. 44; *Jacobs*, Unternehmensbesteuerung (2011), pp. 293 f.

483 Cf. *Jacobs*, Unternehmensbesteuerung (2011), pp. 293 ff.

484 Ibid.

To achieve the allowance of the responsible supervisory bodies, the AIFM has to submit suitable documents that prove her or his qualification and attach suitable information that reveals her or his portfolio strategy. These attachments must include the names of all investors or shareholders who maintain a qualified participation in the fund, the business strategy, including detailed compliance information, detailed information on the features of the fund, contract conditions or statutes of all administrated funds, information on the portfolio strategy and the business objectives of the fund and significant information on the procedure to amend these objectives, information on the assessment procedure and possibly the calculation model for the assessment of these assets, information on the possible outsourcing of services and suitable information on the depositary of the fund assets, the assessment agency and the auditor.[485] Any AIFM who complies with these provisions will be entitled, upon notification to manage or market funds, to professional investors throughout the EU by creating a single regulatory and supervisory regime for all AIFMs, and the AIFMD will contribute to market participants to master the barriers and inefficiencies that result from the current patchwork of national regulation.[486]

The allowance is only given when the responsible authority decides that the AIFM will respect all relevant legal requirements.[487] As an exception to the latest development of the jurisdiction[488] of the ECJ, the allowance furthermore provides that the administrative centre of the AIFM and her or his statute centre are located in the same Member State of the EU.[489] According to Article 6 of the AIFMD, the responsible authorities must correspond to the application if the AIFM is expected to fulfil all legal requirements, avails himself or herself of an adequate capital (Article 6 lit. a AIFM) and adequate references and (practical) experience and – in the case where the investors hold a qualified participation –

---

485 Cf. *Jaskolski/Grüber,* Corporate Finance Law (2010), pp. 188, 193.
486 http://www.aifm.de/tl_files/pdf/MEMO-10-572_EN[1].pdf (requested August/29th/2011.
487 Article 4 AIFMD.
488 *ECJ,* judgment on December/18th/2008, C-210/06 (*Cartesio*), www.curia.europa.eu.
489 Article 4 AIFMD.

this qualified participation is suitable to a solid and cautious conduct of the AIFM. Also, the main administration and the statute centre are located in the same Member State.[490]

1.2.3. Investor protection by transparency and disclosure

According to Walker´s point of view any enhanced regulation of the financial market should secure investment trust and the fact that effective operation of those markets is well-protected in all major markets because the recent financial crisis could have resulted from the failure of investment trust.[491] To realise stronger investor protection, it provides stronger requirements of transparency and disclosure.[492] The AIFMD differentiates between the registration procedure that realises a stronger preventive transparency towards the supervisory authorities, stronger informatory requirements towards creditors, the current informatory requirements towards the financial supervisory authorities and the additional informatory requirements of leveraged funds (Article 25 AIFMD) or funds with a dominating impact (Article 26 ff. AIFMD).[493] Article 21 AIFMD provides additional informatory requirements towards the responsible authorities because any short selling[494] and the most important asset categories have to be announced. These provisions are completed by informatory requirements on the AIFM's most important market places, her or his business tools, her or his most important commitments, her or his most significant earnings and on the essential risk concentration (Article 10 AIFMD).

Under the provision that the AIFM respects the legal requirements of the annual report, the informatory obligations towards investors and towards the responsible supervisory authorities and certain further informatory obligations, the

---

490 Cf. *Heese/Lamsa,* CORPORATE FINANCE law 1/2011, p. 39, 42 f.

491 *Walker,* in: The Future of financial regulation (2010), pp. 179 (195 ff.).

492 Basically the requirements of transparency as the provision of a sustainable and proportional regulation cf. *Bhagat/Romano,* ECFR (2010), pp. 273 ff.

493 Article 1 ff. AIFMD.

494 On the present and future regulation of short selling cf. *Zimmer/Beisken,* WM (2010), pp. 485 ff.

Member States of the EU are entitled to allow the distribution of those AIF in their countries that are administrated by a AIFM who is a resident of a third country.[495]

Because of the European Commission's view that a reliable and objective assessment of assets is decisive for the protection of investors, the AIFM has to ensure that all assets that were purchased by the AIF and the value of the AIF shares are annually assessed.[496] In the case of open funds and an irregular capital increase or decrease, the AIFM also has to implement an additional assessment for periods of less than a year.[497] The assessment underlies the regulatory regime of the resident country.[498]

1.2.4. Strengthening of market integrity and market efficiency

Systemic risks that result from highly leveraged portfolio strategies will be contained by a limitation of leverage. The legal restriction of leveraged portfolio strategies aims directly at the containment of systemic risks and will implement a harmonised regulation for an enhanced market efficiency and market integrity.[499] This requirement is decisive because Walker points out that a well-functioning market provides that all market participants must trust markets to carry out their essential functions, among others. Referring to the author´s point of view, the essential market functions are the allocation of capital, processing information, risk management and wealth creation.[500]

On closer inspection, there is a closer correlation between the key factors of leverage, systemic risk and trust. For instance, a professional fund management company can get into a situation where it cannot fulfil all investor requests to

495 Cf. *Müller/Staub,* GesKR 2/2010, pp. 216, 223; on the future regulatory framework on the distribution of financial products in Germany cf. *Bruchwitz,* BB (2011), pp. 1226 ff.; *Voigt,* BB (2011), pp. 451 ff.

496 http://www.aifm.de/organisation.html (requested on August/31st/2011).

497 http://www.aifm.de/organisation.html (requested August/31st/2011).

498 Ibid.

499 Cf. *Schmuhl,* Corporate Finance biz (2011), p. 139, 140.

500 Cf. *SEC,* The Investor´s Advocate (2013), published under http://www.sec.gov/about/whatwedo.shtml, (requested July/17th/2013).

refund if these are submitted at the same time, as was shown by the 2008 bank runs. Normally, the fund management companies are committed to disclose the relation between their equity position and their leverage in their balance sheets. Thus, each investor can approximately estimate her or his individual risk of investment. A highly leveraged corporation may have the chance of having a comparatively higher yield, but it is also confronted with the higher distrust and reservation among investors that can finally result in a credit gap. Thus, Basel III requires a higher equity position as a shield against bank insolvency, stronger investor trust and the realisation of systemic risks that result from a shortage of credit supply and investor trust.

1.2.5. Monitoring of capital accumulation

Following Walker´s point of view the new financial world brought significant benefit and advance but it also generated new problems and challenges in terms of oversight, control and stability.[501] Thus, an advanced monitoring of credit accumulation must be secured at all times. To prevent a similar scenario such as the recent financial crisis in the future, the AIFM provides a stronger monitoring of capital accumulation.

As it is underlined by the considerations of the European Commission, the AIFMD aims at providing a legal framework for the enhanced monitoring of macro-prudential risks and improving risk management and organisational safeguards to minimise micro-prudential risks. The issue is not only whether investors understand the risk inherent in the CDO products which they are buying, but also that the risks that banks are taking on have to be monitored trhough public authorities being able to verify, without inordinate effort, the true level of the risks to which the bank is exposed.[502] The AIFMD will enhance the protection of the investors, improve public accountability for the AIF holding controlling stakes in companies and develop the single market for AIFM. Thus, the AIFM

---

[501] Cf. *Walker,* in: The Future of financial regulation (2010), pp. 179 (202 f.)

[502] *McIlroy* in Straus, Future of Banking (2009), pp. 119, 125.

has to take suitable measures to ensure that the managed funds appoint an independent and qualified depository that is responsible for the monitoring of the fund's activities and to ensure that the fund's cash and assets are well-protected. Thus, the depositories will be held to a high standard of liability in the case of a substantial loss of assets, and the burden of proof will reside with the depository.[503]

The AIFM has to ensure that the depositary of the fund assets uses generally accepted methods for the assessment of the fund assets to guarantee that all fund assets are assessed in correspondence with the generally accepted standard. In view of the objective of an effective containment of credit fraud and other types of white-collar crime, the AIFM is neither entitled to overtake the function of the depositary itself – she or he has to transfer this function to any credit institute that is registered in the EU – nor is she or he entitled to transfer his principal responsibility to a third person.[504] To build an effective shield against white-collar crime in the segment of alternative investments, it is essential that the future regulatory framework[505] provides a clear definition of responsibilities as one condition for an effective containment of systemic risks. Namely, the FCIC regards those public officers as primarily responsible who should have protected the financial system, those who should have conducted the regulatory agencies and those who wrongfully conducted systemically relevant corporations (manipulation of financial reports, waging of too-strong risks): Who reaches for public accountability and obtains the trust of the public.[506]

---

503 http://www.aifm.de/tl_files/pdf/MEMO-10-572_EN[1].pdf (requested August/29th/2011).

504 *Jaskolski/Grüber,* Corporate Finance Law (2010), pp. 188, 194.

505 On the future regulation of the European financial supervision cf. *Hopt,* NZG (2009), pp. 1401 ff.

506 Cf. *Nationale Kommission zur Untersuchung der Finanz- und Wirtschaftskrise,* Schlussfolgerungen (2009), p. 13.

1.3. Contents of the AIFMD

1.3.1. Fund managers focused approach

First of all, we must define the scope of the directive to gain a clear perspective about what kinds of investments are subject to the AIFMD. The AIFMD is aimed not at the funds themselves but at the fund managers and their current business activities. Its regulatory approach is to be seen in view of the AIFM's widespread economic freedom that results from the BJR.[507] In many cases it is the fund manager who decides on the investment strategy and consequently on its risk profile.[508] Because hedge funds are often located in non-European countries to obtain a greater flexibility under the less-restrictive jurisdiction of offshore-countries – a non-regulated decision of asset classes and the non-regulated use of short selling and leverage can be identified as important criteria for the success of hedge funds – this approach of indirect regulation seems appropriate because a direct access to the regulated funds is often problematic.[509] Any regulation of the investment strategies instead of regulations for fund managers that could be based on the definition of investment limits as – for example – the German approach of the dUBGG[510] could cause enormous restrictions and a decline of the private equity segment.[511] However, does this indirect approach really solve the supposed core problems of the recent financial crisis?

The AIFMD defines an AIFM as a legal or natural person whose regular business activity consists of the administration of one or more alternative investment funds (Article 3 paragraph 1 lit. c AIFM). An alternative investment fund[512]

---

507 On the BJR cf. Second Chapter, 1.3.2.

508 Cf. *Sustmann/Neuhaus/Wieland,* CORPORATE FINANCE law 2/2012, p. 78, 85.

509 Cf. *Schmuhl,* Corporate Finance biz (2011), p. 139, 141.

510 Gesetz über Unternehmensbeteiligungsgesellschaften (dUBGG) as amended and promulgated on September/9th/1998 (Federal Law Gazette I 1998, p. 2765), last time amended by Article 78 of the law of December/17th/2008 (Federal Law Gazette I 2008, p. 2586); on the future of the UBGG in the light of the AIFMD: *Sustmann/Neuhaus/Wieland,* CORPORATE FINANCE law 2/2012, p. 78.

511 Cf. *Swoboda/Schatz,* in: Striegel/Wiesbrock/Jesch, Kapitalbeteiligungsrecht (2009), p. 852.

512 On the definition of the Alternative Investment Fund under the AIFMD cf. *Kind /Haag,* DStR (2010), pp. 1526 ff.

is defined as an organism for the collective financial investment, including its investment branches that do not underlie the Undertakings for Collective Investment in Transferable Securities (UCITS[513]). The AIFMD does not apply to the UCITS funds. As a basis for the transnational distribution of financial products, the UCITS directive aims at the harmonisation registration, supervision, structure, business activities and information of UCITS in the EU.[514]

1.3.2. Regional scope

Regionally, the AIFMD not only applies to those AIFMs that are located in the EU. According to the proposal of the Spanish presidential of the European Council of 1 February 2010, the AIFMD will also apply to those AIFMs who are resident in third countries[515] (e.g., offshore countries[516] such as the Cayman Islands) and who distribute share certificates within the EU.

1.3.3. One-size-fits-all

1.3.3.1. Definition of investment fund

Against the general objective of the European Commission to subject all types of investors and all kinds of financial business activities (the one-size-fits-all approach[517]) that bear a substantial systemic risk and to implement an adequate and harmonised regulation of the financial markets, the AIFMD applies to all kinds of funds.[518] Primarily, in view of this widespread scope of the AIFMD, it is useful to describe briefly the expression "fund". Generally, this legally and

513 Directive of the European Council on the coordination of laws, regulation and administrative provisions relating to untertakings for collective investment in transferable securities (UCITS).

514 Cf. *Müller/Staub,* GesKR 2/2010, pp. 216, 216.

515 http://www.aifm.de/anwendung.html, requested August/31st/2011.

516 The term "offshore" stands for the phenomena that - under the conditions of economic globalisation, the increasing transnational mobility of capital and the digitalisation of information media - numerous microeconomic functions and processes are dislocated into countries where the market participants discover more advantageous frame conditions for their production and less expensive labour costs.

517 Cf. *Schmuhl,* Corporate Finance biz (2011), p. 139, 141.

518 Cf. *Swoboda/Schatz,* in: Striegel/Wiesbrock/Jesch, Kapitalbeteiligungsrecht (2009), p. 852; http://www.aifm.de/hintergrund-detail.html (requested August/29th/2011).

not precisely defined term stands for each kind of collective capital accumulation that is invested and administrated by third persons (fund managers and portfolio manager) for the investors.[519] Funds can be defined as special assets that are separated from the assets of the asset management company and whose objective consists of the collective investment in transferable securities. They were already very well-known as an investment strategy in Great Britain in the second half of the 19th century. Conceptually, these funds followed the idea of opening a profitable investment strategy with a straightforward risk, even for the lower-income brackets. By investing in funds, the lower-income brackets could share the advantages of the capital market and obtain well-designed opportunities of diversification.[520] Due to the batch of numerous small engagements, the asset management company gets into a stronger market position und normally obtains relatively advantageous sales conditions. The investor saves time and transaction costs because the fund manager overtakes the professional choice of assets and the professional market observation.

In particular for the lower-income brackets, investment funds represent a comparatively advantageous investment strategy because the investment is not focused on a single asset but on a portfolio and has to acknowledge the principle of risk spreading. From the investor's perspective, the abovementioned separation of assets conveys an asset shield in the case of the insolvency of the asset management company – even with this perspective the investment risk that results from the participation in a fund is normally comparatively low. However, the investor generally decides on the market segment where the investment takes place. For instance, one can choose between real estate funds, energy funds or commodity funds. Recently, funds are even distributed at the organised markets. Moreover, one can choose the investment style and opt for a cautious, risk-aware or speculative strategy. Nevertheless, the fund manager who has a direct impact on the fund administration is mandatorily committed to the principle of risk

519 Cf. *Böhringer//Funck,* in: Haisch/Helios, Finanzinstrumente (2011), p. 744.
520 Cf. *Volkart,* Corporate Finance (2008), p. 487.

spreading and must not focus on one single asset. To secure an appropriate control and supervision and the steady correspondence with the legal requirements, the fund responsibility is not concentrated with one single person but is allocated within a triangle. If someone decides to invest in a fund, she or he contacts the asset management company that is responsible for the professional and proper administration of the fund and decides on the investment strategy. The safekeeping of the fund assets is allocated at a depositary bank, which even assumes the function of stating the daily acquisition and market price.

1.3.3.2. The Approach of the AIFMD

The one-size-fits-all approach of the AIFMD evidently aims at cutting regulatory gaps. As it is underlined by the European Parliament and the financial supervision in the EU, the AIFMD will abolish trading with any non-regulated financial product.[521] Thus, the AIFMD aims at the regulation of each legal or natural character independent of her or his legal entity responsible for the administration of an AIF that is not subject to the UCITS directive.[522] It covers almost every kind of institutional funds, such as shipping funds. Moreover, it covers real estate funds, commodity funds, currency funds, mezzanine funds, infrastructure funds and other types of credit accumulation, respectively other kinds of institutional[523] funds for alternative assets – independent of their legal entity or structure of organisation.[524]

1.3.3.3. Open and closed investment funds

In particular, the AIFMD applies to open funds and closed funds.[525] In contrast to a closed investment fund, an open investment fund is generally accessible

---

521 http://www.aifm.de/hintergrund-detail.html (requested August/29th/2011).

522 Cf. *Müller/Staub,* GesKR 2/2010, pp. 216, 222.

523 A fund can be qualified as institutional if its main business consists of the undertaking of financial investments, cf. *Kind /Haag,* DStR (2010), pp. 1526, 1527.

524 Cf. *Swoboda/Schatz,* in: Striegel/Wiesbrock/Jesch, Kapitalbeteiligungsrecht (2009), p. 852; http://www.aifm.de/hintergrund-detail.html (requested August/29th/2011).

525 On the recently discussed topic whether the AIFMD is even subject to the so-called family offices cf. *Krause/Klebeck,* BB (2012), pp. 2063 ff.

to anyone who avails himself or herself of the required minimum investment (sometimes €25) and enables the investor to the sale and purchase at any arbitrary point of time. By purchasing the shares of the fund, the investor achieves the legal position of a joint owner of the fund assets and is entitled to participate in the surplus of the fund. In contrast to a participation in a closed-end fund, the investment management company takes the legal position of a formal proprietor of the assets, according to which it is signed in the respective land register.

By request, the fund management company is normally legally committed to resell the fund shares at any point of time at the respective market price, which means that an open fund investment does not result in a restricted cash flow for the depositor/investor: The investor remains liquid because the steady availability of the invested money is secured. General restrictions do not exist. The total investment of an open investment fund is not limited. As a typical feature of open funds, the number of shares is generally not defined and corresponds to the number of requests. In contrast, the number of shares of a closed investment fund is limited, which means that the fund is closed as soon as all available shares are sold. Nevertheless, the "shareholders" of a closed fund are entitled to transfer their shares to another person. At best, in exceptional cases, the access to the fund can temporarily be restricted if the fund is based on shares whose quantity is limited – for example, this can happen at the emerging stock exchange of a small, developing country.

The generally limited investment risk resulting from the portfolio investment can be further limited if the investment is focused on an umbrella fund. An umbrella fund focuses on several further funds, which has the effect that the relevant risks are additionally spread. As a consequence, even the current market developments can be displayed in the development of the fund investment with a significant delay. Thus, not only the investment risk but also the yield of an umbrella fund is typically under average.

From the investor's perspective, another disadvantage of open investment funds can result from those information asymmetries that result from the fact that the asset management company is not committed to deliver more information on its investment strategy than she or he is legally committed to. It is, however, questionable whether those information asymmetries really create a disadvantage for the single investor – if she or he is not a financial expert and only has the objective to earn money but not to take a strategic impact on a certain market development. In this situation, it is necessary to distinguish between the possession of information and the ability to analyse the available information properly, specifically in correspondence with the chosen investment strategy. Normally, the fund management company consists of financial experts who have access to sources of information that are not readily available to each single investor. Furthermore, they operate very close to the markets and can react more speedily than the single investor, which is a great advantage with the conditions of high-frequency trade (HFT).[526]

Another potential disadvantage that should be considered before the investment concerns those practical problems that can arise if a greater number of fund investors decide to disinvest at the same time. If the asset management company cannot fulfil its legal commitment to immediately meet the reclaim by the respective cash flow, the fulfilment of the investor's request can be delayed – thus, this delay can cause capital losses for all fund-participating investors. If the fund is a real estate fund, a synchronised reclaim can cause additional losses for all investors because these assets are typically financed by bank loans – specifically, a synchronised reclaim towards leveraged funds can result in an interest compensation claim.

As an exception, the managers of pension funds and the administrators of non-pooled assets such as foundations, state funds or those investments that are

[526] Latest information on the development of the HFT in view of the often political biased discussion on the introduction of an European financial transaction tax that shall contain systemic risks cf. *Frey/Bruhn,* BB (No. 29/2012), p. 1763; *Hunkemöller,* BB (No. 29/2012), First page.

held by credit institutes, assurance companies and reassurances are also not subject to the AIFMD.[527] Those funds that also aim at a monetary participation of employees (Article 2 paragraph 2 lit. f AIFMD), social assurance and pension funds (Article 2 paragraph 2 lit. e AIFMD) and holdings (Article 3 paragraph 1 lit. r AIFMD) are not subject to the AIFMD.[528] In addition, those fund managers who administrate one or several funds whose only investor is the AIFM itself, its holding company, its affiliate company or other affiliate companies of those holding company as far as none of those investors is an AIF itself, do not underlie the AIFMD (corporate groups privilege). Finally, it is also not subjected to supranational institutions, such as the World Bank, member organisations of the World Bank Group and other entities.[529]

1.3.4. De minimis exemption (quantitative scope)

As another exemption of the general scope of the AIFMD that refers to the business volume of the AIFM, the de minimis exemption eases the future regulatory framework for small accumulations of capital. The de minimis exemption states that AIFMs who administrate an asset volume of not more than €100 million only have to fulfil the requirements of Article 2a paragraph 3 of the AIFMD: They only have to fulfil the requirement of registration and disclosure of their portfolio strategy towards the responsible national supervisory authority. Moreover, when they do not administrate a leveraged portfolio and the investors are not entitled to cancel their investment within five years from the initial launch of the private equity fund, the de minimis exemption goes up to €500 million. This exception aims at the reduction of administration and transaction costs by the financial supervisory authorities. Transaction costs are those that are necessary

[527] Cf. *Swoboda/Schatz,* in: Striegel/Wiesbrock/Jesch, Kapitalbeteiligungsrecht (2009), p. 852.
[528] http://www.aifm.de/tl_files/pdf/MEMO-10-572_EN[1].pdf (requested August/29th/2011).
[529] http://www.aifm.de/tl_files/pdf/MEMO-10-572_EN[1].pdf (requested August/29th/2011).

for the execution of any transaction, such as the costs of information, communication and coordination (e.g., contractual costs).[530]

When an AIFM does not cross the relevant bar of €500 million, she or he must inform the responsible financial authorities about the most important tools, the biggest risks and risk concentration at those funds she or he administrates; this requirement will also contain significant systemic risks.[531] The trigger point of €500 million will exclude many fund managers from venture capital funds from the scope of the AIFMD to ease the access to the capital market, even in times of a generally restricted credit supply.[532]

The de minimis exemption can be seen because systemic risks are a result of the amount of credit accumulation. A certain level of credit accumulation can be seen as a result of a well-functioning competition if it contributes to the general public welfare such as maintaining price stability. However, if it crosses a certain level, it can cause serious risks to the market integrity. Walker identifies the volume of credit accumulation in the financial segment as one core reason for the recent financial crisis. Thus, the de minimis exemption that states an exception for a small AIFM is a consequence of the principle of proportionality.[533] In a way, it respects Walker´s[534] postulation that any sustainable financial regulation must avoid overreaction.

The AIFMD neither precisely defines the procedure for how the relevant business volume should be determined nor does it define the relevant point in time. Because of the principal objective to implement effective investor protection, and in view of the fact that any "portfolio-focused approach" does not contribute to the further objective of legal and planning security, it is preferable to

---

530 Cf. *Dietl,* in: Köhler/Küpper/Pfingsten, Betriebswirtschaft (2007), pp. 1750, 1751; *Jost,* in: Köhler/Küpper/Pfingsten, Betriebswirtschaft (2007) pp. 782, 783.

531 http://www.aifm.de/anwendung.html (recently requested on August/31st/2011).

532 *Tollmann,* Hertz-Eichenrode/Illenberger/Jesch/Keller/Klebeck/Rocholl, Private Equity-Lexikon (2011), p. 4 (5).

533 Cf. third chapter, 1.1.

534 Cf. *Walker,* in: The Future of financial regulation (2010), pp. 179 (202).

focus on the depository obligations of the investors.[535] Referring to the phrase "assets under management", which also covers those deposits that are already performed, it also seems possible to focus on the already-performed deposits.[536]

1.3.5. Administrating activities requirements

In this content, the legal interpretation of the word "administrate", which describes the key element of the alternative fund managers' activity, is not yet clear because Articles 8a-18 of the AIFMD do not include any legal definition. Furthermore, it does not define precisely what measures it takes to fulfil the requirement of "cautious" conduct. Many of the terms that are used by the directive, such as the requirement of honest, cautious, diligent and fair conduct (Article 9 AIFMD), are general principles. They are less concrete, not legally defined and can be qualified as sentences that neither underlie the juridical control nor that can be controlled fragmentarily. Finally, they are subject to national implementing rules that still have to be enacted and that must respect the general objective to protect market integrity and the principle that all investors must be treated justly and equitably (Article 9 paragraph 1 lit. f AIFMD). The principle to treat all investors justly and equitably is concretised at the end of Article 9 paragraph 1 AIFMD, which forbids the AIFM to give any investor special privileges.

The systematic position of the AIFMD in EU law hints at an interpretation that covers services such as the portfolio management, the risk management and the marketing of the fund, whereas any activity that does not include an element of power for strategic decisions cannot be defined as "administration" – thus, only consulting activity of the fund manager cannot be defined under the term "administration".[537] Finally, the interpretation must not neglect the objective of the AIFMD to contain systemic risks. A mere consulting activity that aims at the preparation of portfolio decisions seems insufficient to cause systemic risks because it has no direct impact on the market integrity. Finally, Article 34a of the

535 Cf. *Swoboda/Schatz,* in: Striegel/Wiesbrock/Jesch, Kapitalbeteiligungsrecht (2009), p. 854.
536 Ibid.
537 Cf. *Heese/Lamsa,* CORPORATE FINANCE law 1/2011, p. 39, 41.

latest version of the AIFMD allows this kind of distribution under the provision of suitable tools that guarantee the monitoring of systemic risks in accordance with the international standards and the continuous corporation between the supervisory authorities of the concerned Member State and the third country.[538]

Article 18 of the AIFMD entitles the AIFM to transfer certain administrative tasks to an experienced third person. In the latest version of the AIFMD, the AIFM is entitled to outsource the portfolio management and the risk management to a company in a third country under the provision that this company underlies a (financial) supervision in its function as fund manager, and that the responsible supervisory authority in the third country cooperates with the delegating AIFM.[539] This regulation goes back to the Spanish proposal for an amendment of the AIFMD and can be seen as a consequence of the liberty of economic freedom of organisation that is granted by the ECFR. It is a tribute to the awareness of the enormous transnational mobility of capital. Moreover, the AIFM normally has a strong intrinsic incentive not to lose the "allowance to operate", so that it does not seem very probable that one will abuse one´s economic freedom for an efficient organisation, an (international) division of labour.

Due to Articles 34a-35 of the AIFMD, the distribution of any AIF that is located in third countries and administrated by an AIFM who resides in a Member State of the EU provides that the AIFM fulfils all requirements of the AIFMD except those from the articles on the depository, and, furthermore, that there exists an agreement with the third country which secures an efficient exchange of information with the third-country supervisory authorities.[540]

1.3.6. Equity requirements

Because the European Commission holds a minimum capital of the AIFM as inevitable to contain significant liability risks of the AIFM, Article 14 AIFMD

538 Cf. *Müller/Staub,* GesKR 2/2010, pp. 216, 223.

539 Article 18 paragraph 1 AIFMD in the version of the Spanish proposal, dated March/ 10th/2010.

540 Cf. *Müller/Staub,* GesKR 2/2010, pp. 216, 222.

provides harmonised capital requirements in the EU and will ensure that the AIFM avail himself or herself of adequate capital to fulfil the current contractual obligations.[541] Article 14 of the AIFMD is based on an "impact assessment" approach that will seriously affect the implementation and organisation of an AIFM.[542] Finally, it is seen as a significant barrier for the further development of the European private equity market.[543] The minimum capital requirements that are stipulated by the AIFMD will secure a minimum of liquid assets that are transferable into cash immediately and that do not include speculative elements (Article 6 lit. a paragraph 8 AIFM) and which also aim at a continuous and regular administration of the AIF by its managers.[544]

To secure a continuous and regular administration of the AIF, the AIFM must avail himself or herself of a minimum of capital resources that must be liquid and quickly available. Its volume must cover 25% of the general costs of the last business period – specifically, the business planning but not less than €125,000, €300,000 in the case of an internal AIFM.[545] If the relevant assets go over €250 million, it takes additional capital resources that must correspond to 0.02% of that capital amount, which goes over the relevant amount of €250 million.[546] Effectively, in view of Walker's experience that systemic risks result from the amount of credit accumulation, the total amount of capital resources is limited by €10 million. Finally, the AIFMD entitles the AIFM to deposit 50% of the minimum capital in the form of an assurance or bank guarantee.[547]

1.3.7. Risk management requirements

To lessen the potential for systemic risk, the AIFM has to implement an advanced risk management system that focuses on a functional and hierarchical

---

[541] Cf. *Swoboda/Schatz,* in: Striegel/Wiesbrock/Jesch, Kapitalbeteiligungsrecht (2009), p. 857.
[542] Ibid.
[543] Ibid.
[544] Cf. *Heese/Lamsa,* CORPORATE FINANCE law 1/2011, p. 39, 43.
[545] http://www.aifm.de/eigenkapitalanforderungen.html (requested August/31st/2011).
[546] http://www.aifm.de/eigenkapitalanforderungen.html (requested August/31st/2011).
[547] Ibid.

separation of risk management and portfolio management.[548] An adequate risk management strategy has to ensure that all systemically significant risks are continuously identified, assessed and contained – specifically, that the liquidity profile of the deposits corresponds with the relevant debts.[549]

Although alternative investments can be characterised by certain general features, such as the use of leverage tools, the use of short selling and the fact that they are normally not traded at an organised market, they appear in a very different way as a consequence of their business volume, their structure of investors (e.g., strategic investors or financial investors) and their product placement. As a consequence, the AIFMD does not state detailed requirements for the implementation of the risk management that needs to be established. In view of the principal objectives of the AIFMD (effective containment of systemic risks, effective protection of investors), it is imperative that the AIFM secures the full correspondence between the contractual conditions with the portfolio strategy and its principal objectives.[550] Moreover, it is decisive that all systemically relevant risks and their effect on the portfolio as a whole can be monitored at any time by a suitable "stress test"[551].[552]

The AIFM must ensure that the risk management corresponds to a certain standard. This requires an accurate identification, evaluation and supervision of those risks that result from investments and that directly affect the portfolio as a whole, inclusively the implementation of a "stress test".[553] Furthermore, this must take suitable measures for the compliance of the relevant risk profile in relation with the total business volume, the portfolio structure, the investment strategies and the investment objectives that are defined in the statute, the business prospect and the emission attachments.[554] The AIFM is subject to specific requirements if

548 Ibid.
549 *Jaskolski/Grüber,* Corporate Finance Law (2010), pp. 188, 194.
550 Ibid.
551 Cf. *Walker,* in: The Future of financial regulation (2010), pp. 179 (196).
552 *Jaskolski/Grüber,* Corporate Finance Law (2010), pp. 188, 194.
553 http://www.aifm.de/verhaltensregelungen.html (requested August/31st/2011).
554 Ibid.

the business model should be based on the use of leverage effects.[555] An advanced risk management has to inform all investors about leverage tools, secure a continuous monitoring of the risks of the portfolio as a whole and take suitable measures that these risks are in compliance with the relevant contract conditions and emission prospects.

As a minimum, the required risk management will also have to embrace an adequate, regularly updated due diligence before any investment.[556] A due diligence aims at the exposure of chances and risks of an investment to verify the purchase price. It should be mandatory in view of the normative decision theory,[557] which provides that any investment decision should only be made on the basis of complete information.[558] As we know from the recent financial crisis, we shouldn't purchase a product that we don't understand.

1.3.8. Supervisory requirements

Following Walker´s point of view[559], all financial markets must be subject to an effective oversight and control that refers to the capital and liquidity reserves, risk management, asset valuation and incentives.[560] To secure an effective control of the liquidity reserves, the AIFMD provides an adequate liquidity management that requires regular "stress tests" for usual and unusual liquidity conditions.[561] The regulations on the recall of AIF investments and the investment strategy must correspond with the liquidity demand of the AIF.[562]

---

555 Ibid.

556 Article 11 AIFMD; http://www.aifm.de/verhaltensregelungen.html (requested on August/31st/2011).

557 The normative decision theory faces the question of what it takes to define an optimal decision in a certain situation under all relevant circumstances. It recognises the number of different objectives, the information basis of the market participants concerning the reality (security, risk, uncertainty) and the character of the person who has to drew the decision, cf. *Bamberg,* in: Köhler/Küpper/Pfingsten, Betriebswirtschaft (2007), p. 383 f.; Further information on the decision theory: *Baums,* ZGR (2011), pp. 218 ff.

558 *Liekefett,* Due Diligence (2005), p. 41.

559 Cf. *Walker,* in: The Future of financial regulation (2010), pp. 179 (195 ff. , 202 ff.).

560 http://www.aifm.de/verhaltensregelungen.html (requested August/31st/2011).

561 Ibid.

562 Ibid.

1.3.9. Transparency requirements

Transparency helps to build a "bridge of confidence and trust" as one essential condition for the protection of what is probably the most important capital of a corporation: its reputation. An enhanced transparency contributes to reduce the current transaction costs of a corporation because the investors rely on this reputation. A corporation that voluntarily respects certain transparency standards has a comparatively higher business reputation – not only among customers and investors but also among the financial supervisory authorities and the general public, whose acceptance is significant for the corporation's "license to operate".[563] Furthermore, the general understanding of financial products is one essential condition for the containment of systemic risks because it can be defined as one element of the investors' risk management, where they normally do not intentionally purchase a financial product they don't understand and whose risk they cannot estimate. In particular, compelling legal requirements about the transparency of alternative investments are decisive in view of the fact that those business models – different from the share trade at the organised capital markets – are often based on the obscurity of their portfolio strategy, which leads to their financial supervision become a "fight against windmills". Yields on the basis of non-transparent business models often bear the danger of significant systemic risk.

Because the lack of transparency can be identified as one core reason for the recent financial crisis, the European Commission's approach to contain a similar crisis in the future can be seen as a *"key part of the European Commission's drive to lay the regulatory foundations for a secure financial system that supports and stimulates the Real Economy."*[564]

---

563 Basically the "license to operate" is the synonym for the general acceptance of a corporation under the conditions of economic globalisation cf. *Heap,* Legal framework (2009), p. 171 ff.; *Huber,* in: Straus, Globalized Economy (2009), p. 55 f.; *Türk,* in: Straus, Globalized Economy (2009), pp. 3 ff.

564 http://www.aifm.de/tl_files/pdf/MEMO-10-572_EN[1].pdf (requested August/29th/2011).

Against the highlighted regulatory background, the AIFMD provides stronger transparency requirements (Articles 19-21 of the AIFMD). These include an annual report on the current business activities that has to be drawn up no later than six months after the close of the relevant financial year (Article 19 of the AIFMD). This mandatory report will be submitted to the responsible financial authorities and must contain a balance sheet and an overview of the assets, a list of all yields and expenses, information on the manager's remuneration structure and the carried interest and a report on all business activities in the relevant period.[565] Moreover, the AIFM has to publish the remuneration of those managers whose business activities significantly affect the risk profile of the AIF and – before any investment – the portfolio strategy, possible leverage tools, and the principles in the case of a recall of the investment and the assessment principles.[566] These mandatory information requirements will contribute to a continuous monitoring and analysing of potential systemic risks and are strengthened in the case where the AIFM uses leverage tools. In that case, the AIFM also has to inform the responsible financial authority about the total amount of leverage of each AIF and the source of leverage (credits, lender of shares or derivatives).[567] The comparatively five biggest creditors (share lenders) must be identified.[568]

1.4. Transformation into national law

1.4.1. Regulatory technique

In comparison with the European Legal Ordinance that sets a harmonised and mandatory regulatory framework in all European Member States, the European Directive is only compelling with regard to its regulatory objective. It principally requires the transformation in each Member State into its own national law.[569] Thus, the European directive is the relatively proportional measure to realise the

565 *Jaskolski/Grüber,* Corporate Finance Law (2010), pp. 188, 195.
566 Ibid.
567 Ibid.
568 Article 21 paragraph 4 AIFMD.
569 In particular, on the transformation of the AIFMD into German law cf. *Jesch/Geyer,* BKR (No. 9/2012), p. 359 ff.

superior objective of the common market by respecting national traditions and customs[570] because the Member States as the consignees of the directive have a formal arrangement[571] at its transformation into national law: They must not go below the compelling minimum standard of the directive, but they are free to stipulate stronger rules. Thus, the EU awards a "sovereignty reserve" to the Member States. Functionally, the regulatory technique of the directive principally contributes to the coordination of the different national legal and administrative rules.[572] In view of the principle of practice effectiveness (effet utile)[573] any natural or legal person is entitled to directly invoke the rules of the directive should the time corridor for the national transformation elapse without result.[574] According to the jurisdiction of the ECJ[575], each European Member State is forbidden to interdict the direct invoke on a European directive.

As one consequence of the legal character of each directive, the targets of the AIFMD are mandatory to any European Member State. Each European country has the decision autonomy to implement a regulation for all types of AIF or only for those that cross the relevant bar.[576] However, each European Member State makes the independent decision whether it transfers all relevant articles into national law or only those that go beyond the de minimis exemption.[577]

1.4.2. Time corridor

After the AIFMD was released in the European Gazette, the European Member States had two years to transfer it into their own national laws. These two years began with the first day after the AIFMD became effective, 21 July 2011,

---

570 Cf. *Härtel*, Handbuch (2006), p. 173 (§ 9, bullet 14).

571 Cf. *Hetmeier*, in: Lenz/Borchardt, EGV (2006), § 249, bullet 9.

572 Cf. *Härtel*, Handbuch (2006), p. 173 (§ 9, bullet 14).

573 Cf. *Nagel*, Wirtschaftsrecht (2003), p. 59 ff.

574 Cf. *ECJ*, C-221/88 *(Busseni)*, Collection of decisions (1990), p. I-495 = NJW 1991, p. 1409; *ECJ*, C-91/92 *(Faccini Dori)*, Collection of decisions (1994), p. I-3325; *ECJ*, C-5/83 *(Rienks)*, Collection of decisions (1983), p. I-4223; *ECJ*, C-8/81 *(Becker)*, Collection of decisions 1982, p. 53 = NJW (1982), p. 499.

575 Cf. *ECJ*, at: *Bieber/Epiney/Haag*, EU (2005), § 6, bullet 64.

576 Cf. Proposal of the European Commission, http://register.consilium.europa.eu/pdf/de/10/st06/st06795-re03.de10.pdf, Article 2b (requested August/25th/2011).

577 Cf. *Jaskolski/Grüber*, Corporate Finance Law (2010), pp. 188, 193.

and it ends on 22 July 2013 (Article 66 AIFMD). Within this time period, the European Commission, assisted by the European Securities Supervision (ESMA), will release implementation rules that contribute to the practical implementation of the AIFMD.

1.5. Level 2-Measures (AIFMD-IRR)

1.5.1. Timeline and introduction

To enable any concretisation of the AIFMD by the European Member States, the ESMA[578] has already been requested to work out the so-called "Level 2 Measures" – the consultation of the relevant market participants ended on 14 January 2011. With the "Level 2 Measures" the European Commission is requested to define all kinds of possible conflicts of interests and the organisational and administrative requirements to contain those conflicts of interest prospectively.[579] Additionally, the European Commission must define the criteria of an enhanced risk management[580], such as the liquidity requirements (liquidity management systems, liquidity management procedure and the coherence between investment strategy, liquidity profile and the principles on the recall of investments).[581] The ESMA presented its propositions for suitable implementing rules on 16 November 2011 on time (ESMA recommendations on general provisions, authorization and operating conditions, depositary, transparency requirements and leverage and supervision). Already on 23 February 2012, the ESMA released a discussion paper on key concepts of the AIFMD and types of AIFM, which represented a first step to elaborating the draft regulatory technical standards (RTS) subject to Article 4 paragraph 4 AIFMD. Based at the ESMA-recommendations, the European Commission released implementing rules for the AIFMD-

578 *ESMA,* ESMA's response to the European Commission's provisional request to CESR/ ESMA for technical advice on possible Level 2 measures concerning the Directive for Alternative Investment Fund Managers (AIFM), published under http://www.esma.europa.eu/ system/files/2011_382.pdf.

579 http://www.aifm.de/verhaltensregelungen.html (requested July/6th/2013).

580 Ibid.

581 Ibid.

Supplementing Directive 2011/61/EU of the European Parliament and of the Council with regard to exemptions, general operating conditions, depositaries, leverage, transparency and supervision (AIFMD-implementing rules and regulations, AIFMD-IRR[582]) – on 19 December 2012. The AIFMD-IRR shall be implemented by an additional state law of the European Commission, Nr. 231/2013 (EU), dated 19 December 2012[583].[584]

1.5.2. Legal objectives

In view of the predominating objective of the AIFMD to provide a clear and consistent framework for the regulation and supervision of AIFM in the EU and to ensure a high level of investor protection in the European Union, the AIFMD-IRR shall secure preferably consistent implementation of the AIFMD in the European Member States and, moreover, contribute to the effective containment of systemic risks. In view of these objectives, the AIFMD-IRR shall provide

- Firstly, a common approach to calculate the respective assets under management – AuM – ("issue 1"),
- Secondly, common methods to determine an AIF´s leverage, both as a reflection of the AIF´s "footprint" as a trigger for leverage-related reporting – "substantial use of leverage" – ("issue 2"),
- Thirdly, a common approach on the AIF´s level of additional own funds – operational continuity – ("issue 3"),
- Fourthly, a common approach on the scope of custody and, moreover, the repositories liability to return financial instruments lost in custody ("issue 4"),
- Fifthly, a common approach to AIF´s frequency ("issue 5").

582 Published under http://ec.europa.eu/internal_market/investment/docs/20121219-directive/delegated-act_en.pdf.
583 Official Gazette of the European Union L 83/1 (22 March 2013).
584 Cf. http://ec.europa.eu/internal_market/investment/docs/20121219-directive/delegated-act_en.pdf

1.5.3. Contents at a glance

The AIFMD-IRR embrace comparatively detailed rules that notably concern the calculation of the administrated assets (Article 3 paragraph 6 AIFMD-IRR) and the methods to calculate the leverage (Article 4 paragraph 3 AIFMD-IRR). It prescribes requirements of additional own funds or the professional indemnity insurance (PII[585]), which covers professional liability risks and therefore implicates the level of investor protection achieved by the AIFMD (Article 9 paragraph 9 AIFMD-IRR). Moreover, it prescribes the perimeter of financial instruments that can be registered in a depositary's financial instruments account, which determines the scope of the latter's obligation to return instruments lost in custody (Article 21 paragraph 17 AIFMD-IRR). It also provides the scope of liability for losses that occur while an instrument is held in custody, determining the level of investor protection (Article 21 paragraph 17 AIFMD-IRR), the precise scope of cash monitoring that is important for investor protection (Article 21 paragraph 17 AIFMD-IRR), and reporting frequencies that are decisive to implement adequate monitoring of systemic risks at macro-prudential and micro-prudential level to secure an adequate level of investor protection (Article 24 paragraph 6 Level II measures). It also gives precise requirements for that case that leverage is to be considered to be *employed on a substantial basis* and crucial in triggering the reporting obligations in Article 24 paragraph 4 AIFMD (Article 24 paragraph 6 AIFMD-IRR).

Moreover, the AIFMD-IRR determines conditions and procedures for the determination and authorization of AIFMs, including the capital requirements applicable to AIFMs; operating conditions for AIFMs, including rules on remuneration, conflicts of interest, risk management, liquidity management, investment in securitisation positions, organisational requirements, and rules on valuation; con-

585 The PII, which is known under the expression errors & omissions (E&O), particularly in the USA, represents a form of liability insurance that contributes to protecting professional advice- and service-providing individuals and corporations from bearing the unlimited cost of defending against an omission claim placed by a client, and damages awarded in such a civil lawsuit.

ditions for delegation, including further clarity on the meaning of a letter box entity; rules on depositaries and rules for cooperation arrangements.

1.5.4. Contents in detail

Article 2 AIFMD-IRR demands the AIFM to precisely calculate the total AuM. The AIFM is therefore committed to register all AIF (Article 2 paragraph 1 lit a) AIFMD-IRR). For each administrated fund, one has to register the respective portfolio value according to the binding rules of one´s locating country and, should this be necessary, register the value of the AuM according to valuating rules that are determined by the statutory law of the AIF (Article 2 paragraph 1 lit b AIFMD-IRR).

To calculate the respective assets, these shall be valued without deducting liabilities and assessing the taken financial derivative instruments (FDIs[586]) at the value of an equivalent position in the underlying assets. The FDIs shall be valued under correspondence with the underlying assets acquired by the fund reflects the AIF´s exposure to these assets.

Referring to the leverage ratio (Article 4 AIFMD), the European Commission prefers to combine the "Gross-method" and the "Commitment-method". Resulting from applying the first method, those leverage ratios follow the principal objective of the AIFMD to capture the respective macro-prudential risks early and consistently. The "Commitment-method", meanwhile, has become well established and acknowledged in the asset management segment. Its effects can be readily compared with those for UCITS funds.

In combination with the "Gross-method", the "Commitment-method" provides a good insight into the investment strategies and exposure of those AIF relevant for the respective stakeholders, notably towards investors and supervisors. In case of proven necessity for an additional method to better apprehend

[586] As already mentioned, derivative transactions typically include a broad diversity of financial contracts, such as structured debt obligations and deposits, swaps, futures, options, caps, floors, collars, forwards and various combinations of these.

systemic risk, the ESMA shall be authorized to propose the respective precise parameters. This method would then be adopted by modifying the delegated act. Recourse to an advanced method must not obviate the calculation of leverage according to the "Gross-method" and the "Commitment-method" – both remain mandatory to all AIFM. According to the author ´s point of view, these leverage conditions could nevertheless result in the disclosure of figures that do not properly represent the true leverage of the fund and, moreover, cause significant confusion to investors.

According to the aforementioned ESMA-recommendations, the AIFM should calculate any additional fund based on the variable AuM and, moreover, combine additional own funds and PII subject to certain conditions (General operating conditions).[587] Thus, any additional own fund cover professional liability risks up to a volume of 0.01% of the AuM, calculated on gross assets valuing derivatives at market price. Alternatively, any PII with coverage of 0.9% of AuM for aggregate of claims/year and 0.7% of AuM per individual claim seem to be appropriate to protect investors from damages that result from the AIFM's professional failures. This approach differs from the ESMA recommendation for a minimum threshold and a cap on the PII. The European Commission regards this proposal as being inconsistent with the absence of any cap in calculating additional own funds.

Concerning the custody requirements, the European Commission holds the view that, following the option to consistently register systemically relevant financial means (transferable securities, money market instruments[588], units in collective investment undertakings) belonging to an AIF, shall be held in custody. Even this approach differs from the ESMA-recommendation to the extent that AIF assets may not be excluded from the scope of custody since they are subject of a security interest collateral arrangement. Should any AIF provide its assets as collateral to collateral takers, the AIFMD requires that these assets remain in cus-

[587] Cf. http://www.esma.europa.eu/system/files/2011_382.pdf
[588] Definition money markets cf. Annotation No. 48.

tody – except if the AIF transfers ownership of the collateralised assets to the collateral taker (title transfer collateral arrangement).

Custody of the collateralised AIF assets can be ensured either through the process that the collateral taker is appointed custodian over the collateralised AIF's assets or the AIF's depositary appoints a sub-custodian that acts for the collateral taker. Alternatively, collateralised assets remain with the AIF's depositary and are 'earmarked' in favor of the collateral taker. Anyway, the aforementioned custody design reflects industry practice and ensures that the depositary is not liable for the return of those assets that do not underlay its "control". Moreover, the proposed approach that corresponds with the AIFMD Level 1-measures does not require that a central counterparty (CCP) becomes a sub-custodian.

Concerning depositary and the definition of an "external event", the European Commission shares the recommendations of the ESMA and advises to deem any event that does not relate to the operational sphere of a depositary or its appointed network of sub-custodians (custody operations fraud, operational failures or any lack of compliance with the respective AIFMD's legal operational provisions) as an external event. In case of insolvency of any sub-custodian, possibly operational mistakes by the sub-custodian, like its lack of ability to organize the segregation requirement, is not qualified as an "external event". As a consequence, external events would be natural disasters or acts of state or government measures (e.g. market closures).

Concerning the scope of cash monitoring, the European Commission prefers to assign the mandatory commitment to the depository to perform ex-post periodic reconciliations of AIF's cash flows. This would enable the depositary to identify cash flows that obviously do not comply with the investment strategy of the AIF. Furthermore, it could notify the AIFM and, if the discrepancies are not resolved, the responsible authority would be informed. On the one hand, this approach could effectively minimize those significant expenses that possibly result from delays in AIF's transactions in the case of an ex-ante cash monitoring regime. On the other hand, a cash monitoring regime that reduces the function of the depositary on verifying that the AIFM or any third party has procedures in place to reconcile the AIF's cash flows and monitoring the outcomes of the reconciliations is considered less effective and robust than the preferred option. The effectiveness of this approach would entirely depend on the effectiveness and the accuracy of the cash monitoring and reconciliations by the AIFM itself with the inherent conflicts of interest. Since the AIFM or any third party are not legally required to perform the reconciliations, the verification regime also entails legal uncertainty as to whether the reconciliations would be performed at all and whether the depositary has duly discharged its cash monitoring obligations. Providing legal certainty and containing operational weaknesses and risks of fraud were the main reasons for deviating from the regime based on verification of procedures as proposed by the ESMA.

Concerning the reporting requirements, following the recommendations of the ESMA and realizing adequate regulatory reporting standards in a major non-EU AIFM jurisdiction, the AIFM shall be generally committed to quarterly reporting. Should the respective AuM reach a total volume of more than 1 billion Euros, semi-annual reporting is mandatory. Moreover, the AIFMD-IRR prescribes annual reporting for AIFM with AuM below the AIFMD-threshold. Against the background of the characteristic investment policy of private equity and venture capital and to effectively contain non-proportional administrative burdens for smaller AIFMs, managers that "rule" non-leveraged AIFs which invest in non-registered corporations and issuers in order to acquire control only have to perform annual reporting.

Furthermore, As the European Commission underlines, an AIF would be ideally considered to be employing leverage on a substantial basis when its exposure, as calculated using the before-mentioned "Commitment-method", exceeds three times the net asset value (NAV[589]) of the AIF. This shall provide the preferably best trade-off between adequate reporting on leverage and the administrative effort on the AIFM and the responsible authorities. A threshold that covers three times that of the NAV would realize leverage related reporting by AIFMs that employ higher levels of leverage while exempting AIFMs, whose leverage is similar or close to those employed by UCITS. This approach would even require one level playing field and, moreover, legal certainty to AIFMs due to their reporting obligations. The significance of legal certainty was probably the predominating cause for the differences from the ESMA-recommendation that proposes self-assessment by the AIFM.

1.6. Review

As the first attempt to establish a harmonised European regulation of the private equity segment, the AIFMD tries to close a threatening gap in the financial market regulation. It shall close this gap by stipulating an equal regulatory framework that is mandatory for various kinds of alternative investments. It focuses on the alternative fund manager who avails himself or herself of a widespread economic freedom and who has responsibility for the liquidity management and the risk management of the AIF. The AIFMD will abolish trading with any non-regulated financial product. Also, the equal treatment shall enhance the neutrality of economic decisions.

The AIFMD contains detailed requirements on the registration, the administration, the portfolio strategy, and the annual reporting to strengthen investor protection, market integrity and market efficiency. Moreover, to reduce current information asymmetries and in view of the awareness that the financial crisis of 2008/2009 revealed a widespread failure of investment trust, the AIFMD puts one major focus on the transparency of the administrated financial product, the

589 In general, the NAV can be defined as the mutual fund's price per share or exchange-traded fund's (ETF) per-share value. In both cases, the per-share dollar amount of the fund is calculated by dividing the total value of all the securities in its portfolio, less any liabilities, by the number of fund shares outstanding, cf. http://www.investopedia.com/terms/n/nav.asp.

investment strategy and the remuneration of the involved fund managers (Articles 19-21) to enhance the protection of investors and depositors ("good conduct"). It will contribute to the establishing of an advanced monitoring of the alternative investment circulation as one essential provision for the early identification of systemic risks and, moreover, the implementation of an enhanced financial supervision. Furthermore, the AIFMD aims at the strengthening of the equity position of the AIFM (Article 14 AIFMD). Thus, it requires an annual assessment of all relevant assets and a limitation of leverage. In correspondence with Walker´s awareness that systemic risks result from a too-strong credit accumulation, it implements a "de minimis exemption" that excludes those investment funds that do not cover more than €100 million, specifically €500 million: A sustainable financial regulation should avoid over-reaction and unnecessary regressive response.

The current 28 European Member States are being given until 21 July 2013 to transform the AIFMD into their own national laws. Due to the legal character of a European directive, the AIFMD is only mandatory in terms of its objective (Article 288 paragraph 3 TFEU) and leaves a "sovereignty reserve" to each European Member State. As one consequence, in many European countries it is not yet clear whether this will happen through the integration into an existing law – in Germany the integration into the German Investmentgesetz (dInvG[590]) is being discussed – or through the creation of a particular private equity law.

2. Evaluation of the AIFMD: The AIFMD as an appropriate reaction to the recent financial crisis

2.1. Is the AIFMD a complete solution or merely a single-focused solution?

In view of the increased complexity of the financial crisis of 2008/2009, the editors of the AIFMD obviously neglected the principle of risk diversification

[590] Investmentgesetz (dInvG) of December/12th/2003 (Federal Law Gazette I 2003, p. 2676), lately amended by Article 5 of the law dated February/13th/2013 (Federal Law Gazette I 2013, p. 174).

that is well-known to each retail investor. If one concentrates on one specific risk profile by neglecting other risk profiles, one does not minimise but increase the risk of a total loss of the whole investment. Thus, it seems questionable if the regulatory focus on the AIFMs is a suitable approach to contain future systemic risks. Furthermore, the one-size-fits-all focus of the European Commission bears the risk that many financial market participants that do not really bear a systemic risk will suffer a serious profit collapse and receive incentives to leave the EU, choosing instead offshore countries like the Cayman Islands. A regulatory approach that produces an exodus of capital instead of a sustainable containment of systemic risk does not contribute to the common good, is not proportional and should be omitted. The common good does not require any kind of overregulation but requires precise incentives for a sustainable economic growth.

Because the economic depression that followed the financial crisis of 2008/2009 was a crisis of liquidity and trust among investors and at the interbank market, precise incentives require the safeguarded perspective of a steady and reliable credit supply of the real economy, including courageous start-up corporations and a steadily well-functioning monitoring of credit accumulation. Any non-proportional credit accumulation bears not only systemic risks but also aggravates the access to affordable (venture) capital as a consequence of a market concentration on the supply side. Thus, a sustainable legal approach should not follow a one-size-fits-all perspective. It seems preferable to design a regulatory framework that matches the specific shape of an (alternative) investment.

2.2. Critical reflection on the AIFM-focused approach

In opposition to Walker, the regulatory focus on the AIFM instead of the AIF seems proportional and sustainable because many significant systemic risks are caused by the managers who are resident in the few global centres of finance and therefore more easily approachable than the administrated AIF that are predominantly resident in the off-shore centres such as the Cayman Islands.[591] A regulation of the AIFM also seems preferable as the relevant supervisory information if this information is often only available from these managers.[592]

2.3. Evaluation of selected contents

2.3.1. Critical reflection on the one-size-fits-all approach

The essential question is whether all types of alternative investments should be regulated equally. If it is the objective of the AIFMD to reduce the systemic risk but not the "breath" of private entrepreneurship, which requires a steady supply of private capital, it may be a risk to regulate the activities of private equity without considering the principle of proportionality. Also, the Basel Capital Accord requires a precise analysis of risk and a realistic access of risks as one condition of a proportional and sustainable regulation.

With regard to the significance of private equity to the credit supply of private business activities and the economic growth of the national economy, any overregulation can harm the attractiveness of the European capital market. Private equity is not severe at all. For example, the private equity investor can have a direct impact on the operative and strategic decisions of the management of the target corporation to enhance the discipline of its managers and reduce the moral hazard. Thus, the use of private equity gives the managers of the target corporation a strong incentive to spend the capital resources more efficiently.[593] In addition, private equity contributes to reducing the agency costs.[594] Agency costs that can be seen as a direct consequence of the principle-agent conflict can be defined as the tangible and intangible expenses borne by shareholders because of the self-serving actions of managers. This includes the explicit costs over the out-of-

591 Cf. *Koller,* Bankenstabilisierung (2011), pp. 97, 134.
592 Ibid.
593 *Jaskolski/Grüber,* Corporate Finance Law (2010), pp. 188, 189 f.
594 Ibid.

pocket expenses (direct agency costs) to the more implicit ones (implicit agency costs).[595]

Moreover, the use of private equity can minimise the tax and increases the amount of capital that is available for future investments.[596] The on-going economic globalisation strengthens the competition among private corporations and among the national economies. This competition concerns not only the price and the quality of products but also the speed and minimises the time that is left to a corporation to face unexpected developments. A sufficient reaction towards unexpected market developments requires a sufficient availability of capital and a current supply of private capital. A sufficient regulation of the alternative fund managers' activities should not only consider the risks of this capital branch. It must also focus on its chances and its future perspectives, with regard to the legal framework of private equity, and on the emerging markets such as Brazil. Thus, it is the objective of this analysis to face the question of whether the AIFMD is really a sufficient compromise between the concern to minimise systemic risks and that potential that private equity offers to private corporations and to the welfare and growth of the European national economies. It might be seen as an invitation to the European Commission to reflect on its approach once more.

Against the abovementioned background, the one-size-fits-all approach of the European Commission that treats almost each kind of alternative investment equally is a breach of the principle of proportionality anchored in the European Charter. One cannot say that every type of alternative investment bears the same risk profile. Many of these funds – such as private equity funds, closed real estate funds and special funds – do not really bear a systemic risk.[597] By covering each kind of fund, the AIFMD not only affects the market integrity that actually should be promoted but also the efficiency of public resources. As already discussed, a well-functioning private equity contributes to public wealth, innovation

595 *Lee/Lee,* Finance (2006), p. 11.
596 *Jaskolski/Grüber,* Corporate Finance Law (2010), pp. 188, 189.
597 Cf. *Koller,* Bankenstabilisierung (2011), pp. 97, 133.

and to the monetary capital and the intellectual resources of a corporation.[598] Any sustainable regulation cannot neglect these functions. Thus, the AIFMD causes a significant amendment of the regulatory framework for fund managers in the EU and consequently results in an undifferentiated supervisory treatment of different types of alternative investments.[599] In view of their contribution to general welfare, it would be desirable that actively administrated certificates, "managed futures" and "index bonds" would also not be subject to the AIFMD.

In referring to its core approach, one cannot doubt that the AIFMD aims at hedge funds and private equity. The one-size-fits-all approach embraces a broad variety of different investment types and therefore realises a uniform regulation concept that neither considers their different features nor the different economic arrangements designed by the market participants.[600] Financial experts, financial associations, financial consults[601] and financial institutions such as the German association of closed funds, or VGF, consequently complain that the AIFMD embraces many kinds of credit accumulation that do not really bear a systemic risk.[602] Instead of covering all types of AIFM, it is preferable to avoid any exception and to set the focus on all systemically relevant AIF to promote the financial market stability.[603]

Moreover, one cannot find any coherence between the AIFMD and other directives of the EU. Therefore, it is not really surprising that an opinion poll by Pregin – an independent research institute with a focus on alternative forms of investment – came to the conclusion that that 89% of the interviewed fund man-

598 Cf. *Jordan,* Private Equity (2007), p. 1, 2.

599 *Cf. Müller,* Hedgefonds (2011), pp. 243 (281).

600 Cf. *Swoboda/Schatz,* in: Striegel/Wiesbrock/Jesch, Kapitalbeteiligungsrecht (2009), p. 891 (1.3.: objectives of the Directive).

601 Overview on the relevant questions from the perspective of the consulting practice: Cf. *Bernhard/Mark,* in: Festschrift für Schwark (2009) p. 349 ff.

602 Cf. *Schmuhl,* Corporate Finance biz (2011), p. 139, 147; http://www.aifm.de/hintergrund-detail.html (requested August/29th/2011).

603 Cf. *Schmuhl,* Corporate Finance biz (2011), p. 139, 147; On the impact of the European legislation on the German "Finanzmarktstabilisierungsgesetz" cf. *Horn,* BB (2009), pp. 450 ff.

agers admit that the AIFMD is not necessary.[604] In view of the central objective of the AIFMD to establish an effective, harmonised investor protection scheme, the one-size-fits-all approach seems questionable.

Finally, the questionability of the EU Commission's approach is even shown in the time period between submitting the application for the authorisation of the AIFM and the final decision by the responsible supervisory authority. Because many investors will not accept the uncertainty that results, a schematic approach may be suitable in the meantime for many asset classes but not for private equity funds.[605]

2.3.2. Critical reflection of the quantitative scope/De minimis exemption

It also carries negative weight that the de minimis exemption seems too low and does not correspond to the real stability requirements, as it does not prevent the regulation of almost each AIFM who has not recently been subjected to the Directive of the European Council on Undertakings for Collective Investments in Transferable Securities (Directive 85/611/EWG, dated 20 December 1985) – UCITSD.[606, 607] Therefore, it goes far beyond those regulatory postulations of the G20[608] that were released for systemically relevant hedge funds.[609] Although the credit accumulation of many hedge funds can be identified as one core reason for the recent financial crisis, one cannot deny that these funds have created a widespread transnational wealth, and that they fulfil an essential function for the

604 Cf. *Heese/Lamsa,* CORPORATE FINANCE law 1/2011, p. 39, 39.

605 Cf. *Swoboda/Schatz,* in: Striegel/Wiesbrock/Jesch, Kapitalbeteiligungsrecht (2009), p. 856.

606 The UCITSD defines specific requirements on the coordination of the different rules of the European Member States on funds, other common investments and the permitted portfolio strategies (*eligible assets*). It is concretised in the European Directive 2007/16/EG that states rules on the implementation of the UCITSD.

607 For further information on the latest version of the UCITSD see *Patzner/Kempf,* EWS (2010), pp. 366 ff.

608 The G-20 represents the informal association of the 19 most important industrial countries (United States of America, Japan, Germany, United Kingdom, France, Italy, Canada, South Korea, Australia, Mexico) and emerging countries (China, Brazil, Russia, India, Turkey, Indonesia, Saudi Arabia, Argentina, South Africa) plus the EU that aims at the implementation of a steady panel for corporation and consultation in terms of the international financial system.

609 Cf. *Koller,* Bankenstabilisierung (2011), pp. 97, 134.

credit supply of the real economy. Because the European Member States themselves cannot fulfil each function and that their enormous (public) debts consequently caused the recent Euro crisis, one should treat their functions sophistically. One should abandon the widespread belief that their business policy only follows the mantra of "Buy it, strip it, flip it[610]", which means a business strategy that imposes enormous debt to corporations, reduces the number of working places and causes a decline in taxes.

Should the principal objective of the AIFMD really consist of the promotion of financial stability, a bar of US$1,000 million (€750 million) should actually be sufficient. Thisis in view of the fact that, in 2008, 1% of the hedge fund managers administrated 75% of the total assets and simultaneously 3% of the hedge fund managers covered assets of more than US$1 billion. A regulatory framework at a bar of €750 million would embrace widely more than 80% of the hedge fund assets – more than enough to contain significant systemic risks.[611] This underlines that the AIFMD does not fulfil Walker's requirement of a proportional approach.

In view of the increasing importance of an effective risk management and compliance, it is expected that these privileged "small" AIFMs will also respect all requirements of the AIFMD: For an increasing number of investors, it is becoming more important that the target corporation avails itself of an effective risk management.[612] On the one hand, an effective risk management might result in higher transaction costs, and thus reduce the yield. On the other hand, it reduces the risk of a total loss of the investment.

2.3.3. Critical reflection of the European passport

The European passport is an element of the "core field harmonisation", creates a "level playing field" and directly results in the European freedom of

610 Cf. *Jordan,* Private Equity (2007), p. 1, 2.
611 Cf. *Koller,* Bankenstabilisierung (2011), pp. 97, 134.
612 Cf. *Heese/Lamsa,* CORPORATE FINANCE law 1/2011, p. 39, 42.

movement of capital and the European freedom of movement of employees. Because Walker identified the volume of credit accumulation as one core reasons for the recent financial crisis, it applies to a credit accumulation of €1 million (de minimis exemption). As Schmuhl[613] states, the introduction of a European passport for an AIFM can contribute to the investment volume in the AIF segment, enhance the transparency of the venture capital market[614] and the willingness of those investors to venture an investment, but also stimulate the inner European market by simplifying the AIF commerce. Under the conditions of economic globalisation, the European passport of the AIFM can be seen as a seal of quality that stands for a high level of investor protection.

3. Interim result

As already mentioned, the AIFMD can be seen as another attempt towards an international regulation of collective deposits, respectively collective investment whose effectiveness depends on the development of the international financial markets. It sets a contrast to the Guidelines for Disclosure and Transparency in Private Equity[615] that has been submitted by Walker. These guidelines prefer a more voluntary regulation at the basis of private corporations (comply or explain) that goes back to the initiative of the British Venture Capital Association (BVCA).

Due to the background of the increasing (economic) impact of the emerging markets and that of the BRIC states and the increasing transnational mobility of capital that is promoted by the development of the new media of information and communication, the national governments seem to be driven by the international financial markets. They react towards the international market development, but they do not really act because the increasing significance of the financial markets

613 Cf. *Schmuhl,* Corporate Finance biz (2011), p. 139, 148.

614 The venture capital market contributes to the financing of "young" corporations in the high-technology segment with an over-averaged capital request that results from research intensity, cf. *Lenenbach,* Kapitalmarktrecht (2010), p. 1469.

615 Guidelines for disclosure and transparency in Private equity, http://walker-gmg.co.uk/sites/10051/files/wwg_report_final.pdf (requested July/17th/2013).

makes it increasingly complicated to take any legal measure at the national level. As a consequence, the regulation of alternative investments is also regulation under extreme uncertainty. Thus, it would be a wise decision to limit its validity for a certain period of time and to decide on its prolongation as soon as it is possible to deduce any conclusion on its effectiveness on the basis of the real financial market development.

Under the conditions of economic globalisation, any regulation of the financial markets – seen from the investor's perspective – is not more than a product because of the international competition of economic locations.[616] If one wants to ease this competition that often results in a "race to the bottom", it is inevitable for each national body to strengthen the efforts towards internationally compelling standards of financial regulation.

616 On the structure of an economic constitution beside those of the national states: *Renner,* Transnationales Recht (2011), p. 1 ff.

Fifth Chapter:

Alternatives to the AIFMD/alternative approaches to the recent financial crisis

1. Legal approaches

1.1. General annotations

1.1.1. Risks of a one-sided focus

In view of the enormous mobility of (private) capital, any approach that is suggested as a response to the financial crisis of 2008/2009 should consider that any legal regulation of alternative investments is an essential location factor. Under the circumstances of a globalised economy, any financial investor has the economic freedom of action to decide where to place her or his investment. Any too-strong level of legal regulation, at the national and even at the European level, can directly cause an exodus of capital towards the offshore countries, which usually results in welfare losses. For example, since the liberalisation of the British capital market in the late 1970s, many investors left their original countries and opted to operate in the City of London[617], which probably has become the most significant financial centre in the EU.

Thus, any regulation of alternative investments should not only focus the containment of (macro-prudential) systemic risks and the protection of deposi-

[617] According to the *Global Financial Centres Index, which* compares the competitiveness (availability of qualified labour forces, quality of the labour market, economic framework, market access, infrastructure and general competitiveness) of the 75 globally most significant financial places, published twice a year by the *City of London Corporation*, London reaches the position as a financial global leader before New York City, Hong Kong and Singapore. For further information on the ranking of the global financial Centers see cf. http://www.cityoflondon.gov.uk/business/economic-research-and-information/research-publications/Documents/research-2010/Global%20financial%20centres_7.pdf. (requested October/24th/2012).

tors.[618] It should set one major focus at the steady credit support of the real economy, which is essential to a continuous and sustainable economic growth.[619] Therefore, one should not only discus the risks of alternative investments and other financial innovations but also focus on its contribution to public welfare in view of the recent Euro and debt crisis.[620] Many market participants do not trust these innovations because they do not understand its general functions and place too much trust in a negative report in the mass media. The initial hypothesis of alternative approaches instead of the AIFMD should therefore consist of a careful analysis of the effect and contribution of alternative investments. Any legal response should not dry out the public contribution of these financial innovations.

1.1.2. Regulation of the product instead of the fund manager

If one discusses alternative legal approaches for the sustainable containment of systemic risks, one does not have to focus on the fund managers as the administrators and distributors of the fund. In opposition to the AIFMD, it seems reasonable to set the focus on the fund itself, the depositors or the specific risk profile of a financial product. Instead of being subject to all the different types of alternative investments (open funds, closed funds etc.) regardless of their specific risk profile, a more proportional regulation would aim at the systemic significance of a specific type or group of investments. For example, one could realise this by the legal requirement of a license or certification that has to be proved by the editor before the launch of the financial product. A certification in this spirit could ease the supervision,[621] create a bigger level of (public) transparency and reduce the public costs.

---

618 On the protection of investors and depositors by key investor information and comparable documents: Cf. *Podewils,* ZBB (2011), p. 169 ff.; *Casper,* BB (20/2011), Die Erste Seite; *Steffen/Sachse,* ZBB No. 1/2011, pp. 33 ff.

619 On the expected economic growth in the business period 2012 cf. *Dams,* DIE WELT (September /21st/2011), p. 10.

620 On the future treatment of "debt sinners" in view of the recent European developments: *Greive,* DIE WELT (September /21st/2011), p. 10.

621 Until 2011 there was no independent financial supervision at the European level, cf. *Baur/Boegl,* BKR 2011, p. 177 (177).

However, one should consider that a regulation of the fund instead of the fund manager could easily be avoided by shifting a single feature of the financial product. Noteworthy difficulties of hedge fund regulation result from the restricted nature of the direct regulation on hedge funds which can be seen as one consequence that an internationally generally acknowledged legal definition of hedge funds does not exist.[622] Regardless of some typical characteristic features, such as the use of leverage, derivatives[623] and short selling that are typical for most hedge funds, a general definition of hedge funds does not exist.[624] Moreover, in financial practice, there is no clear separation between hedge funds and private equity.[625] The lack of a legal definition may cause legal insecurity among investors, but it contributes to the major public interest because any legal definition could easily be circumvented – thus, does a legal regulation enable a suitable approach at all? In general, there should be a revision of the current definitions to make sure that they definitely embrace all different kind of funds.[626]

Finally, any legal regulation of alternative investments could cause a footrace between the other involved market participants and the legislators. Though the European Commission or the responsible ministry could react more speedily and flexibly towards an amendment of the relevant product than the parliamentary legislator, it is usually the editor who wins this race – also under the comitology procedure.[627] Thus, in view of the enormous mobility and flexibility of capital, any regulation of the fund contributes to the fund managers, but not to the public and is therefore not a suitable approach.

622 On the definition of hedge funds cf. Connor/Woo, Hedge Funds, pp. 5 ff.

623 General annotation on the regulation of credit derivates in view of the financial crisis of 2008/2009: *Litten/Bell,* BKR (2011), pp. 314 ff.

624 Cf. *Faber,* in: Hommelhoff/Hopt/Werder, Corporate Governance (2009), p. 223; *Buck-Heeb,* Kapitalmarktrecht (2011), p. 277 (bullet No. 653).

625 Cf. *Faber,* in: Hommelhoff/Hopt/Werder, Corporate Governance (2009), p. 223.

626 Cf. Connor/Woo, Hedge Funds, pp. 1 ff. (33).

627 As a part of the so-called "Lamfalussy Process" the comitology procedure represents a special legislation at the European level: The European Commission concretises the regulatory frame that is given by directives of the European Parliament and the European Council by detailed provisions, cf. *Jung,* in: Schulze/Zuleeg/Kadelbach, Europarecht (2010), § 20, Bullet No. 3.

1.1.3. Necessity of an international benchmarking

Any legal approach should always consider the prospective consequences to the allocation of private capital, its supply to the real economy and general public welfare. As it is shown by the recent Euro and debt crisis, financial regulation is often an action of uncertainty.[628] To reduce the risks of uncertainty one possible solution is to undertake an international benchmarking and focus the legal framework of comparable industrial countries, regions or communities of states like the *NAFTA*[629] (North American Free Trade Agreement).

Under the conditions of a globalised economy and an enormous mobility of capital, no country is enabled to maintain its public welfare by measures of protectionism. The Contract on the World Trade Organisation (WTO Contract[630]) that is based on David Ricardo's idea of the comparative advantages of costs[631] generally forbids any protectionist measures. To keep a substantial piece of the global value-added chain, each country needs to steadily monitor the scenery at the foreign markets, including its legal and infrastructural framework.

Under the provision of the necessary financial and economic facilities, each market participant opts for that country that offers the comparatively best conditions contributing to his economic objective. Normally, she or he chooses the country that offers the highest gross margin.[632] The gross margin approximately corresponds to the Internal Rate of Return (IRR)[633] that is calculated at the basis of that weighted average cost of capital that leads to a Net Present Value (NPV)[634] at the level of zero.[635] The benchmarking can be described as a proce-

---

628 On economic and investment decisions as decisions under uncertainty: *Baums,* ZGR (2011), pp. 218 ff.; *Pacces,* ECFR (2010), pp. 479 ff.

629 Cf. *Nowrot,* in: Tietje, Internationales Wirtschaftsrecht (2009), § 2, ann. 38.

630 Agreement of the World Trade Organisation (WTO), dated April/15th/1994, Federal Law Gazette 1994 II, p. 1625 = Official Journal of the European Communities (EU) 1994 L /336/3, effective January/1st/1995.

631 On David Ricardo´s theory of comparative advantages cf. Second Chapter, 1.6.2.

632 Cf. *Spengel,* ifo Schnelldienst (13/2004), pp. 3, 4.

633 Profit on capital investments or securities, cf. *Lee/Lee,* Finance (2006), p. 231.

634 The net present value, respectively the net benefit of an investment is the present value of a project's cash flows minus its costs, cf. *Lee/Lee,* Finance (2006), p. 189.

dure to identify the international decisive factors of success and consists of a comparison of the framework for alternative investments.[636] It requires a comparative analysis that follows a clearly determined reference value that makes it easier to identify and to adapt the respective best practices. By undertaking a benchmarking of the international different regulation of alternative investments, the regulating country can reduce the public costs of regulation and its public transaction costs. Furthermore, it can take measures against welfare losses. It is an integral element to analyse the economic consequences of a legal regulation.

1.2. International and European level

1.2.1. Separation of commercial banks and investment banks

An approach that is seriously discussed as a legal approach at the European level consists of the separation of commercial banks and investment banks.[637] It is an open secret that the objective of an equity return of 25% that was operated by Deutsche Bank is only realistic if the credit institute focuses on strong investment banking, which means its financial engagement in big industrial companies. Primarily, the proposal to separate commercial banks and investment banks (a separate banking system) goes back to the American Glass-Steagall Act[638] of 16 June 1933 – one American response to the worldwide economic depression that started in October 1929.[639]

On the one hand, this proposal faces the challenge of containing systemic risks effectively because those risks even result from overflowing investment banking. On the other hand, it seems to ignore the necessity of a well-

---

635 Cf. *Hasselbach/Rödding,* in: Eilers/Rödding/Schmalenbach, Unternehmensfinanzierung (2008), p. 803 f.; *Volkart,* Corporate Finance (2008), p. 198.

636 Cf. *Behrends*, Managementsysteme (2005) p. 105 (referring to the use of benchmarking systems in the building sector).

637 On this proposition cf. *Steinberg/Somnitz,* ZfBW 6/2012, pp. 384 ff.; *Rexer,* DIE WELT (October/18th/2011), p. 9.

638 The Banking Act of 1933 is most commonly known as the Glass-Steagall Act whose name results from its legislative sponsors, *Carter Glass* and *Henry B. Steagall*, cf. *Kroszner/ Rajan*, Glass-Steagall Act, 1993, p. 1 ff.

639 *Sinn,* Kasino-Kapitalismus (2009), p. 90.

proportioned portfolio and a diversification of risks.[640] It belongs to the very first lesson of any investor in shares that it is essential to acquire shares of a different class of risks: small risks ("cautious investment"), middle risks ("decided investment") and comparatively big risks ("speculative investment"). If one decides only to take small risks, there is hardly any chance to earn money. If one decides only to take big risks, the probability to lose money is comparatively large. This lesson should also be considered in the discussion of a separation of commercial banks and investment banks. What it takes is a well-proportioned diversification of risks – otherwise, a credit institute loses its attractiveness to investors and its competitive position. The proposed separation can aggravate a pronounced anti-cyclical portfolio strategy and, therefore, can even minimise a credit institute's immunity against systemic risks.

The Glass-Steagall Act probably forced the recent financial crisis because the forwarding of savings by the capital markets was overestimated.[641] Although the separate banking system was successively transformed after the legal compulsion to decide for one of these business models was abolished in 1999, and many commercial banks cautiously approximated towards the investment banking, the separate banking system still remains after the breakout of the financial crisis.[642]

The proposal to separate commercial banks and investment banks is not an appropriate response to the recent financial crisis. Moreover, in view of the principle of risk diversification, it could emerge as a boomerang under certain circumstances.

1.2.2. Good conduct of rating agencies

Until the outbreak of the financial crisis of 2008/2009, the managers of many rating agencies often used mathematical applications instead of their common sense to estimate the relevant risks – thus, their risk management often turned

---

640 In Germany § 2 paragraph 5 InvG requires that assets for the common capital investment are subject to the principle of risk spreading.
641 *Sinn,* Kasino-Kapitalismus (2009), p. 90.
642 Ibid.

into a risk justification[643] As the FCIC points out, they overrated mortgage securitised instruments by using wrongfully designed computer models and by underlying the pressure of financial corporations that paid for the ratings – against the background of fighting for market quotes.[644] Against this background, notably Walker pointed out the significance of properly rated financial products and structured financial products.[645] The European Commission enacted the VO 1060/2009 regulation that states minimum requirements for the rating agencies. According to its Article 1, this regulation will contribute to integrity, transparency, responsibility, good governance and reliability of the rating agencies and improve the quality of financial ratings in the EU. The term "good governance" refers to the analysis and organisation of processes and structures to enhance a corporation's ability to solve the problems that result from its public institutional and interactive engagement.[646]

1.2.3. Propositions of the G20

In view of the financial crisis of 2008/2009, the Member States of the G20 Summit that took place in London on 2 April 2009 proposed a consistent international supervision that no longer neglects any financial market participant, financial product or financial region.[647] In compliance with the regulatory intention of the European Commission, the direct supervision will remain with the national supervisory authorities.[648] Nevertheless, the G20 states agreed to implement common international standards, a tight corporation of the national authorities and an enhanced function of the IMF.[649]

643 Cf. *FCIC,* Financial Crisis Inquiry Report (2011), pp. 19, 72 f., 149.
644 Cf. *Nationale Kommission zur Untersuchung der Finanz- und Wirtschaftskrise,* Schlussfolgerungen (2009), p. 8.
645 Basically on structured financial instruments: *Wolf/Hill/Pfaue,* Strukturierte Finanzierungen (2011), p. 1 ff.; see also *De Vries Robbé,* Structured Finance (2010), pp. 1 ff.
646 Cf. *Budäus/Hilgers,* in: Hommelhoff/Hopt/Werder, Corporate Governance (2009), p. 885.
647 Cf. *Lenenbach,* Kapitalmarktrecht (2010), p. 1497 (15.79 f.).
648 Ibid.
649 Ibid.

Together with the IMF,[650] the Financial Stability Board (FSB) – one essential element of the new European financial supervision[651] – has undertaken collaborative early-warning measures to strengthen the assessment of systemic risks and to identify possible regulatory controls and supervisory practices as a response to the changing face of systemic risks in financial markets.[652] Another comparatively suitable tool to identify hidden risk potentials of a credit institute or any other financial investment is the leverage ratio:[653] When the leverage ratio shifts by more than 5%, the German capital market law states a mandatory obligation on the part of the credit institute to inform the public (§ 15 of the German Security Trading Act, Wertpapierhandelsgesetz – dWpHG[654]).

The G20 states authorise the FSB to design international financial standards for an enhanced control of systemic risks and a more effective oversight of the global financial system and to devise more effective international regulatory frameworks that durably link micro-prudential supervision with broader macro-prudential systemic concerns.[655] Its focus on macro-prudential regulatory involves devising regulatory standards to measure and limit leverage levels in the financial system as a whole. This requires financial institutions to have enhanced liquidity reserves against short-term wholesale funding exposures and counter-cyclical capital regulation, whereby capital requirements are linked to points in the macro-economic and business cycle.

1.2.4. Systemic risk containment by the Financial Transaction Tax

Another measure that is currently discussed to contain systemic risks that result from the international cross-linking of financial market participants is the

650 On the current assessment of the global economy by the IMF under its chief secretary *Christine Lagarde* Cf. *Dams,* DIE WELT (September /21st/2011), p. 10.
651 On the new European financial supervisory architecture: *Lehmann/Manger-Nestler,* ZBB No. 1/2011, p. 2 ff.
652 Cf. *Alexander,* ZBB/JBB (2011), p. 337 (343).
653 *Lenenbach,* Kapitalmarktrecht (2010), p. 1495 (15.73).
654 Wertpapierhandelsgesetz (dWpHG) as amended on the bulletin dated September/9th/1998 (Federal Law Gazette I 1998, p. 2708), last amended by Article 10 paragraph 1 of the law of February/13th/2013 (Federal Law Gazette I 2013, p. 174).
655 Cf. *Alexander,* ZBB/JBB (2011), p. 337 (343).

(global) taxation of financial transactions by the FTT – an international tax for financial transactions. The FTT is also known as Tobin Tax, which represents one specific type of transaction tax.[656]

A tax rate of only 0.1% on each financial transaction could significantly contribute to the national budget of the benefited countries – financial experts expect a plus of several thousand million Euros. In addition, they expect that the FTT would significantly contain speculative financial transactions and the derivative commerce. However, financial experts expect a serious exodus of capital towards offshore countries. Regarded comprehensively, the FTT could make the intense financial cross-linking less attractive and minimise the total volume of financial transactions.

Financial experts expect that the FTT could dry out the HFT that is normally based on a complex algorithm and results in information advantages that enable the market participants to realise better-than-average profits. The FTT could substantially harm this business model because the yield of a single HFT transaction normally does not go beyond a few cents.[657] The proposition to contain the HFT is to be seen against the flash-crash[658] that happened at the New York Stock Exchange on 6 May 2010 when the Dow Jones Index declined by some 1,000 points within a few minutes without any obvious reason – the Securities and Exchange Commission (SEC[659]) came to the result that this incident resulted from a computer-based transaction at the volume of several thousand million US$.[660] Nevertheless, the United States and Great Britain reject any financial market transaction tax, so that it is expected that the FTT will be subject to the European continental states – the United States prefers a bank levy on its biggest credit institutes

656 On the international taxation by the Tobin Tax that aims at the taxation of global financial transaction (Financial Market Transaction Tax) cf. *Rosen,* BB 3/2010, p. I.

657 Cf. *Kaiser,* DIE WELT (November/5th/2011), p. 21.

658 This term describes the phenomena of an enormous slump in prices that happens within a very small time period.

659 On the latest SEC requirement concerning the remuneration of managers in the United States: *Lander/Flägel,* RIW No. 7/2011, pp. 425 ff.

660 Cf. *Kaiser,* DIE WELT (November/5th/2011), p. 21.

to ensure that these institutes contribute to the financing of the response to the financial crisis of 2008/2009.[661]

The introduction of a FTT could consequently result in an exodus from the organised financial markets into the OTC commerce and other types of shadow banking and aggravate the present lack of transparency in the financial segment. The OTC commerce[662] is neither executed at the stock exchange nor at other organised financial markets. It can be described as a telecommunication network of dealers who provide liquidity to investors by their willingness to "make markets" in particular securities: When an investor wants to purchase a security, a dealer firm will sell it from its own inventory of securities – if an investor wants to sell, the dealer will purchase the security and hold it in inventory.[663] The abovementioned exodus should be contained in view of the awareness of the FCIC that the rise of the shadow banking system, which could easily compete with the traditional banking system, was accompanied by widespread short-term debts.[664] On the eve of the financial crisis of 2008/2009, key segments of the financial market – such as the Repo-market,[665] off-balance business units[666] and off-balance derivates – were kept invisible and free from suitable protection measures that had been implemented to prevent financial „meltdowns".[667] In view of this

661 Cf. *Goffart,* HANDELSBLATT (November/4th/2011), p. 16.

662 On the draft of the European Commission on the future regulation of the OTC commerce cf. *Diekmann/Fleischmann,* WM (2011), p. 1105 ff.

663 *Lee/Lee,* Finance (2006), p. 199.

664 Cf. *FCIC,* Financial Crisis Inquiry Report (2011), pp. 27 ff.

665 Repo is the abbreviation for repurchase agreement, which signifies the regular auction of a central bank which contributes to providing the commercial banks with short-term liquidity. Conceptionally, the central bank purchases assets from the commercial banks that are resold to the central bank after the elapse of the respective Repo transaction, cf. Hertz-Eichenrode/Illenberger/Jesch/Keller/Klebeck/Rocholl, Private Equity-Lexikon (2011), p. 158.

666 Financial structures that are not reported in the balance sheet of a corporation, such as ABS and SPVs, and that aim at achieving a better rating by „hiding" the debts of a corporation, cf. cf. Hertz-Eichenrode/Illenberger/Jesch/Keller/Klebeck/Rocholl, Private Equity-Lexikon (2011), p. 132.

667 Cf. *FCIC,* Financial Crisis Inquiry Report (2011), pp. 20 ff.

awareness, the FCIC regards the US Government as primarily responsible for the financial crisis because it opted for the deregulation of OTC-transactions.[668]

Because the OTC commerce has risen by a volume of US$60 billion in only the year 2010 and because an inclining number of hedge funds and speculators try to concentrate "their" risks in the OTC commerce and other models of shadow banking, the G20 decided to also extend bank supervision to these business models.[669] Since Germany liberalised the investment restrictions for special assets, it is no longer forbidden for investment companies to take part in the OTC commerce.[670] If one considers that OTC transactions can reach a total business volume of approximately €6 billion, it is easy to understand that – under the conditions of international financial cross-linking and the international securitisation of risks – OTC transactions can easily cause fatal chain reactions. Nevertheless, it does not seem a proportional response[671] if one forbids these transactions – in view of their contribution to the immediate credit supply of corporations. A proportional approach consists of an enhanced transparency, including of these transactions. The FTT is, therefore, no suitable legal tool to contain systemic risks.

1.3. National level

1.3.1. Interdiction of short selling

As another response to the financial crisis of 2008/2009 and because (uncovered) short selling can bear a substantial systemic risk, the German government decided to amend its dWpHG in 2010 by placing a general interdiction of these financial transactions. Under the law for the prevention against abusive trading of securities and derivatives (Gesetz zur Vorbeugung gegenüber missbräuchliche

668 Cf. *FCIC,* Financial Crisis Inquiry Report (2011), pp. 24 ff., 74 ff.; *Nationale Kommission zur Untersuchung der Finanz- und Wirtschaftskrise,* Schlussfolgerungen (2009), p. 10.

669 Cf. *Goffart,* HANDELSBLATT (November/4th/2011), p. 16.

670 Cf. *Möllers,* BKR (2011), p. 353 (353).

671 On the principle of proportionality cf. Third Chapter, 1.1.

Wertpapier- und Derivategeschafte[672]), uncovered short selling in shares and other debt certificates (state bonds) must not be transacted any longer at any German stock exchange. The German government and the German Federal Agency for Financial Market Supervision (BaFin) holds the view that the non-regulated trade with CDS that is not motivated by a security interest represents a potential risk for the stability of the financial system as a whole.[673]

Because the use of short selling and derivatives is one typical feature of hedge funds and private equity funds, the European Commission also presented a draft for an order that refers to the regulation of CDS on debt certificates of the EU Member States.[674] This legal order consists of information requirements for the case of uncovered short selling on debt certificates of EU Member States and an authorisation of the national supervision authorities to effect a limited restriction of certain CDS.[675] In comparison to the German regulatory approach, the European approach does not generally forbid uncovered short selling.[676]

1.3.2. The "integrated approach" by the German Investmentgesetz

The AIFMD is an isolated solution because it sets the focus only at the regulation of alternative investments as its own segment. Instead of choosing an isolated solution, Germany has given an example for an "integrated solution" with the German InvG. By separating the fund administration from the fund safekeeping by the implementation of a depository bank as a relatively independent instance, the legal conception of the InvG not only institutionally secures the position of the special assets and the investors and protects them against any abuse of

672 Gesetz zur Vorbeugung gegenüber missbräuchliche Wertpapier- und Derivategeschafte (dVmWDG), as amended on July/21st/2010 (Federal Law Gazette I 2010 dated June/14th/ 2010, p. 786).

673 Cf. *Litten/Bell,* BKR (2011), p. 314, 314.

674 Cf. Draft for an order of the European Parliament and the European Council on short selling and certain other aspects of CDS (September/15th/2010), KOM (2010), p. 482.

675 Cf. *Litten/Bell,* BKR (2011), p. 314, 320.

676 Ibid.

the investment company, but it also creates legal security for each single investor.[677]

Its regulatory approach sets the focus on different types of investment (§ 1 dInvG) covering public funds inclusively its organization, registration, prospect requirements, disclosure requirements[678] and portfolio restrictions – although it covers some specific features with regard to tools to enhance the leverage, short selling and prime brokers.[679] It is significantly different from other regulatory concepts that cover a specific approach to alternative investments, normally different from the regulation of traditional investment funds that are made for retail investors.[680] Retail investors are private depositors with a comparatively small investment volume (private customers, manufacturers with small income, small corporate clients) who are subject to standardised financial products that do not have to be explained in each case.[681]

1.3.3. Bank licenses of industrial companies

As one first step against an overflowing capital accumulation and towards a bigger independence of the real economy, one can mention the "bank licenses" that can be acquired through the central supervisory authority: in Germany, the BaFin.[682] These bank licenses contribute to a more decentralised grant of credits by industrial companies with a minimum investment volume of €5 million. For example, big German companies such as Siemens acquired a bank license and thereby contribute to the economic independence of subcontractors whose function is essential to keep the value-added chain alive for the final good. These

677 Cf. *Möllers,* BKR (2011), p. 353 (355).
678 Cf. *Pütz,* in: Striegel/Wiesbrock/Jesch, Kapitalbeteiligungsrecht (2009), pp. 486 ff.
679 Cf. *Dornseifer,* in: Leible/Lehmann, Hedgefonds (2009), pp. 77, 82.
680 Ibid.
681 *Hockmann/Thießen,* Investmentbanking (2009), p. 563.
682 According to the regulatory intention of the European Commission the direct supervision shall remain at the national authorities while enhancing the corporation between them, creating uniform supervisory standards and giving the definitive decision to the European authorities in the case of different opinions, cf. *Lenenbach,* Kapitalmarktrecht (2010), p. 1496 (15.77); on the question whether corporations of the Real Economy are subject to the legal framework of banking supervision cf. *Wieland,* BB (2012), p. 917.

companies have comparatively better facilities to properly rate the creditworthiness of their subcontractors. Therefore, a bank license can be seen as an appropriate measure towards an overflowing capital accumulation, an enhanced rating of creditworthiness and enables a suitable compromise between the two superior objectives, the preservation of freedom of economic action and the effective containment of systemic risks.

1.3.4. US Private Fund Investment Advisors Registration Act of 2009

In view of the recent financial crisis in 2008, the Obama administration introduced the draft of the Private Fund Investment Advisors Registration Act of 2009 on 15 July 2009. This regulatory draft is subject to any fund that covers a minimum of US$30 million and states the binding obligation to the fund advisors to inform the SEC on the total volume of administrated assets, lenders of off-balance-sheet obligations and other positions that are essential to rate the impact of their operative business on the financial stability as a whole.[683] It is being considered to transfer this information to the Federal Reserve to fulfil its function as supervisor of systemic risks and to identify the possible need for further regulation of the relevant funds.[684] This American draft for the regulation of alternative investments aims at the quick identification of systemic risks but not at the registration of private equity investments by the supervisory authorities.[685]

1.4. Harmonisation versus regulatory competition

1.4.1. Introduction and overview

The AIFMD harmonizes the licensing requirements of AIFM in the European Member States and follows a direct approach by facing the entities instead of the products. In view of this approach it seems appropriate to discuss whether one supranational uniform legal solution is a more suitable response to the financial crisis of 2008/2009 and to what extent this approach is economically more pref-

683 Cf. *Swoboda/Schatz,* in: Striegel/Wiesbrock/Jesch, Kapitalbeteiligungsrecht (2009), p. 851.
684 Ibid.
685 Ibid.

erable than any regulatory competition. Since any regulation that does not focus on the current situation of financial markets and corporations could fail the target to effectively contain systemic risks, there is the need to discuss the economic contributes of harmonisation over regulatory competition.[686] Already in June 1985, the European Commission released a White Paper[687] that contained a broad program of rules to harmonise the national law on the supervision of financial institutes[688] and to strengthen the protection of depositors. The White Paper followed a new harmonisation concept that set on the harmonisation of significant rules and standards concerning supervision and licensing and the mutual acknowledge how to transform these into national law. The White Paper consequently contained a harmonisation concept that set on the realization of a minimum coordination of the nationally different rules and the mutual acknowledgement of the differing national rules.

1.4.2. Definition

Conceptually, harmonisation is based on the successive adjustment of the capital law of the European Member States. Harmonisation means the adjustment of nationally differing legal requirements of the European Member States, the (partial) deletion of differences in their legal situation.[689]

Thereby, one can distinguish technical measures such as the Level 2-measures and political measures of harmonisation. At the European level, the

686 Critically on the legal concept of harmonization: *Anzinger,* StuW (3/2002), pp. 261 ff.; *Brüggelmann,* ifo Schnelldienst (11/2004), pp. 5 ff.; *Fuest,* Steuerharmonisierung (2006), pp. 1 ff.; *Herzig,* StuW (2006), pp. 156 ff.; *Hey,* Unternehmensbesteuerung (1997), pp. 1 ff.; *Jacobs,* ifo Schnelldienst (11/2004), pp. 3 ff.; *Meitinger,* Schutz von Geschäftsgeheimnissen (2001), pp. 1 ff. *Ruffner,* FS Zaech, S.409 ff. *Spengel,* ifo Schnelldienst (13/2004), pp. 3 ff.; *Spengel/Braunagel,* StuW (2006), pp. 34 ff.

687 White Paper from the European Commission and the European Council on "Completing the Internal Market", published under http://europa.eu/documents/comm/white_papers/pdf/com1985_0310_f_en.pdf.

688 As *Walter* underlines, it particularly takes one coherence of micro-prudential and macro-prudential supervision, equal starting conditions and adequate protection of the financial consumers against unfair business practices, cf. *Walter,* in: Bechtold/Jickeli/Joachim/Rohe, FS Möschel (2011), pp. 969, 973.

689 Cf. *Herrnfeld,* in: Schwarze, Europarecht (2012), AEUV, Article 114, bullet No. 29.

harmonisation of the financial regulation can notably concern the licensing requirements or the equity capital requirements. Stability and competitiveness of the financial services segment essentially depend on adequate equity to steadily cover losses of unexpected dimension.[690] Directives such as the AIFMD represent probably the most important technical measures of harmonisation.

Notably, the change towards the Lamfalussy process is accompanied by a change from partial towards full harmonisation, notably to adopt international standards and to strengthen the Common market by the unification of requirements.[691] It was primarily driven by the fact that the European Commission successively followed not only the superior target of market integration but even regulative and supervisory objectives – as one consequence, the respective directives currently reached full harmonisation and the European Member states lost any right to influence a legal relationship by unilateral declaration.[692] Against the background that banks are economically essential for the macro-economic commerce of goods, services and financial deposits. Notably the effective containment of systemic risks and the conservation of financial market stability successively came into the legal focus of the European Commission.[693]

Based on a fourth-step procedure, the Lamfalussy process gives the European Commission more legislative power by simultaneously reducing the legislative power of the European Parliament and minimizing the transformation scope of the European Member States. To reach a maximum level of approximation of laws, it shall realize the concept of full harmonisation.

1.4.3. Legal objectives

By name, the European legislation is faced with the regulatory challenge that the financial commerce is widely decentralized, with the consequence that it is practically almost impossible to consistently control the contracts of credit insti-

690 Cf. *Walter,* in: Bechtold/Jickeli/Joachim/Rohe, FS Möschel (2011), pp. 969, 974.
691 Cf. *Ohler,* in: Ruffert, Europäisches sektorales Wirtschaftsrecht (2012), § 10, bullet 38.
692 Cf. *Moloney,* CMLRev. (2010), pp. 1317, 1356.
693 Cf. *Ohler,* in: Ruffert, Europäisches sektorales Wirtschaftsrecht (2012), § 10, bullet 79 ff.

tutes, security houses and assurance companies. Due to the fact that any market-based financial system can only function as long as the performance of those market participants who take on economic risk correspond to the probability of the respective risks , it is the primary target of the regulatory framework to create those conditions that enable the market participants to identify and to access their respective risks.

Under the scope of Article 114 TFEU, the European Commission is principally free to opt for any legal approach and set the respective rules as it sees fit since the principle of subsidy does not unfold any significant force to financial markets regulation.[694] As Herrnfeld points out, the harmonisation subject to Article 114 TFEU is not "end in itself", but it shall contribute to reaching specific legal objectives of the European primary law as the effective functioning of the Single Market, the effective practice of fundamental rights and the minimizing of distortions of competition resulting from the application of different national rules.[695]

By opting for the legal measure of a directive, the European Commission has chosen an approach that normally leaves a transformation scope to the European Member States. At the latest, since the beginning of the new millennium, the European Commission changed from the committee process towards the Lamfalussy process. The Lamfalussy process is named after Alexandre Lamfalussy, chairman of the Committee of Wise Men, and shall accelerate and adapt the whole regulatory process in particular by a better coordination between the EU-directives and the factual market developments. It was confirmed by the European Council in 2001 and based on four steps: Firstly, the governing political bodies decide on principal topics; secondly, the comitology process recruiting from the CESR (Committee of European Securities Regulators[696]) and the ESC

694 Cf. Fleischer/Schmuhl, NZG (2010), pp. 1241, 1245.
695 Cf. *Herrnfeld,* in: Schwarze, Europarecht (201), AEUV, Article 114, bullet No. 1.
696 Cf. http://www.esma.europa.eu/.

(European Securities Committee[697]) clears the respective technical questions; thirdly, national supervisory bodies overtake the coordination of the directives in the single European Member States; fourthly, the European Commission controls that the directive is properly transferred into national law on time.

1.4.4. Harmonisation of the licensing and capital requirements

Concerning the licensing requirements that are significantly amended by the legal validity of the AIFMD, the European law significantly contributed to one harmonised legal framework that preventively aims at the realization of the directive objectives to allow the market access only to those corporations that prospectively secure the steady fulfillment of a good corporate conduct[698] and the careful handling of the entrusted assets.[699]

In contrast, the harmonised equity requirements are based on adequate and actual available equity capital to enable the steady functionality of the financial markets and the protection of consumers who serve as the debt capital creditors of the respective financial institutions.[700] The harmonisation of equity capital requirements shall flank the realization of the single European market for financial services and follows the idea to economically consolidate the confidence into the performance of the respective credit institutes by providing an (additional) security for the primary creditors for the case of their possible insolvency.[701]

Moreover, the harmonised equity requirements limit the leverage of financial institutes and even the volume of its business operations since they are generally calculated at a percent basis in addition to the balance assets and other decisive risk factors.[702] Under the provision that any credit institute only avails of a certain

697 Cf. http://ec.europa.eu/internal_market/securities/esc/index_de.htm
698 Cf. Fifth chapter 1.2.2.
699 Cf. *Ohler,* in: Ruffert, Europäisches sektorales Wirtschaftsrecht (2012), § 10, bullet 82.
700 Cf. *Ohler,* in: Ruffert, Europäisches sektorales Wirtschaftsrecht (2012), § 10, bullet 86.
701 Cf. *German Central Bank,* Monthly Bulletin January 2012, p. 43; generally on the confidence into the economic rationality cf. *Dullen,* ZfBW special edition „Verdient der Markt noch unser Vertrauen“ (2013), pp. 23 ff.
702 Cf. *German Central Bank,* Monthly Bulletin December 2006, p. 70.

amount of equity at a certain point of time, this amount represents the calculative cap for its total business volume and effectively limits its risks.[703] Under the impression of the financial crisis of2008/2009, Basel III proposed a harmonised regulatory framework of the financial markets to limit the acknowledgeable equity elements to deposited share capital and actual realized earnings, limit the use of hybrid financial means[704] and significantly enhance the equity ratio from currently 8 percent.[705] According to the view of Walter, Basel III would not endanger the ability of the banking segment to supply the real economy with financial means as one provision of provision of economic growth and innovation.[706]

1.4.5. Positive effects of harmonisation

On the one hand, a maximum level of harmonisation can principally contribute to higher legal security, enhances reliability to corporations locating in the European Union and contributes to the outstanding legal target of general freedom of movement of capital (Article 63 TFEU). The superior European target to establish a common market for all commercial goods (Article 26 TFEU) is comparatively widely realized in the segment of financial services, primarily as a consequence of the immaterial character of capital whose exchange only depends on contracts.[707] By intensifying and accelerating the transnational commercial streams between the European Member States, it contributes to the general wealth and can be seen as one essential condition for steady economic growth and one measure to maintain their competitiveness towards other economic power centers like the BRIC-states.

---

703 Cf. *Ohler,* in: Ruffert, Europäisches sektorales Wirtschaftsrecht (2012), § 10, bullet 86.

704 Hybrid securities such as convertible bonds combine two or more different financial means and therefore avail of both debt and equity characteristics. Convertible bonds avail of features of an ordinary bond but are significantly impacted by the price movements of the stock into which it is convertible, cf. http://www.investopedia.com/terms/h/hybridsecurity.asp.
Cf. Second Chapter 1.8.2.

705 Cf. *Ohler,* in: Ruffert, Europäisches sektorales Wirtschaftsrecht (2012), § 10, bullet 88.

706 Cf. *Walter,* in: Bechtold/Jickeli/Joachim/Rohe, FS Möschel (2011), pp. 969, 974.

707 Cf. *Ohler,* in: Ruffert, Europäisches sektorales Wirtschaftsrecht (2012), § 10, bullet 32.

The economic integration of all European Member States is economically and politically desired since some financial experts assume that big financial markets are more liquid and therefore more stable, which was clearly demonstrated during the financial crises of 2008/2009.[708] In addition, the competitive pressure between the different providers of financial services is stronger under the conditions of a higher level of economic integration. Resulting from the higher competitive pressure among the providers of financial services, there would be more options for the financial consumer and even a higher level of risk diversification, better capital allocation and more economic growth.[709] Finally, the financial integration eases the operation of a European monetary policy by the ECB since the monetary incentives are more equally adapted by the commercial banks.[710]

From this perspective, a strong level of legal harmonisation can be seen as one condition to strengthen welfare in the European Member States. Against the background of the financial crisis of 2008/2009, the original legislative target to ease the transnational activities of banks and credit institutes and to harmonise the equity capital requirements turned into the primary target of keeping stability of the financial system, which means the public interest as well as a stable and functioning credit institutes and markets.[711]

1.4.6. Negative effects of harmonisation

On the other hand, the concept of full harmonisation bears some risks that should be taken seriously in view of the legal objective of the European Union to effectively contain system risks in the future. Namely, the reverse of the bigger European financial market has the consequence that local and regional crises can

---

708 *ECB,* Monthly bulletin (April 2011), pp. 61 ff.

709 *European Commission,* SEC (2007) 1696 - final edition -, European Financial integration Report (2007), p. 8.

710 Cp. *Alexander,* ERA Forum 2011, pp. 229, 232.

711 Cf. *Ohler,* in: Ruffert, Europäisches sektorales Wirtschaftsrecht (2012), § 10, bullet 2.

easily expand (harmonisation as a "risk amplifier") and geographically reach a wider diffusion.[712]

Secondly, one should not neglect that any full harmonisation approach could aggravate cyclical effects. If nearly all financial market participants in the European Union is subject to the same regulation and almost each legal option to circumvent that regulation is abandoned, the economic effects of an unexpected financial crisis could be comparatively more massive than those of the financial crisis of 2008/2009. Thus, any full harmonisation could amplify negative economic effects – in particular, should the ESRB fail, its objective to identify early future systemic risks on time, like the drying shrinkage of any single market or another serious lack of liquidity.

As Romano points out, any full harmonisation approach such as the Basel Capital Accord bears the significant risk that, when that business strategy fails catastrophically, the crisis was not restricted to one nation and a few institutions, but spread worldwide.[713] Principally, one could compare the basic line of Romano's point of view to the principle of risk diversification. Since historical data can only be transferred to novel and unknown risks of the future a very limited level, it generally takes a broad scope to effectively face those risks.[714]

Any economic decision and, notably any decision of a corporation, is a decision under uncertainty[715] and therefore it bears the risk that its assumptions do not materialize but instead are refuted by real economic developments. To minimize the respective risks, corporations do not set everything on the same card but follow the principle of risk diversification. Any harmonised approach that does not follow the principle of risk diversification enhances the risk of a total loss. In view of this awareness, Romano emphasizes that any globally harmonised framework can dramatically increase systemic risk if regulators make an error in

712 Cf. *Ohler,* in: Ruffert, Europäisches sektorales Wirtschaftsrecht (2012), § 10, bullet 34.
713 Cf. *Romano,* Yale Law & Economic Research Paper No. 414, p. 17.
714 Cf. *Ohler,* in: Ruffert, Europäisches sektorales Wirtschaftsrecht (2012), § 10, bullet 100.
715 On the uncertainty of economic actions and notably those of a corporation cf. Cf. *Pacces,* ECFR (2010), pp. 479 ff.

their regulatory approach.[716] Therefore Romano holds the view that the more plausible serious source of catastrophic systemic risk was an international regulatory harmonisation, rather than diversity in regulatory regimes. This is because of the perpetual uncertainty regarding how best to measure institutions' and instruments' risk and contribution to systemic risk, particularly because such risk dynamically changes over time as the business environment changes.[717] All in all, a preferably broad diversity in regulatory regimes seems essential since systemic risks are regionally, temporarily and objectively extremely variable and require one preferably flexible approach.[718] Moreover, the respective uncertainty exacerbates the risk that regulators will get things seriously wrong, and with any harmonised regulation, regulatory error is much more costly, as it will ripple across the global financial system.[719]

In contrast to the concept of harmonisation, with a diversity of regulatory regimes[720], there was at least a chance that not all regulators underlay the same mistake and – accordingly – would not incentivize all financial institutions to follow the same flawed strategy.[721] The diversity of financial market regulations always leaves the option for regulatory arbitration[722]. Thus, as Romano additionally points out, regulatory arbitrage was a "key driver" of financial innovation – by name, the impressive innovation in U.S. derivative products[723] has been facili-

716 Cf. *Romano,* Yale Law & Economic Research Paper No. 414, p. 17.
717 Cf. *Romano,* Yale Law & Economic Research Paper No. 414, p. 17.
718 Cf. *Ohler,* in: Ruffert, Europäisches sektorales Wirtschaftsrecht (2012), § 10, bullet 100.
719 Cf. *Romano,* Yale Law & Economic Research Paper No. 414, p. 18.
720 Nevertheless, according to the concept of harmonization, there is a diversity in the financial market supervision expressed by the "division of labor" between the Committee of European Securities Regulators - an independent expert group for securities markets that is recruited by high-level representatives of the national supervisory bodies -, the European Securities Committee (ESC), the Committee of European Insurance and Occupational Pensions Supervisors (CEIOPS), the ESMA, the EBA, the ESRB and the European Insurance and Occupational Pensions authority (EIOPA).
721 Cf. *Romano,* Yale Law & Economic Research Paper No. 414, p. 18.
722 Arbitration can be defined as a process in which a disagreement between two or more parties is resolved by impartial individuals ("arbitrators") in order to avoid costly and lengthy litigation, cf. http://www.investorwords.com/249/arbitration.html.
723 A derivative such as options, forwards and futures can be defined as financial instrument whose value depends upon the value of an underlying security, cf. *Grabaravicius Dierick,* ECB-Occasional Paper No. 34 (August 2005), p. 59.

tated by the US-American regulatory regime's fragmentation, which spurs firms to devise new products that avoid the less favorable and the more expensive regulator's jurisdiction and, in addition, correlatively creates an incentive for more efficient regulation as regulators respond to firms' jurisdiction-shifting decisions.[724]

The "invisible hand[725]" that was confirmed by Adam Smith as the healthful force of competition can even contribute to finding the most suitable financial market regulation.[726] Thus, the aforementioned financial innovations, on balance, have even generated substantial social value by lowering transaction costs and permitting efficient risk-sharing. All in all, in any regime of global harmonisation, regulatory error could result in heightened systemic risk, as regulatory incentives lead financial institutions worldwide to adopt similar business strategies – when such strategies fail, they could do so catastrophically, as witnessed in the recent financial crisis.[727] Against the background that regulatory arbitrage as a "byproduct" of regulatory diversity can definitely contribute to building a valuable hedge against the realization of systemic failure, it would be a profound mistake to view it as a weed that needs to be eradicated in order to have a more well-manicured garden.[728]

Thus, any full harmonisation approach could foil the superior legal target to effectively contain systemic risks. As mentioned before, should the financial markets be affected by any regulatory competition problem that bears the risk that the collapse of single corporations or markets can also affect other market participants – against this background, it is one important target of the financial

---

724 Cf. *Romano,* Yale Law & Economic Research Paper No. 414, p. 18.

725 On the conception of the invisible hand that significantly bases on the teachings of Adam Smith, cf. Van *Suntum,* Unsichtbare Hand (2001), pp. 1 ff.

726 Critically on the conception of the invisible hand cf. *Dullen,* ZfBW special edition (2013), pp. 23 ff.; *Horn/Klodt/Preissl,* ZfBW special edition (2013), pp. 2 ff.; *Nullmeier,* ZfBW special edition (2013), pp. 34 ff.

727 Cf. *Romano,* Yale Law & Economic Research Paper No. 414, p. 20.

728 Cf. *Romano,* Yale Law & Economic Research Paper No. 414, p. 20 f.

market regulation to take suitable measures to overwatch the functioning of the financial markets even in critical situations.[729]

Under the provision that one defines harmonisation as one complete respectively partitial equalization of regulatory framework, it creates pressure towards the economically less powerful countries like, for example, the new European member state Croatia to reach the average economic strength of the European Member States and to steadily fulfill the convergence criteria that are legally defined in Article 140 paragraph 1 sentence 3 TFEU (price stability; equilibrium of public earning and debts; stability of exchange rates; stability of public interests). The objective to steadily fulfill the convergence criteria could increase the demand for additional capital, notably venture capital. If the regulated banks cannot correspond to the increasing demand for capital since they are subject to the respective equity requirements and other legal provisions, the harmonisation can create more economic incentives towards shadow banking that, as already before-mentioned, often bears serious systemic risks, notably as one consequence of an expanded line of credit intermediation. Under this provision, harmonisation of the capital market law can generate additional systemic risks since countries with economically different frame conditions are subject to the same legal framework. Therefore, it seems very questionable if the AIFMD, which sets on a strong level of harmonization, represents an adequate response to the financial crisis 2008/2009. Any legal approach that neglects the specific economic requirements, which are very different between the currently 28 European Member States, neglects the principle of proportionality.

Thirdly, any full harmonisation bears the risk of losing national "chambers of experience", which contribute to finding the most effective approach to effectively containing systemic risks – in particular, in view of the background that the European Union is not a federal state but a supranational confederation that is based on the principles of subsidy (Article 5 paragraph 3 TEU) and the limited

729 Cf. *Ohler*, in: Ruffert, Europäisches sektorales Wirtschaftsrecht (2012), § 10, bullet 6.

single authorization (Article 5 paragraph 2 sentence 1 TEU). According to the principle of limited single authorization, the European Union must not act out of the expressive responsibilities and competences that are transferred by the European Member States and written in the primary European law. The actions of the European Commission are not based on a parliamentary mandate but on an authorization by the national head of states. In case of doubt, these competences must be outlaid restrictively.

In Germany, there is currently a pending action at the BVerfG as to whether the ECB is authorized to the unlimited purchase of bonds.[730] In critical situations, if the interbank market fails or the deposit business dries out, the ECB generally overtakes the primary source of liquidity.[731] In view of the experience that the drying shrinkage of any single market is one essential symptom for the assumption of a systemic crisis, it is currently the principal approach of the ECB to take suitable measures against lacks of liquidity and to supply the respective credit institutes adequate central bank money, to reduce the respective requirements for credit securities and to purchase assets. On the one hand, against the background that the easy money policy is one probable source of the financial crisis of 2008/2009, any legal measure that is taken as a response to the financial crisis of 2008/2009 must correspond to the outstanding objective to enhance the resistivity of the international financial system.[732] On the other hand, credit institutes must strengthen their "defense line" against shocks of liquidity by adequate devise and business models (e.g. own customer deposits), adequate equity and remuneration systems.[733]

730 The first senate of the BVerfG is currently involved with the question whether the unlimited purchase of bonds by the ECB (Outright Monetary Transaction-Program, OMT) corresponds with the German constitutional provisions, cf. http://www.bundesverfassungsgericht.de/pressemitteilungen/bvg13-029; critical on the commitment of the state cf. *Graf,* in: Studiengesellschaft für Wirtschaft und Recht, Finanzmarktregulierung (2012), pp. 105 ff.

731 Cf. *Ohler,* in: Ruffert, Europäisches sektorales Wirtschaftsrecht (2012), § 10, bullet 14.

732 Cf. *Walter,* in: Bechtold/Jickeli/Joachim/Rohe, FS Möschel (2011), pp. 969, 973.

733 Cf. *Walter,* in: Bechtold/Jickeli/Joachim/Rohe, FS Möschel (2011), pp. 969, 973.

According to this point of view the rescue of suffering banks is primarily the task of the investors and depositors since they have chosen for the respective engagement. The recapitalization of the central banks is nevertheless a commitment of the European Member States whose budget is financed by the tax payer who does not automatically have a contractual link to the suffering bank. It should be one principal target of any legislation to take suitable measures against a nationalization of losses. Besides the question of keeping those limits set by the principle of limited single authorization, one should not neglect that any unlimited purchase of bonds may contribute to system dependability but even to "moral hazard" since the expectation of any final rescue sets the false incentive to underestimate the respective risks.[734]

Any full harmonisation approach could result in the loss of diversity of different legal approaches, which contributes to the effective containment of systemic risks as long as the provisions of a systemic crisis are not definitely explained. The resulting standardization minimizes individual financial innovations and even individual defense strategies of financial corporations.[735] According to the author´s point of view, this loss is a severe development as individual solutions are one essential provision of any market-based order.

In view of the enormous acceleration of the economic development in the industrial states that is driven by the economic globalization, it seems very questionable whether anyone will be able to find a really satisfactory response to the financial crisis of2008/2009. Due to the ongoing process of financial innovations that could generate new, so far unexpected and probably more severe systemic risks, a diversity of different legal approaches seems desirable. As it is shown by designing any investment strategy, where the diversity of risks creates a shield against the realization of unexpected risks, the diversity of legal national approaches in the regulation of financial markets can build a shield against the realization of systemic risks.

---

734 Cf. *Ohler,* in: Ruffert, Europäisches sektorales Wirtschaftsrecht (2012), § 10, bullet 6.
735 *Walter,* in: Bechtold/Jickeli/Joachim/Rohe, FS Möschel (2011), pp. 969, 975.

1.4.7. Interim result

As the AIFMD follows a direct regulatory approach facing the AIFM instead of the AIF and, moreover, it shall consistently cover these entities, it could be revealed as one pro-cyclical risk amplifier that bears the questionable incentive to transfer capital outside of the European Union and thereby contribute to those global disequilibria of commerce that stood at the beginning of the financial crisis of 2008/2009. Should the AIFMD consequently cause a capital exodus towards financially less regulated countries, it could contribute to future liquidity gaps that were essential drives of the financial crisis of 2008/2009. If one takes these serious doubts into consideration, one cannot access the AIFMD as a satisfactory response to the financial crisis 2008/2009 and as one adequate approach to contain the realization of systemic risks in the future. Public wealth as one essential consequence of economic growth depends on financial innovations, whose realization is endangered by any harmonised approach that takes many market players the "air to breathe", which means the short-term and steady supply with liquidity.

Finally, it is important to submit the question as to whether the European Commission opts for the legal measure of a directive if the European "government" intends to reach a maximum level of harmonisation of the capital market law. Why has the European Commission not chosen the legal measure of statutory regulation – in particular, against the background that an accelerated response seems essential to effective containment of systemic risks? Why does the European Commission leave any transformation scope to the European Member States if full harmonisation is the superior legal target, which could be realized as more effective, less expensive and more accelerated by statutory law?

1.5. Further Discussion

In view of the various different legal approaches, it must be discussed whether it is preferable to set the regulatory focus on the fund managers, the investors or the product. In a global comparison, the regulatory frameworks for alternative investments differ significantly – a circumstance that is essential in view of the fact that hedge funds[736] and private equity funds act globally and can opt for another country at any point of time because the legal requirements in the origin country are either too restrictive or not practical enough.[737] Thus, the omission of an international harmonisation of regulatory concepts can cause a "race to the bottom" – a race that contributes to the country with the most liberal legislation.

2. Voluntary approaches

2.1. General annotations

2.1.1. Market-based intervention

Within a competitive market order the probably less expensive and even the most effective containment of systemic risks consists of a "market based intervention" that is rudimentary realised by the IFRS setting on a high level of transparency towards market participants.[738] A market-based intervention" means a direct control by the market participants. According to the author´s point of view it is probably the most proportional approach since direct regulation is (only) useful where market processes fail, although any "market based intervention" may underlay certain limitations in terms of incentive, cost, efficiency, moral hazard and liquidity.[739] It is the comparatively best approach because it is the most immediate, flexible, responsive and cost-effective solution and contributes to avoiding (several) associate information problems.[740] Finally, a "market based

736 Cf. §§ 112 ff. of the German InvG.

737 Cf. *Dornseifer,* in: Leible/Lehmann, Hedgefonds (2009), pp. 77, 82.

738 On the IFRS cf. Second Chapter 1.3.3.; cf. *Walker,* in: The Future of financial regulation (2010), pp. 179 (202 f.).

739 On the requirement of a proportional approach to the effective containment of systemic risks cf. Third Chapter, 1.1.

740 According to the author´s point of view, any response that is given to the financial crisis 2008/2009 and to contain future systemic risks should even consider the resulting costs that are decisive in the competition of financial corporations and, of course, have a strong impact on the yield and consequentially even on the steady liquidity towards market participants.

intervention" seems conclusive because the access and the costs of the relevant market information can often be identified as the origin of a market dysfunction.

A market-based intervention that focuses on the capital and credit accumulation is probably the less expensive and the more effective control because almost each market participant has her or his own interest in affordable consumer credits and a steady credit supply and the steady availability of affordable venture capital. As a consequence of the international securitisation of credit risks and the transnational entanglement and cross-linking of credit institutes that normally increase with the (concrete) volume of credit accumulation, the level of systemic risks increases with the volume of capital and credit accumulation.

On the one hand, the international entanglement and cross-linking that is promoted by the international liberalisation of commercial streams resulting from the WTO efforts contributes to the public welfare of many – not only industrial countries. By creating a corrective in those times where the domestic demand decreases, the international commercial entanglement and cross-linking creates a kind of (anti-cyclical) buffer[741], which minimises a country's credit risks and which helps to keep its level of creditworthiness. It helps to optimise a country's risk diversification. Thus, the international commercial entanglement and cross-linking contributes to a country's public welfare and wealth.

On the other hand, the international entanglement and cross-linking makes it increasingly complicated to isolate a dysfunction that probably affects the whole system. For example, a dysfunction in Russia[742] may directly infect the financial market integrity in the United States Also the Basel III Committee[743] came to the conclusion that the intense commercial relations and an often non-proportional cross-linking between the systemically relevant credit institutes intensified the

741 The Basel III-Convention also aims at the strengthening of the cyclical immunity of (private) credit institutes by a mandatory anti-cyclical equity buffer that can be seen as a complementary tool of its risk-prevention and that shall neutralise unexpected losses, cf. http://www.bis.org/publ/bcbs189.pdf (requested October/24th/2012).

742 As one of the so-called BRIC-states Russia is expected to enter the WTO at the end of 2011, cf. *Goffart,* HANDELSBLATT (November/4th/2011), pp. 16 (16).

743 On the respective conclusions of the Basel III Committee cf. *Basel Committee on Banking Supervision,* Basel III (2011), pp. 1 ff.

global dimension of the financial crisis 2008/2009.[744] The danger that a dysfunction of any single credit institute directly leads to a global financial collapse increases with the volume of a single bank's capital and credit accumulation because its international financial engagement makes it complicated to supervise and control the resulting risks – because even under the WTO regime sufficient international standards, on a credit institute's equity equipment or a (sufficient) international monitoring of credit risks do not exist. Under these conditions, a well-functioning market-based intervention requires a better coherence between micro-prudential risk management and the macro-prudential monitoring of systemic risks. This coherence requires a better disclosure and transparency towards investors.

The international financial cross-linking has the tendency to strengthen the capital concentration at the financial markets. It let the total volume of financial transactions and consequently also the yield of the internationally engaged corporations increase. In any case, one has to state that with the increasing international financial cross-linking, even the volatility that expresses the number of financial transactions in the stock index increases enormously. Also, the Member States of the G20 that recently met at their summit agreed that the 29 biggest and systemically relevant credit institutes worldwide will widen their equity position by 1-1.5% by 2016 – an equity requirement that goes beyond those equity requirements of Basel III that demanded a (regular) equity position of 7%.[745]

---

744 Also the Basel III-Convention aims at the strengthening of the cyclical immunity of (private) credit institutes by a mandatory anti-cyclical equity buffer that can be seen as a complementary tool of its risk-prevention and that shall neutralize unexpected losses, cf. *Basel Committee on Banking Supervision,* Basel III (2011), pp. 5 ff.

745 Cf. *Goffart,* HANDELSBLATT (November/4th/2011), p. 16 f.

2.1.2. Further Requirements

Whereas financial analysts find it comparatively easy to identify (potential) systemic risks, with the value-at-risk-coefficient[746] that also remains a significant indicator in times of a declining proper trade, the general public and also the majority of (small and mid-size[747]) corporations find it complicated to identify systemic risks precociously. Normally, corporations need a special department or external analysts for the precocious identification of relevant systemic risks, which causes them relatively high costs of transaction and information. Finally, these costs minimise the effectiveness of direct control from the market participants instead of state regulation. Nevertheless, the market participants, specifically the counterparties of the systemically relevant credit institutes, have a direct interest in containing the capital and credit concentration because it usually directly results in a rise in prices of credits. Under the conditions of a market economy, each market participant has a vital interest to earn money and save the income source.[748] In the financial segment, a concentration of market power enables the benefited market participant to decide on the (general) price level.

As a consequence of this concentration process, the credit prices increase whereas the availability of venture capital decreases. The reduced availability of venture capital can restrain the implementation of industrial projects and other innovations that are essential for a country's future. Finally, it can cause significant welfare losses. Thus, it is essential to implement measures to keep a well-balanced competitive structure in the financial segment that contributes to the containment of systemic risks and the steady availability of affordable credits for start-up companies. The question that has to be discussed is what measures it takes to establish this competitive structure.

---

746 Value-at-risk is a procedure for estimating the maximum loss associated with a security or portfolio over a specific period of time, associated with a given confidence level, cf. *Lee/Lee,* Finance (2006), p. 283.

747 On the consistent assessment of equity capital by risk premiums depending on ratings: *Gleißner/Knoll,* BB (2011), pp. 2283 ff.

748 Cf. *Baetge,* Bilanzanalyse (2004) p. 2.

If one agrees with Walker and focuses on a direct control by the market participants and the market counterparties, it requires an enhanced transparency and disclosure that reduces their information costs and that can be seen as one essential provision of a more effective "self-supporting" market control. Thus, an adequate response to the financial crisis 2008/2009 as well as an instrument to effectively contain future systemic risks particularly requires incentives to a higher level of market discipline as an integral component of a well-functioning risk management.[749] Market discipline requires the proper evaluation of assets, a well-proportioned risk diversification and a clear coherence between chances and risks – specifically, a strict liability concept.

From the author´s perspective market discipline can particularly generated by effective counterparty risk management, internal risk management, market controls on specific exposures (leverage ratio, concentration and asset composition), disclosure and liquidity and an efficient and effective infrastructure oversight.[750] In addition, one enhanced risk management[751] requires some adequate market directives to take sure that funds and even fund managers operate prudentially and effectively in terms of the respective operational issues, management and internal controls, client relations, valuation, risk management, regulation, documentation and business consistence.[752] The requirement of an enhanced transparency concerns the balance sheet, the structure of the investment fund manager's remuneration and the relevant risks. Another step towards a direct control by the market counterparties consists of a reform of the rating agencies, which have to convey all significant information to the market participants necessary to identifying systemic risks precociously.

749 Cf. *Labonte,* Systemically (2013), pp. 1 ff. (13 ff., 35 ff.).
750 Cf. *Labonte,* Systemically (2013), pp. 1 ff. (13 ff., 35 ff.).
751 On the requirements of an enhanced risk management cf. fourth chapter, 1.3.7.
752 On respective requirements of advanced risk management cf. *AIRMIC,* Structured approach, pp. 1 ff.

2.2. The Basel III Capital Accord

The Basel III[753] capital requirements[754] that are based on the Basel equity recommendations (Basel Convention) released in 2004 can be seen as a response to the financial crisis of 2008/2009. As probably the most important and influential international regulatory framework, the Basel Capital Accord sets regulatory capital standards for banking institutions and for establishing the principle of consolidated supervision based on home country control and mutual recognition, as set forth in the Basel Concordat.[755] In comparison with Basel II, they aim at a more exact calculation of risk positions than the provision of equity equipment that corresponds with the real risk position of a corporation.[756] Basel III focuses on a stronger self-regulation by enhanced methods to verify the risk of a corporation and the consideration of credit risk minimisations, by securitisation and transfer of credit risks.[757]

Basel III, which requires a core capital, specifically a tier 1-capital,[758] is only mandatory to the Basel III Member States, which only make up a relatively small part of global financial commerce. To minimise the risks of the transnational cross-linking, the Basel III Committee decided to face potential systemic risks by capital incentives for the credit institutes to wind up OTC and derivate transactions with the support of central counterparties,[759] stronger capital requirements for specific financial transactions (derivative transactions, securitisations and off-balanced transactions), and stronger capital requirements for the interbank market. In particular, due to the legal character of Basel III as non-binding "soft

[753] For further information on the Basel Capital Accord see footnotes 171, 257 f. and 577.

[754] Critical reflection of the strengthened capital requirements by the European Commission: *Jost/Rexer,* DIE WELT (October/19th/2011), p. 10.

[755] Cf. *Alexander,* ZBB/JBB (2011), p. 337 (340).

[756] Cf. *Jung,* in: Schulze/Zuleeg/Kadelbach, Europarecht (2010), § 20, ann. 109.

[757] Ibid.

[758] The term "tier 1 capital" is used synonymously for the core capital quote that describes those assets that are covered by (own) capital resources of the corporation, credits ("going concern capital"), cf. *Basel Committee on Banking Supervision,* Scope of Application/Part I/I. B. 1.; published under http://www.bis.org/publ/bcbs189.pdf (requested October/24th/ 2012).

[759] Cf. *Basel Committee on Banking Supervision,* Basel III (2011), pp. 2 ff.

law[760]", the credit institutes will decide how to calculate their individual equity demand: Either they opt for their own models and create a default buffer that corresponds to their specific risk positions, or they use the standard approach that is based on the results of the rating agencies.[761] This option has become essential because systemic risks result from the default risk of state bonds, as it is shown by the recent Euro and debt crisis: 54 of the 90 biggest credit institutes use exception clauses to remove themselves from the requirement of building a risk buffer against the default of state bonds.[762]

2.3. Discussion

It is questionable whether the AIFMD is a suitable approach to face systemic risks as they result from a too-large volume of credit accumulation. According to Hilmar Kopper, former president of Deutsche Bank – the balance sheet of which almost corresponds to the German GDP – less than 5% of the staff of a systemically significant credit institute such as Deutsche Bank create that (financial) innovation that is necessary to maintain their competitive position on the international capital market. Those human resources are extremely rare. Because of the increasing international competition for "high potential" and capital, it is unavoidable for any credit institute to set substantial incentives to hire these labour forces. Those incentives can be of an economic, financial or other nature. The recent Euro crisis has shown that many economic decisions are decisions made under extreme uncertainty.

An economic crisis of a similar dimension like that of 2008/2009 has never happened in history. Because a flexible response to an economic crisis without such a precedent in history needs a minimum of freedom of economic action, and the state supervisory authorities generally do not have a superior economic expertise, one should consider a voluntary approach as a serious alternative to any legal regulation. Thus, financial institutes that are resident in countries with a

---

760 Cf. *Alexander*, ZBB/JBB (2011), p. 337 (338).

761 Cf. *Osman*, HANDELSBLATT (November/4th/2011), p. 42 (42).

762 Ibid.

comparatively liberal regulation will have the comparatively better possibilities to hire that staff they need to create financial innovation, to maintain their international competitive position and to generate a welfare surplus. They are in a comparatively better position because the range of freedom of economic action is an essential competitive feature, also in the international competition for labour forces. Therefore, a more voluntary approach can face the exodus not only of capital. It is a measure to prevent the escape of qualified labour forces that it takes to develop the comparatively best solutions to economic crises without any historic example, to prevent welfare losses and to maintain a country's position under the conditions of economic globalisation. Instead of a non-proportional legal regulation of economic freedom, it takes legal measures against an overflowing capital accumulation that can be identified as the "superior" core reason of the recent financial crisis because it directly infect other parts of the national economy.

Sixth Chapter:
Conclusions

1. Outlook

The AIFMD sets the regulatory focus on the activities of the fund managers instead of the funds. On the one hand, this is a sophisticated idea because the funds as special assets are unable to act and primarily underlie the design of the fund managers. As it was pointed out in this thesis, there is no clear definition of hedge funds or private equity. Among investors and corporations, the lack of a clear definition may cause legal insecurity. Nevertheless, because of the conditions of a speedily changing market, any legal definition of these business models could have the effect that the legal requirements could easily be overcome. The significant systemic risks whose realisation contributed to the financial crisis of 2008/2009 do not result from the mere existence of special assets but from the tools the fund managers chose to administrate these assets.

The FCIC comes to the conclusion that the most serious crisis since the „Great Depression" of 1929/1930 was evitable. It was evitable because it was the result of the actions of human beings („anomaly").[763] As the FCIC points out, the involved persons were warned by the rapid distribution of risky and second-rated mortgage loans and its securitisation, the rapid incline of real estate prices, reports on relentless credit-lending practices and a significant increase of private mortgage debts.[764] Between the year 2001 and the year 2007, the national mortgage debt almost doubled, and the amount of mortgage debt per household rose more than 63% from US$91.500 to US$149.500, even while wages were essentially stagnant.[765] Unfortunately, these warning signs, primarily as a result of

763 Cf. *FCIC,* Financial Crisis Inquiry Report (2011), p. 17, 22 ff.
764 Cf. *FCIC,* Financial Crisis Inquiry Report (2011), p. 17, 20, 23.
765 Cf. *FCIC,* Financial Crisis Inquiry Report (2011), p. 20.

blind trust and an insufficient control were ignored. The FCIC speaks of a „21st-century financial system with 19th-century safeguards".[766] In view of this awareness, it seems arguable and coherent to set the regulatory focus on the fund managers instead of the funds. The market-based control that should be strengthened by the AIFMD is optimised by the separation of fund administration and the deposition of the assets. This separation strengthens the market-based control of the relevant assets, minimises conflicts of interests and reduces the danger of any market abuse.

However, it neither seems proportional nor sustainable and, moreover, it contradicts the ideas of Basel III that based on a precise identification of the individual risk profile that the AIFMD subjects all to different kinds of alternative investments. The neglect of the individual risk profile of the funds reduces the possible economic growth in the segment of alternative investments, stimulates the capital exodus towards the offshore countries and can cause significant welfare losses. A capital exodus as a consequence of the one-size-fits-all approach can result from higher organisational requirements concerning financial transactions, compliance and information. As it is pointed out by Kee-Meng Tan, European chief of the financial consulting firm Knight Capital, there are no principal complaints against any financial market regulation as long as they do not cause higher costs.[767] The higher costs that result from the legal effect of the AIFMD will probably cause a rise of credit costs, contradictory to the central regulatory objective to secure the steady credit supply of the real economy and can reduce the availability of venture capital. Within the global competition of economic locations, an adequate availability of venture capital is essential to realise locational advantages any country needs to keep its public welfare. Thus, the AIFMD neither seems a proportional nor sustainable approach. It may help the supervisory authorities to reduce the costs of administration and control. The neglect of the individual risk profile of the administrated funds by using a more general,

766 Cf. *FCIC,* Financial Crisis Inquiry Report (2011), p. 20; cf. *Nationale Kommission zur Untersuchung der Finanz- und Wirtschaftskrise,* Schlussfolgerungen (2009), p. 6.

767 Cf. *Kaiser,* DIE WELT (November/5th/2011), p. 21.

wholesale and exhaustive approach not only contradicts the more market-based Basel III but – following the experience of Kee-Meng Tan[768] – it also reflects that many governmental officials, at the European level and at the national level, do not really understand the commerce of the alternative investments.

Instead of facing all the different types of alternative investments without regard to their (precise) risk profile, it is preferable – following Alexander[769] – to implement an effective international regulatory reform that is based on a more macro-prudential approach to regulation, supervision and crisis management that will necessarily require enhanced measures to control excessive risk-taking whilst mitigating and paying for the tremendous social costs imposed by financial crises. What it takes is a stronger coherence between micro-prudential and macro-prudential risk management, monitoring and supervision. Under the provision of a clear regulatory framework and the absence of any monopolist or oligopoly structures, as a consequence of their superior expertise (private) corporations have the comparatively better facilities to quickly identify systemic risks. A market-based approach such as Basel III seems a comparatively better approach than any paternalist legal approach.

Any legal regulation represents a narrowing of liberty. Following Immanuel Kant, liberty should always be interpreted as liberty for bearing responsibility – under the conditions of a market economy. Responsibility means responsibility for the next generation. The principle of sustainability according to the ideas of Brundtland, the former Norwegian ministry president, says that each generation should always respect the requirements of the next generation. If everyone respects these comparatively easy principles and tries to act following a perspective that covers a period of more than one single business period, one probably needs less legal regulation. Any regulation can be identified as a consequence of the community that mandates the state to establish equilibrium of interests towards the omission of individual responsibility.

[768] Ibid.
[769] Cf. *Alexander*, ZBB/JBB (2011), p. 337 (344).

Thus, the intensity of legal regulation correlates to the ability of the individual to control her or his actions and to evaluate these actions critically. Applied to the financial markets, this means that any corporation could be subject to a more liberal legal regulation that respects its individual freedom of action if it shares the principles of "good corporate governance". As it is shown in HFT, the corporations often avail themselves of an expertise that makes it ambitious to the supervisory authorities to control the financial markets exhaustive.

On the one hand, financial innovations such as HFT or the increasing shadow banking has opened enormous yield expectations to financial corporations. On the other hand, these financial innovations make confidence and trust among the other market participants and among the state supervisory authorities decline. This decline of confidence and trust that is confirmed by recent opinion polls from autumn 2011 not only effects higher transaction costs for almost each financial corporation but has also led to the claim of the G20-Summit in Cannes for a global taxation of any financial transaction – the FTT could cause the end of the HFT – and an update of the European Financial Market Directive (MiFID 2). This update will implement more effective supervisory systems against any market abuse, annual mandatory information on the credit institute's business strategy towards the regulatory agencies and an interdiction towards these institutes to withdraw from the (organised) markets in times of market turbulence.[770]

Because an interdiction like this will probably cause financial losses for the concerned corporations, the strengthening of the European Financial Market Directive could cause another exodus of capital which endangers the essential capital supply of the real economy and substantial welfare losses. This underlines the significance of adequate transparency and disclosure which ensures confidence and trust among the market participants. It underlines the initial hypothesis based on Kant's ideas. Private responsibility among the financial market participants enables these to use their expertise to implement profitable but even sustainable

[770] Cf. *Kaiser,* DIE WELT (November/5th/2011), p. 21.

solutions instead of suffering the consequences of any non-proportional legal regulation.

According to Kay Swinburne, British member of the European Parliament, who is significantly involved in designing the MiFID 2, many representatives of the European supervisory bodies would not understand enough of the financial innovations like the HFT.[771] Adequate voluntary information, transparency and disclosure could save the concerned corporations from any strengthening of legal regulation. It saves confidence and trust among market participants, contributes to reduce the relevant transaction costs and sets the provision for a market-based approach as proposed by Walker. Any regulation sets on a retrospective view and can be seen as a reaction towards a social, economic or even financial development. To establish a more proportional and sustainable solution, the legislator should strengthen his focus on the future developments and the practical consequences of his decisions. In the final communiqué of the G20-Summit in Cannes, its participants underline that they renew their commitment to cooperate, and that they have drawn decisions to strengthen economic growth, labour markets, financial security and social integration to secure that globalisation contributes to human beings. The future will demonstrate whether these confirmations will become reality.

2. Closing comments

The financial crisis of 2008/2009 was an incident of an unprecedented global dimension and complexity. In particular, in view of the current global entanglement of the financial segment, the crises can be compared with the global economic depression that began with the collapse of the New York Stock Exchange on 29 October 1929. Thus, the identification of a suitable response to the financial crisis of 2008/2009which promises the containment of systemic risks in the next future is a pioneering work. It requires the detailed analysis of its history, its

771 Ibid.

symptoms and its supposed core reasons. Any hasty reaction of legislators is counterproductive. Thus, this thesis tried to convey a brief overview of the abovementioned parameters and introduced the AIFMD as the legal approach of the European Commission towards the financial crisis of 2008/2009. By discussing the overriding question as to whether the AIFMD can be identified as an appropriate approach towards the financial crisis of 2008/2009, it highlighted the issue of the AIF-directed focus and the one-size-fits-all perspective. It also reveals that the approach chosen by the European Commission will probably not solve the problem of a steady and affordable access of the real economy towards venture capital. The administrative requirements posed by the AIFMD will probably cause enormous agency and transaction costs. Finally, these costs will be turned over to the side of credit demand. Any appropriate response to the financial crisis of 2008/2009 requires legal means to contain any non-proportional capital accumulation and to establish an enhanced monitoring of credit accumulation. In view of this awareness, this thesis closes with the introduction and discussion of alternative responses towards the financial crisis of 2008/2009, such as the taxation of financial market transactions by the FTT, the conception of bank licenses and the interdiction of short selling. It closes with an outlook.

Bibliography

Adrian, Tobias/Ashcraft, Adam B.: Shadow banking regulation, Staff Report, Federal Reserve Bank of New York vol. 559.

Alexander, Kern: Rebuilding International Financial Regulation and Basel III, ZBB/JBB (2011), pp. 337–344.

- *Selfsame* -: Reforming European financial supervision, ERA Forum 2011, Journal of the Academy of European Law Vol. 12 (2), S. 229–252.

Anzinger, Heribert M.: Harmonisierung der Zinsbesteuerung in der EU: Quellensteuer, Abgeltungsteuer, Informationsmodell – nur eine Frage des tragfähigen Kompromisses? StuW (3/2002), pp. 261 ff.

Assies, Paul H./Rösler, Patrick: Handbuch des Fachanwalts Bank- und Kapitalmarktrecht, Third Edition, Cologne 2012.

Association of Insurance and Risk Managers (airmic): A structured approach to Enterprise Risk Management (ERM) and the requirements of ISO 31000, London, published under http://theirm.org/documents/SARM_FINAL.pdf (requested July/17th/2013)

Avgouleas, Emilios: The Global Financial Crisis and the Disclosure Paradigm in European Financial Regulation: The Case for the Reform, ECFR (2009), pp. 440–475.

Baetge, Jörg: Bilanzanalyse, Second Edition, Düsseldorf (2004).

Balling, Stephan: „Die kurzfristige Refinanzierung ist immer die Ursache für Finanzkrisen“ – Gespräch mit Prof. Dr. Douglas Diamond, Universität Chicago –, in: Auszüge aus Presseartikeln No. 37/2010, edited by Deutsche Bundesbank, pp. 7–9.

Bauer, Georg/Boegl, Martin: Die neue europäische Finanzmarktaufsicht – Der Grundstein ist gelegt –, BKR (2011), pp. 177–186.

Baums, Theodor: Risiko und Risikostreuung im Aktienrecht, ZGR (2011), pp. 218–274.

Basel Committee of Banking Supervision: Basel III – A Global regulatory framework for more resilient banks and banking systems, Basel (2011), published under http://www.bis.org/publ/bcbs189.pdf (requested July/17th/2013).

Basel Committee of Banking Supervision: Consultative Document – Revisions on the Basel Securitizations Framework, Basel (2013), published under http://www.bis.org/publ/bcbs236.pdf (requested July/17th/2013).

Becker, Hans Paul: Investition und Finanzierung – Grundlagen der betrieblichen Finanzwirtschaft, Second Edition 2008.

Beckstein, Günther: The Challenge of Globalization and the Response of Politics, in: The Role of Law and Ethics in the Globalized Economy, edited by Josef Straus, Berlin/ Heidelberg 2009, pp. 9 ff.

Behrends, Jens: Bewertung von Managementsystemen in der Bauwirtschaft – Ableitung strategischer Handlungsfelder –, Wuppertal (2005).

Bengtsson, Elias: Shadow banking and financial stability – European money market funds in the global financial crisis (2009).

Berger, Hanno/Steck, Kai-Uwe: Regulierung von Hedgefonds in Deutschland – zugleich ein rechtsvergleichender Blick auf die USA, Luxemburg und die Schweiz, –, ZBB 2003, pp. 192–202.

Bernhard, Michael/Mark, Christine: "Private equity goes public", Beteiligung an börsennotierten Unternehmen durch Finanzinvestoren – ein Überblick über die rechtlichen Fragestellungen aus der Sicht der Beratungspraxis –, in: Festschrift für Eberhard Schwark, edited by Stefan Grundmann/Christian Kirchner/Thomas Raiser/Hans-Peter Schwintowski/Martin Weber and Christine Windbichler, Munich 2009, pp. 349–374.

Bhagat, Sanjai/Romano, Roberta: Reforming executive Compensation: Simplicity, Transparency and Committing to the Long-term, ECFR (2010), pp. 273–396.

Bieber, Roland/Epiney, Astrid/ Haag, Marcel: Die Europäische Union – Europarecht und Politik –, Sixth Edition, Baden-Baden (2005).

Bloss, Michael/Ernst, Dietmar/Häcker, Joachim/Sörensen, Daniel: Financial Engineering, Munich 2011.

Bonar, James: "The theory of moral sentiments by Adam Smith", Journal of Philosophical Studies, I (1926), pp. 333–353.

Boyson, Nicole M. Stahel, Christof W./Stulz, René M.: Hedge fund contagion and liquidy shocks, Journal of Finance (January 2010), pp. 1789 ff., published in the internet under http://papers.ssrn.com/sol3/papers.cfm?abstract_id=884202.

Brähler, Gernot: Steuerlich optimale Gestaltung von grenzüberschreitenden Umstrukturierungen, Wiesbaden (2006).

Briggs, Thomas W.: Corporate Governance and the new hedge fund Activism – An Empirical Analysis, Journal of Corporate Law (2007) pp. 681–738, published in the internet under http://papers.ssrn.com/sol3/papers.cfm?abstract_id=911072

Bruchwitz, Sebastian/Voß, Thorsten: Der Regulierungsentwurf für ein Gesetz zur Novellierung des Finanzanlagenvermittler- und Vermögensanlagerechts, BB (2011), pp. 1226–1234.

Brüggelmann, Ralph: Sollte die Unternehmensbesteuerung innerhalb der EU harmonisiert werden, ifo Schnelldienst (11/2004), pp. 5–8

Busack, Michael/Kaiser, Dieter G.: Handbuch Alternative Investments Vol. 1 (Alternative Investments I), First Edition Wiesbaden 2006

- *Selfsame -/- Selfsame -:* Handbuch Alternative Investments Vol. 2 Alternative Investments II), Second Edition Wiesbaden 2006.

Calliess, Christian/Ruffert, Matthias: EUV/EGV – Das Verfassungsrecht der Europäischen Union mit Europäischer Grundrechtecharta –, Commentary, Third Edition, Neuwied/Kriftel (2007)

- *Selfsame -/Schoenfleisch, Christopher:* Auf dem Weg in die Europäische „Fiskalunion“? Europa- und verfassungsrechtliche Fragen einer Reform der Wirtschafts- und Währungsunion im Kontext des Fiskalvertrages, JZ (No. 5/2012), pp. 477–487.

Calmés, Christian/Théoret, Raymond: The impact of off-balance-sheet activities on banks returns: An application of the ARCH-M to Canadian data, Journal of Banking & Finance Vol. 34 (July 2010), pp. 1719–1728.

Casper, Matthias: Zu Risiken und Nebenwirkungen, BB (20/2011), Die Erste Seite.

Cheffin, Brian R./Armour, J.: The eclipse of private equity, EGGI law working paper No. 082/2007 (2007), available at: http://ssrn.com/abstract=982114, requested: July/30rd/2010.

Commission of the European Communities: Commission staff working document accompanying the proposal for a Directive of the European Parliament and of the Council on Alternative Investment Fund Managers and amending Drafts 2004/39/EC and 2009/…/EC, available at: http://ec.europa.eu/internal_market/investment/docs/alternative_investments/fund_managers_impact_assessment.pdf, requested: June/24th/2010.

- *selfsame -:* Commission staff working document accompanying the proposal for a Directive of the European Parliament and of the Council on Alternative Investment Fund Managers and amending Drafts 2004/39/EC and 2009/…/EC, Executive summary of the impact assessment, available at: http://ec.europa.eu/internal_market/investment/docs/alternative_investments/fund_managers_executive_summary_en.pdf, requested: June/24th/2010.

- *Selfsame* -: Directive of the European Parliament and of the Council on Alternative Investment Fund Managers and amending Drafts 2004/39/EC and 2009/…/EC, available at: http://ec.europa.eu/internal_market/investment/docs/alternative_investments/fund_managers_proposal_en.pdf, requested: June/24th/2010.

Connor, Gregory/Who, Mason: An Introduction to Hedge Funds, International Asset Management/The London School of Economics and Political Science, London, published under http://eprints.lse.ac.uk/24675/1/dp477.pdf (requested July/17th/2013).

Cuny, Charles J./Talmor, Eli: A theory of private equity turnarounds, working paper (2006), available at: http://papers.srrn.com/sol3/papers.cfm?abstract_id=875823.

***D**am, Kenneth W.:* The Subprime Crisis and Financial Regulation: An International Perspective, in: The Role of Law and Ethics in the Globalized Economy, edited by Josef Straus, Berlin/ Heidelberg 2009, pp. 95–106.

Dams, Jan: IWF sieht schwarz für die Weltwirtschaft – Die Industriestaaten werden 2010 voraussichtlich wesentlich langsamer wachsen –, DIE WELT (September/21st/2011), p. 10.

Deloitte: Global Systemic Risk Regulation since the Financial Crisis – A Framework for understanding the effectiveness, impacts and harmonization of macroprudential regulation, published in the internet.

De Vries Robbé, Jan Job: Structured Finance – On from the Credit Crunch – The road to Recovery, Austin/Boston/Chicago/New York (2009).

Deutsche Bundesbank: Die Banknotennachfrage während der Finanzkrise, in: Monatsbericht No. 6/2009, pp. 56–57.

Diekmann, Hans/Fleischmann, Dermot: Der Verordnungsentwurf der Europäischen Kommission für den OTC-Derivatemarkt, WM (2011), pp. 1105–1109,

Dobelli, Rolf: Die Kunst des klaren Denkens – 52 Denkfehler, die Sie besser anderen überlassen –, Munich 2011.

Dombret, Andreas/Engelen, Christian: Internationale Finanzarchitektur: Reformprojekte bis zur IWF-Frühjahrstagung 2013, Kreditwesen 22/2012, pp. 1156–1157.

Dornseifer, Frank: Bedarf es einer Regulierung von Hedgefonds und Private Equity? Eine Replik auf die Maßnahmen der Bundesregierung, in: Hedgefonds und Private Equity – Fluch oder Segen? Bayreuther Studien zum deutschen, europäischen und internationalen Wirtschaftsrecht Band 2, edited by Stefan Leible and Matthias Lehmann, pp. 77 ff., Jena 2009.

Dullen, Sebastian: Umbau der Finanzmärkte: Übermäßiges Vertrauen in die Marktrationalität hält an, Wirtschaftsdienst (ZfBW) Special Edition „Verdient der Markt noch unser Vertrauen"(2013), pp. 23–29.

Eilers, Stephan/Rödding, Adalbert/Schmalenbach, Dirk: Unternehmensfinanzierung, Munich (2008)

Eilmannsberger, Thomas/Holoubek, Michael/Kalss, Susanne/Lang, Michael/ Lienbacher, Georg/Lurger, Brigitta/Potacs, Michael/Rebhahn, Robert: Finanzmarktregulierung – WiR – Studiengesellschaft für Wirtschaft und Recht, Vienna 2012.

Enrich, David/ Paletta, Damian: Basel Panel strikes deal on bank risk, The Wall Street Journal (July/27/2010), p. 19.

Grabaravicius, Tomas/Dierick, Frank: Hedge funds and their implications for financial stability, Occasional Paper No. 34, edited by the European Central Bank, Frankfurt am Main (August 2005).

Ferran, Eilis: Regulation of private equity – backed leverage buyout activity in Europe, ECGI – Law working paper No. 84/2007 (May 2007), available at: http://srrn.com/abstract=989748, requested: July/27th/2010.

Financial Services Authority (FSA): The Turner Review – A regulatory response to the global banking crisis, March 2009, published in the internet, last time requested on February/18th/2013.

- *Selfsame -:* Hedge funds – A discussion of risk and regulatory engagement, Discussion Paper 05/4, published under http://www.fsa.gov.uk/pubs/discussion/ dp05_04.pdf.

Fischer, Alexander: Regulierung von Schattenbanken – Europäische Kommission auf dem falschen Weg, Kreditwesen 10/2012, pp. 485-486.

Fischer, Lutz/Kleinedamm, Hans-Jochen/Warneke, Perygrin: Internationale betriebswirtschaftliche Steuerlehre –, Fifth Edition, Berlin (2005).

Fischer, Ralf: Blick nach Brüssel: Hedgefonds und Private Equity – Parlament erzwingt Richtlinienvorschlag –, NZG (2009), pp. 703.

Fleischer, Holger: Zukunftsfragen der Corporate Governance in Deutschland und Europa – Aufsichtsräte, institutionelle Investoren, Proxy Advisors und Whistleblowers –, ZGR (2011), pp. 155–181.

Foxon, Timothy J./Köhler, Jonathan/Michie, Jonathan/Oughton, Christine: Towards a new complexity economics for sustainability, Cambridge Journal of Economics Vol. 37, January 2013, pp. 187–208.

Freshfields: EU draft directive on alternative investment fund managers, available at: http://www.freshfields.com/publications/pdfs/2009/jul09/26360.pdf, requested: June/23rd/2010.

Frey, Johannes/Bruhn, Stephanie: Die Finanztransaktionssteuer – Allheilmittel oder untauglicher Versuch? BB (No. 29/2012), pp. 1763–1768.

Fuest, Winfried: Steuerharmonisierung und Steuerwettbewerb – Zur Unternehmensbesteuerung in der Europäischen Union –, Beiträge zur Ordnungspolitik aus dem Institut der deutschen Wirtschaft Cologne, Cologne 2006.

Gärditz, Klaus Ferdinand: Schwerpunktbereich – Einführung in das Klimaschutzrecht, in: Juristische Schulung (2008), pp. 324–329.

Gorton, Gary: Slapped in the face by the Invisible hand. Banking and the panic of 2007, prepared for the Federal Reserve Bank of Atlanta´s 2009 Financial Markets Conference: Financial Innovation and Crisis, 11.–13.05.2009, Version of May/5th/2009, pp. 23–29.

Gorton, Gary/Metrick, Andrew: Regulating the Shadow Banking System, Working Paper Yale and NBER, October 2010.

Gennaioli, Nicola/Shleifer, Andrei/Vishny, Robert W.: A model of shadow banking, NBER Working paper series Vol. 17115 (June 2011), http://www.nber.org/papers/w17115.

Gerke, Wolfgang: EU-Kommissionsvorschläge sind nicht zielführend, BB 2012, p. I.

Gifis, Steven H.: Law Dictionary, New York 1996.

Gleißner, Werner/Knoll, Leonhard: Konsistente Bewertung von Eigen- und Fremdkapital durch ratingabhängige Risikozuschläge: Ein Vorschlag für KMU, in: BB No. (2011), pp. 2283–2285.

Göppert, Jan: Die Reichweite der Business Judgment Rule bei unternehmerischen Entscheidungen des Aufsichtsrats der Aktiengesellschaft, Abhandlungen zum Deutschen und Europäischen Gesellschafts- und Kapitalmarktrecht Band 28, Berlin (2010).

Goffart, Daniel: G20 nimmt Banken in die Pflicht, HANDELSBLATT (November/4th/2011), p. 16.

Gottschalg, Olivier/Phalippou, Ludovic: The performance of private equity funds: another puzzle? Working Paper (2007) available at: http://ssrn.com/abstract=4, requested: July/27th/2010.

Grabaravicius, Tomas/Dierick, Frank: Hedge funds and their implications for financial stability (2005), European Central Bank occassional paper No. 34, published in the internet under http://www.ecb.int/pub/pdf/scpops/ecbocp34.pdf

Greive, Martin: Euro-Länder sollen an die Kette gelegt werden – IfW-Studie: Schuldenregel für jedes Land –, DIE WELT (September/21st/2011), p. 10.

Gronewold, Lars: Investitionen von Kapitalanlagegesellschaften in strukturierte Finanzprodukte, Dissertation, Münster 2008, published in the Internet under http://miami.uni-muenster.de/servlets/DerivateServlet/Derivate-5665/diss_gronewold.pdf, requested on October/24th/2012.

H*ärtel, Ines:* Handbuch europäische Rechtssetzung, Berlin/Heidelberg (2006).

Haisch, Martin L./Helios, Marcus: Rechtshandbuch Finanzinstrumente, Munich 2011.

- Selfsame -/Helios, Marcus: Investmentsteuerrechtsreform aufgrund AIFMD und KAGB, BB (No. 1/2013), pp. 23–31.

Haede, Ulrich: Wahl und Ernennung des Präsidenten der Europäischen Zentralbank, EWS (2011), pp. 173–175,

Halstrick, Philipp: Tighter Bank Rules Give Fillip to Shadow Banks, Frankfurt am Main (20.12.2011).

Hartmann-Wendels, Thomas: Geringe Eigenkapitaldecke, mangelnde Transparenz und Fehlanreize –, Bankenkrise – Ursachen und Maßnahmen –, Wirtschaftsdienst 2008, pp. 707–711.

Hayek, Friedrich August von: Prices and production, Vienna 1935.

Heap, Brian: In need of an ethical and legal framework, in: The Role of Law and Ethics in the Globalized Economy, edited by Josef Straus, Berlin/ Heidelberg 2009, pp. 171–173.

Heese, Burc/Lamsa, Michael: Die Richtlinie über die Verwalter alternativer Investmentfonds (AIFM-Richtlinie) – Ein erster Überblick über die bevorstehende Regulierung insbesondere von Private Equity-Investoren in Deutschland –, CORPORATE FINANCE law 1/2011, pp. 39–47.

Hermalin, Benjamin E./Weisbach, Michael S.: Transparency and Corporate Governance, NBER working paper No. 12875 (National Bureau of Economic Research 2007).

Hertz-Eichenrode, Albrecht/Illenberger, Stefan/Jesch, Thomas A./Keller, Harald/ Klebeck, Ulf/Rocholl, Jörg: Private Equity-Lexikon, Stuttgart 2011.

Herzig, Norbert: Harmonisierung der steuerlichen Gewinnermittlung in der Europäischen Union, StuW (2006), pp. 156–164.

Heun, Werner: Finanzaufsicht im Wandel, JZ (No. 5/2012), pp. 235–242.

Hey, Johanna: Harmonisierung der Unternehmensbesteuerung in Europa, Vol. 7, Cologne 1997.

Hirte, Heribert/Bücker, Thomas: Grenzüberschreitende Gesellschaften – ein Praxishandbuch –, Second Edition, Cologne/Berlin/Munich (2006).

Hockmann, Heinz-Josef/Thießen, Friedrich: Investmentbanking, Second Edition, Stuttgart 2007.

Hördahl, Peter/King, Michael R.: Developments in Repo Markets During the Financial Turmoil (2008), BIS Quarterly Review, December: pp. 37–53.

Hommelhoff, Peter/Hopt, Klaus J./Werder, Axel v.: Handbuch Corporate Governance, Second Edition, Munich 2009.

Hopt, Klaus: Auf dem Weg zu einer neuen deutschen und europäischen Finanzmarkarchitektur, NZG (2009), pp. 1401–1408.

Horn, Gustav/Klodt, Henning/Preissl, Brigitte: Verdient der Markt noch unser Vertrauen? Wirtschaftsdienst (ZfBW) Special edition, Verdient der Markt noch unser Vertrauen" (2013), pp. 2–7.

Horn, Jens: Einfluss der EU-Vorgaben bei Anwendung des Finanzmarktstabilisierungsgesetzes, in: BB (2009), pp. 450–454.

Horn, Karen Ilse: Die Soziale Marktwirtschaft – Alles, was Sie über den Neoliberalismus wissen sollten –, Frankfurt am Main 2010.

Huber, Bertram: Corporate Responsibility – Essential!, in: The Role of Law and Ethics in the Globalized Economy, edited by Josef Straus, Berlin/Heidelberg 2009, pp. 55–56

Huertas, Thomas F.: Crisis, Cause, Containment and Cure, Basingstoke 2010.

Hull, John: Risikomanagement – Banken, Versicherungen und andere Finanzinstitutitonen –, Second Edition, Munich 2011.

- *Selfsame -:* Risk Management and Financial Institutions, Second Edition, Munich 2011.

Hunkemöller, Manfred: Frische Euros für nicht ganz so frische Euro-Fischer? BB (No. 29/2012), First Page.

Jacobs, Otto H.: Internationale Unternehmensbesteuerung – Deutsche Investitionen im Ausland, ausländische Investitionen im Inland –, Seventh Edition, Munich (2011).

- *Selfsame -:* Internationale Unternehmensbesteuerung – Deutsche Investitionen im Ausland, ausländische Investitionen im Inland –, Sixth Edition, Munich (2007).

Jacobs, Otto H.: Sollte die Unternehmensbesteuerung innerhalb der EU harmonisiert werden, ifo Schnelldienst (11/2004), pp. 3–4.

Jaskolski, Torsten/Grüber, Stephan: Regulierungsaspekte des Private Equity-Markts und der Richtlinienentwurf der Europäischen Union zur Regulierung alternativer Investmentfonds, AGENDA „Regulierung des Private Equity-Marktes“, Corporate Finance Law (2010), pp. 188–196.

Jenkins, T.: How is private equity changing public equity changing public equity markets? Presentation at the SIFR Conference „The Economics of Private Equity“ held on August/30–31/2007.

Jesch, Thomas A./Striegel, Andreas/Boxberger, Lutz: Rechtshandbuch Private Equity, München 2010.

- *Selfsame -/Geyer, Frank:* Die Übergangsbestimmung der AIFM-Richtlinie, BKR (No. 9/2012), pp. 359–363.

Jordan, Thomas: Private Equity – Gibt es speziellen Regulierungsbedarf? Veranstaltung "Deutschland – Schweiz, Partner im Dialog", Berlin 09.05.2007, published in the Internet under http://www.snb.ch/de/mmr/speeches/id/ref_20070509_tjn/souce/ref_20070509_tjn.de.pdf, requested September/1st/2011.

Jost, Sebastian/Rexer, Andrea: Reguliert Europa eine Kreditklemme herbei? – Banker warnen vor dramatischen Folgen schärferer Kapitalregeln. Die Experten raten, die Vorgaben der EU-Kommission zu überdenken –. Finanzminister für Gespräche offen –, DIE WELT (October/19th/2011), p. 10.

Kaiser, Heiko: Die Konstruktion von Finanzprodukten – Eine Analyse aus interner und externen Perspektive, Dissertation, Zurich 2007, published in the Internet under http://www.bf.uzh.ch/publikationen/dis/abstracts/003.pdf, requested October/24th/2012.

Kaiser, Tina: Blitzschnelle Händler unter Beobachtung – Ein Blick hinter die Kulissen der Hochfrequenz-Branche –, DIE WELT (November/5th/2011), p. 21.

Kahan, Marcel/Rock, Edward B.: Hedge funds in corporate governance and corporate control, Law Review (May 2007), pp. 1021–1093, published in the internet under http://papers.ssrn.com/sol3/papers.cfm?abstract_id=919881.

Kind, Sebastian/Haag, Stephan Alexander: Der Begriff des Alternative Investment Fund nach der AIFM-Richtlinie – geschlossene Fonds und private Vermögensanlagegesellschaften im Anwendungsbereich? DStR (2010), pp. 1526–1530.

Kindler, Peter: Finanzkrise und Finanzmarktregulierung – Ein Zwischenruf zum 68. Deutschen Juristentag –, NJW (2010), pp. 2465–2469.

Kirchner, Christian: Risse in der Drei-Säulen-Struktur des deutschen Finanzsystems – Argumente für die Öffnung des öffentlich-rechtlichen Sparkassensektors –, in: Festschrift für Eberhard Schwark, edited by Stefan Grundmann/ Christian Kirchner/Thomas Raiser/Hans-Peter Schwintowski/Martin Weber and Christine Windbichler, Munich 2009, pp. 475–485.

Klebeck, Ulf/Zollinger, Felix: Compliance-Funktion nach der AIFM-Richtlinie, BB 9/2013, pp. 459–464.

Köhler, Richard/Küpper, Hans-Ulrich/Pfingsten, Andreas: Handwörterbuch der Betriebswirtschaft, Sixth Edition, Stuttgart (2007).

Koller, Werner: Bankenstabilisierung in Europa (2011), pp. 97–151.

Kopp, Lothar: Eurozone in der Dauerkrise – Deutschlands Weg in den Staatsbankrott? NVwZ (No. 24/2011), pp. 1480–1485.

Kramer, Robert/Recknagel, Ralf: Die AIFM-Richtlinie – Neuer Rechtsrahmen für die Verwaltung alternativer Investmentfonds, DB (37/2011), p. 2077–2084.

Krause, Martin/Klebeck, Ulf: Family Office und AIFM-Richtlinie – Zugleich eine Studie nach dem Regelungsadressat der AIFM, BB (2012), pp. 2063–2066.

Kroszner, Randall S./Rajan, Raghuram G.: Is the Glass-Steagall Act Justified? A Study of the U.S. Experience with Universal Banking before 1933, Chicago 1993, published in the internet under http://faculty.chicagobooth.edu/ raghuram.rajan/research/papers/randy1.pdf

Kübler, Friedrich: Die Krise der amerikanischen Hypothekenverbriefungen – Ursachen und Herausforderungen , in: Festschrift für Eberhard Schwark, edited by Stefan Grundmann/Christian Kirchner/Thomas Raiser/Hans-Peter Schwintowski/Martin Weber and Christine Windbichler, Munich 2009, pp. 499–510.

Lackhoff, Klaus: Ist der Forderungseinzug durch den Originator einer True-Sale-ABS-Transaktion ein Finanztransfergeschäft? Kreditwesen 10/2012, pp. 503–504.

Labonte, Marc: Systemically important or „Too Big to Fail" Financial Institutions, Congressional Research Service, June/19th/2013, published under http://www.fas.org/sgp/crs/misc/R42150.pdf (requested July/17th/2013).

Lander, Guy/Flägel, Peter: Neue Vorschriften der US Securities and Exchange Commission zur Managementvergütung – „Say-on-Pay" und „Say-no-Golden-Parachutes" –, RIW No. 7/2011, pp. 425–428.

Lee, Cheng-Few/Lee, Alice C.: Encyclopaedia of Finance, New York 2006.

Lehmann, Matthias/Manger-Nestler, Cornelia: Das neue Europäische Finanzaufsichtssystem, in: ZBB No. 1/2011, pp. 2–24.

Lewis, Mervyn K.: The origins of the sub-primie crisis – Inappropriate policies, regulations or both? Accounting Forum Vol. 33 (2009), pp. 114–126.

Leible, Stefan/Lehmann, Matthias: Hedgefonds und Private Equity – Fluch oder Segen? Bayreuther Studien zum deutschen, europäischen und internationalen Wirtschaftsrecht Band 2, Jena 2009.

Le Maux, Laurent/Scialom, Laurence: Central banks and financial stability: Rediscovering the lender-of-last-ressort practice in a finance economy, Cambridge Journal of Economics Vol. 37, January 2013, pp. 1–16.

Lenenbach, Markus: Kapitalmarktrecht und kapitalmarktnahes Gesellschaftsrecht, Second Edition, Cologne 2010.

Lenz, Carl Otto/Borchardt, Klaus-Dieter: EU- und EG-Vertrag, Fourth Edition, Cologne (2006).

Levin, Carl/Coburn, Tom: Wall Street and the financial crisis; Anatomy of a Financial Collapse – Majority and Minority Staff Report, Washington D.C., April/13th/2011, published in the internet *www.hsgac.senate.gov/download/*, last time requested on February/18th/2013.

Liekefett, Kai Haakon: Due Diligence bei M&A-Transaktionen: Voraussetzungen und Grenzen bei Börsengängen, Fusionen, Übernahmen, Beteiligungskäufen, Private Equity und Joint Ventures, Berlin (2005).

Litten, Rüdiger/Bell, Matthias: Kreditderivate – Neue Dokumentations-Standards als Reaktion auf die globale Finanzmarktkrise, WM (2011), pp. 1109–1117.

- *Selfsame -/- Selfsame -:* Regulierung von Kreditderivaten im Angesicht der globalen Finanzmarktkrise, in: BKR (2011), pp. 314–321.

Ljungqvist, A./Richardson, M.: The investment behaviour of private equity fund managers, RICAFE working paper No. 005 (October 2003), available at: http://ssrn.com/abstract=482546 or DOI: 10.2139/srrn.482546, requested: July/27th/2010.

Loff, Detmar/Klebeck, Uwe: Fundraising nach der AIFM-Richtlinie und Umsetzung in Deutschland durch das KAGB, BKR (No. 9/2012), pp. 353–359.

Lorz, Alexander/Sauer, Heiko: Ersatzunionsrecht und Grundgesetz, DÖV No. 5/2012, p. 573 ff.

Lux, Thomas: Effizienz und Stabilität von Finanzmärkten: Stehen wir vor einem Paradigmenwechsel, Wirtschaftsdienst (ZfBW) Special edition „Verdient der Markt noch unser Vertrauen“(2013), pp. 16–23

Maerker, Klaus: Zur Funktionsweise von Lehman-Zertifikaten – zugleich eine Besprechung zum OLG Düsseldorf, Urteil v. 16.12.2010, I 6 U 200/09, BKR (2011), pp. 147–150.

Mayer/Brown: The AIFM-Directive in the context of national regulation, available at: http://www.mayerbrown.com/public_docs/AIFM-1-context-national-regulation.pdf, requested: June/23rd/2010.

McCreevy, Charlie (European Commissioner for Internal Market and Services): Private equity, speech to Allied Irish Banks, London, February/8th/2008, available at: http://europa.eu/rapid/pressReleasesAction.do?reference=SPEECH/08/68&format=HTML&aged=0&language=EN, requested July/27th/2010.

McCulley, Paul: Teton reflections (August/September 2007), published under http://www.pimco.com/EN/Insights/Pages/GCBF%20August-%20September%202007.aspx.

McIlroy, David H.: The future of banking Regulation, in: The Role of Law and Ethics in the Globalized Economy, edited by Josef Straus, Berlin/ Heidelberg 2009, pp. 119–129.

Meitinger, Ingo: Der Schutz von Geschäftsgeheimnissen im globalen und regionnalen Wirtschaftsrecht – Stand und mögliche Entwicklungen der Rechtsharmonisierung –, Bern 2001.

Moe, Thorvald Grung: Shadow banking and the limits of central bank liquidity support: How to achieve a better balance between global and official liquidity, Working paper, Levy Economics Institute Vol. 712 (2012).

Möllers, Thomas M. J.: Umfang und Grenzen des Anlegerschutzes im Investmentgesetz – Der Trennungsgrundsatz und die Grenzen der Aufrechnung im InvG –, in: BKR 9/2011, p. 353–366.

Moloney, Niamh: EU Financial Market Regulation after the Global Financial Crisis: “More Europe” or more Risks? CMLRev. Vo. 47 (2010), pp. 1317–1383.

Müller, Thomas S./Staub, Christian: Neuerungen im europäischen Anlagefondsrecht – Chance oder Risiko für den Fondsstandort Schweiz? GesKR 2/2010, pp. 216–223.

Müller-Franken, Sebastian: Eurobonds und Grundgesetz, JZ (No. 5/2012), pp. 219–225.

N.N.: A single rulebook – De Larosière`s ambitious, sensible plan should be enacted, in: Auszüge aus Presseartikeln No. 10/2009, edited by Deutsche Bundesbank, pp. 8.

N.N.: Die Finanzkrise wäre vermeidbar gewesen – Amerikanische Untersuchungskommission kritisiert dreißig Jahre der Deregulierung –, in: Auszüge aus Presseartikeln No. 5/2011, edited by Deutsche Bundesbank, pp. 12–13.

N.N.: Economic Growth Strategies to Expand role of Capital Market, published under http://www.sc.com.my/eng/html/cmp2/separated/chapter3.pdf (requested July/17th/2013).

N.N.: Gespenst des Zahlungsausfalls der USA – Ratingagentur S&P droht Amerika mit radikaler Herabstufung der Anleihen auf schlechte Bonitätsnote „D" –, in: DIE WELT (July/1st/2011), p. 15.

N.N.: Larosière-Gruppe für Evolution – Experten gegen Superbehörde für Finanzaufsicht –, in: Auszüge aus Presseartikeln No. 10/2009, edited by Deutsche Bundesbank, pp. 7–8.

N.N.: Lessons for monetary policy from financial crisis – Keynote speech by Prof. Dr. Axel Weber, at the XII Annual Inflation Targeting Seminar of the Banco Central do Brasil, in Rio de Janeiro, May 14, 2010 –, in: Auszüge aus Presseartikeln No. 5/2010, edited by Deutsche Bundesbank, pp. 5–7.

N.N.: Regulierung der Finanzmärkte – Rede von Prof. Dr. Franz-Christoph Zeitler, anlässlich des Seminars er Münchener Juristischen Gesellschaft, in: Auszüge aus Presseartikeln No. 8/2011, edited by Deutsche Bundesbank, pp. 16–20.

N.N.: Umsetzung der G20-Agenda für das Finanzsystem: Wo stehen wir? Rede von Prof. Dr. Axel Weber bei der International Chamber of Commerce (ICC) in Berlin, am 18. Mai 2010, in: Auszüge aus Presseartikeln No. 5/2010, edited by Deutsche Bundesbank, pp. 3–5.

Nagel, Bernhard: Wirtschaftsrecht der Europäischen Union – Eine Einführung –, Fourth Edition, Baden-Baden (2003).

Nietsch, Michael/Graef, Andreas: Aufsicht über Hedgefonds nach dem AIFM-Richtlinienvorschlag, ZBB (2010), pp. 12–20,

Nullmeier, Frank: Die Legitimation der Marktwirtschaft, Wirtschaftsdienst (ZfBW) Special edition „Verdient der Markt noch unser Vertrauen" (2013), pp. 34–40.

*O**ECD:* The Implications of Alternative Investment Vehicles for Corporate Governance. A synthesis of research about private equity firms and activist hedge funds, issued by the OECD Steering Group on Corporate Governance, July 2007, available at: http://www.oecd.org/dataoecd/60/28/39005553.pdf, 2007a, requested: July/27th/2010.

- Selfsame -: The Implications of Alternative Investment Vehicles for Corporate Governance. A survey of Empirical Research, a report prepared for the OECD Steering Group on Corporate Governance by M. Wright/A. Burrows/R. Ball/L. Scholes/M. Meuleman and K. Amess (Centre for Management Buy-out Research, Nottingham University Business School 2007) – 2007b, requested: July/27th/2010.

Oehlrich, Marcus/Baltes, Anamaria/Geldermann, Juliane/Helmer, Kristina/Hempel, Christin/Sautter, Andrea: Finanzmarkkrise damals und heute – Über den Sinn einer umfassenderen Regulierung der Unternehmensführung –, ZRP (2011), pp. 40–44.

O'Neill, Sian: Global Financial Crisis – Navigating and Understanding the Legal and Regulatory Aspects –, London 2009.

Ordonez, Guillermo: Sustainable shadow banking, NBER Working paper series 2012, http://www.nber.org/papers/w19022, Cambridge May 2013.

Osman, Yasmin: Risikopapier Staatsanleihe, HANDELSBLATT (November/4th/2011), p. 42–43.

- Selfsame -/Riecke, Torsten/Afhüppe, Sven: Streit im Turm zu Basel, HANDELSBLATT (July/28th/2010), pp. 34–35.

***P**acces, Alessio M.:* Consequences of Uncertainty for Regulation: Law and Economics of the Financial Crisis, ECFR (2010), pp. 479–511.

Pagano, Marco: Credit Ratings Failures and Policy Options, London (2009), published under http://www.italianacademy.columbia.edu/publications/working_papers/2008_2009/pagano_volpin_seminar_IA.pdf (requested July/17th/2013).

Patzner, Andreas/Kempf, Ludger: Die OGAW IV-Richtlinie, EWS (2010), pp. 366-368,

Party of the European Socialists (PES), Socialist Group in the European Parliament: Hedge funds and private equity – a critical analysis –, PES Group Report (2007).

Pozsar, Zoltan/Adrian, Tobias/Ashcraft, Adam/Boesky, Hayley: Shadow Banking, Federal Reserve Bank of New York Staff Report No. 458 (July 2010 – revised February 2012).

Paul, Stephan: Europäische Bankenaufsicht – Schnelligkeit vor Genauigkeit? Wirtschaftsdienst (ZfBW) 1/2013, pp. 2–3.

Perotti, Enrico: The Roots of Shadow Banking, DSF Policy Paper No. 24 (June 2012).

Podewils, Felix: Beipackzettel für Finanzprodukte – Verbesserte Anlegerinformation durch Informationsblätter und Key Investor Information Documents, in: ZBB 2011, pp. 169–179.

Prüm, Thomas/Thomas, Sven: Die neuen Rahmenbedingungen für Verbriefungen, BKR (2011), pp. 133–143,

Pütz, Achim/Schmies, Christian: Die Umsetzung er neuen rechtlichen Rahmenbedingungen für Hedgefonds in der Praxis, BKR (2004), pp. 51–60.

R*enner, Moritz:* Zwingendes transnationales Recht – Die Struktur der Wirtschaftsverfassung jenseits des Staates, Internationale Studien zur Privatrechtstheorie Band 11, Dissertation Baden-Baden 2011.

Rexer, Andrea: Politik diskutiert Zerschlagung von Banken – Aufspaltung in Geschäfts- und Investmentbanken soll internationale Finanzbranche stabilisieren. Finanzminister für Gespräche offen –, DIE WELT (October/18th/2011), p. 9.

Ricke, Markus: Stichwort: Hedgefonds, BKR (2004), pp. 60–65.

Romano, Roberta: Against Financial Regulation Harmonization: A Comment, Yale, 20. November 2010, published under http://papers.ssrn.com/sol3/papers.cfm?abstract_id=1697348##.

Rosowski, Oliver: Die rechtlichen Rahmenbedingungen für Hedgefonds – Unter Berücksichtigung des Primebrokerage –, Studien zur Rechtswissenschaft Band 235, Hamburg 2009.

Rudolph, Bernd: Die international Finanzkrise: Ursachen, Treiber, Veränderungsbedarf und Reformansätze, ZGR (2010), pp. 1–47.

Rudolph, Bernd: Funktionen, Risiken und Regulierung von Schattenbanken, ZfbF 12/2012, pp. 846–867.

- *Selfsame -:* Zur Regulierung von Schattenbanken, Kreditwesen 13/2012, pp. 650–652.

Ruffner, Markus: Die EG-Harmonisierungs- und Liberalisierungsrichtlinien – Blaupause und Regelungsstandard für das schweizerische Telekommunikationsrecht am Beispiel der Interkonnektion, in: Festschrift für Zaech, pp. 409–427.

S*aenger, Ingo/Aderhold, Lutz/Lenkaitis, Karlheinz/Speckmann, Gerhard:* Handels- und Gesellschaftsrecht – Praxishandbuch –, Second Edition, Baden-Baden 2011.

Sester, Peter: Die Rolle der EZB in der europäischen Staatsschuldenkrise – Bausteine einer Fiskalunion: SMP, EFSF, ESM, Fiskalpakt? EWS (No. 3/2012), pp. 80–90.

Soltysinski, Stanislaw: Global Tax Competition and Tax Corporation, in: The Role of Law and Ethics in the Globalized Economy, edited by Josef Straus, Berlin/Heidelberg 2009, pp. 83–88.

Shadab, Houman B.: The challenge of hedge fund Regulation, Regulation Spring Vol. 30 No. 1 (2007), pp. 36–41, published under http://www.cato.org/sites/cato.org/files/serials/files/regulation/2007/3/v30n1-1.pdf (requested July/17th/2013).

Spengel, Christoph: Sollte die Unternehmensbesteuerung innerhalb der EU harmonisiert werden? In: ifo Schnelldienst (13/2004), p. 3 ff.

- Selfsame -/Braunagel, Ralf U.: EU-Recht und Harmonisierung der Konzernbesteuerung in Europa, StuW (2006), pp. 34–49.

Spindler, Gerald/Bednarz, Sebastian: Die Regulierung von Hedge-Fonds im Kapitalmarkt- und Gesellschaftsrecht – Teil 1: Die Rechtslage –, WM 2006, pp. 553-600.

- Selfsame -/- Selfsame -: Die Regulierung von Hedge-Fonds im Kapitalmarkt- und Gesellschaftsrecht – Teil II: Der Stand der Reformdiskussion –, WM (2006), pp. 601–607.

Schalast, Christoph: Schattenbanken – Regulierung durch wen, warum und wieweit? BB Die erste Seite 2012.

Schmidt, Christoph: Finanzierungsstrategien mittelständischer Unternehmen vor dem Hintergrund von Basel III, in: BB (2011), pp. 105–109.

Schmolke, Klaus Ulrich: Die Regelung von Interessenkonflikten im neuen Investmentrecht – Reformvorschläge im Licht des Regierungsentwurfs zur Änderung des Investmentgesetzes –, WM 2007, pp. 1909–1917.

Schricker, Gerhard/Henning-Bodewig, Frauke: Elemente einer Harmonisierung des Rechts des unlauteren Wettbewerbs in der Europäischen Union, WRP (2001), pp. 1367 ff.

Schrooten, Mechthild: Schattenbanken gehören abgeschafft, Wirtschaftsdienst (ZfBW) 1/2012, pp. 4 ff.

Schulze, Reiner/Zuleeg, Manfred/Kadelbach, Stefan: Europarecht – Handbuch für die deutsche Rechtspraxis –, Second Edition, Baden-Baden 2011.

Schwindt, Hans-Dieter: Kriminologie – Eine praxisorientierte Einführung mit Beispielen –, 19th Edition, Heidelberg 2009.

Sinn, Hans-Werner: Kasino-Kapitalismus – Wie es zur Finanzkrise kam, und was jetzt zu tun ist –, Berlin 2009.

Steffen, Peggy/Sachse, Timm: Mehr Anlegerschutz zu Lasten der Rendite von Investmentfonds? Eine kritische Analyse mit dem Vorschlag der EU-Kommission zur Änderung der Anlegerentschädigungsrichtlinie 97/9/EG, in: ZBB No. 1/2011, pp. 33–45.

Steinberg, Philipp/Somnitz, Caroline: Wege zu einer stärkeren Trennung von Investment- und Geschäftsbanking, Wirtschaftsdienst (ZfBW) 6/2012, pp. 384–391.

Striegel, Andreas/Wiesbrock, Michael R./Jesch, Thomas A.: Kapitalbeteiligungsrecht – Kommentar zum Private-Equity-Recht: WKBG, UBGG, Risikobegrenzungsgesetz, Nebengesetze und AIFM-Richtlinie, Stuttgart 2009.

Sustmann, Marco/Neuhaus, Martin/Wieland, Andreas: Die Zukunft des Unternehmensbeteiligungsgesellschaftsgesetzes (UBGG) vor dem Hintergrund der anstehenden Umsetzung der AIFM-Richtlinie, CORPORATE FINANCE law 2/2012, pp. 78–90.

Theewen, Eckart: Bank- und Kapitalmarktrecht – Handbuch für Fachanwaltschaft und Bankpraxis –, Cologne 2010.

Theisselmann, Rüdiger: Corporate Financial International: Marktanalyse 2011, CORPORATE FINANCE law 1/2011, pp. 1–3.

Thomsen, Steen: Should Private Equity Be Regulated? European Business Organizations Law Review (EBOR 10:1/2009), pp. 97–114.

Tietje, Christian: Internationales Wirtschaftsrecht, Berlin 2009

Türk, Danilo: Globalization and the Responsible Political Decision Making, in: The Role of Law and Ethics in the Globalized Economy, edited by Josef Straus, Berlin/ Heidelberg 2009, pp. 3–8.

United Nations: Report of the World Commission on Environment and Development – Our common future ("Brundland-Report"), New York (1987), published in the internet under http://conspect.nl/pdf/Our_Common_Future-Brundtland_Report_1987.pdf, requested February/18th/2013.

U.S. House of Representatives/Committee of Financial Services: Public Policy Issues raised by the report of the Lehman bankruptcy Examiner, Hearing before the Committee on Financial Services U.S. House of Representatives, 20 April 2010, published in the internet under http://financialservices.house.gov/media/file/hearings/111/printed%20hearings/111-124.pdf, requested: February/18th/2013.

Utzig, Siegfried: Shadow Banking – Hintergründe und Herausforderungen (1), Die Bank 10/2012, pp. 80–83.

Van Suntum, Ulrich: Die unsichtbare Hand – Ökonomisches Denken gestern und heute, Second Edition, Berlin/Heidelberg (2001).

Vinten, Frederik: The performance of private equity buyout fund owned firms, working paper (2007), available at: http://ssrn.com/abstract=1114603, requested: July/24th/2010.

Voigt, Daniel: Vertriebsstrukturen für Beteiligungen auf dem Prüfstand – ein Vergleich mit Neuregelungen der Financial Services Authority –, BB (2011), pp. 451–453.

Volkart, Rudolf: Corporate Finance, Grundlagen von Finanzierung und Investition, Fourth edition, Zurich (2008).

Volpin, Paolo/Pagano, Marco: Credit Ratings Failures and Policy Options, London (2009), published under http://faculty.london.edu/pvolpin/ratings_failure.pdf.

Walker, George Alexander: Basel III Market Compromise, JBR (September 2010), Editorial 1–5.

- *Selfsame -:* Credit crisis: regulatory and financial systems reform, Butterworth's Journal of International Banking and Financial Law (BJIBF) No. 11/2007, pp. 567–572; published in the internet under http://www.law.qmul.ac.uk/events/docs/walker_jibfl_(credit_crisis).pdf; requested on October/25th/2012.

- *Selfsame -:* European Banking Law – Policy and Program Construction, Sir Joseph Gold Memorial series Vol. 6, published by the British Institute of International and Comparative Law, London (2007).

- *Selfsame -:* Financial Crisis Cause and Correction, Financial Regulation International (December 2008), pp. 1–2.

- *Selfsame -:* Global Credit Crisis and Regulatory Reform, in: The Future of financial regulation, Contribute No. 11, pp.179–204, published by Iain MacNeil and Justin O ´Brian, Conference paper, Oxford/Portland (2010).

Walter, Norbert: Lehren aus der Finanzkrise – Ein neuer Ordnungsrahmen für robustere Finanzsysteme, in: Recht, Ordnung und Wettbewerb, Festschrift für Wernhard Möschel zum 70. Geburtstag, edited by Stefan Bechtold, Joachim Jickeli and Matthias Rohe, pp. 969–976, First edition, Baden-Baden (2011).

Webel, Baird: Troubled Asset Relief Program (TARP) – Implementation and Status TARP, (October/19th/2012), published in the internet under https://www.fas.org/sgp/crs/misc/R41427.pdf, requested on February/19th/2013.

Weber, Albrecht: Die Europäische Union auf dem Wege zur Fiskalunion? DVBl. (2012), pp. 801–806.

Weber, Martin: Die Entwicklung des Kapitalmarktrechts im Jahr 2010, NJW (2011), pp. 273–282.

Weiser, Benedikt/Jang, Jin-Hyuk: Die nationale Umsetzung der AIFM-Richtline und ihre Auswirkungen auf die Fondsbranche in Deutschland, BB (2011), pp. 1219–1226.

Wentrup, Christian: Die Kontrolle von Hedgefonds, Abhandlungen zum Deutschen und Europäischen Gesellschafts- und Kapitalmarktrecht Band 21.

Weitnauer, Wolfgang: Die AIFM-Richtlinie und ihre Umsetzung, in: Zeitschrift für Bank- und Kapitalmarktrecht – BKR – (2011), pp. 143–147.

Wieland, Andreas: Unternehmen der „Realwirtschaft" als Adressaten des Bank- und Finanzaufsichtsrechts – Teil 1: Hintergründe und Fragen der Erlaubnispflicht, BB (2012), p. 917.

Wolf, Birgit/Hill, Mark/Pfaue, Michael: Strukturierte Finanzierungen – Grundlagen der Corporate Finance, Technik der Projekt- und Buy-out-Finanzierung, Asset-Backed Securities –, Second Edition, Stuttgart 2011.

Wüpper, Gesche: Ein Quadratmeter für 8000 Euro – Preise für Altbauwohnungen in Paris steigen auf Rekord. Ende des Trends nicht vor 2010 –, DIE WELT (July/30th/2011), p. 20.

Wymeersch, Eddy: The reforms of the European Financial Supervisory System – An Overview –, *Wymeersch,* ECFR (2010), pp. 240–265.

Y*eoh, Peter:* Should private equity funds be further regulated? Journal of Asset Management (2007), pp. 215–225.

Z*etsche, Dirk:* Die europäische Regulierung von Hedgefonds und Private equity – Ein Zwischenstand –, NZG (2009), pp. 692–697.

Zimmer, Daniel/Beisken, Thomas A.: Die Regulierung von Leerverkäufen de lege lata und de lege ferenda, WM (2010), pp. 485–491.

Zimmermann, Guido: Die Finanzkrise – im Kern eine Einlagenkrise der Schattenbanken, Wirtschaftsdienst (ZfBW) 2/2012, pp. 105–109.

Zülch, Henning/Hoffmann, Sebastian/Detzen, Dominic: ESMA – Die neue europäische Wertpapier- und Kapitalmarktaufsicht, EWS (2011), pp. 167–173.

EINZELSCHRIFTEN

Klaus Nathusius
Engagement of Entrepreneurs in Universities
Lohmar – Köln 2013 • 272 S. • € 44,- (D) • ISBN 978-3-8441-0245-1

Yuanfei Shi
Die verkehrliche und technisch-betriebliche Bedeutung der Integration des Eisenbahn- und Luftverkehrs in China
Lohmar – Köln 2013 • 232 S. • € 56,- (D) • ISBN 978-3-8441-0248-2

Jörn-Axel Meyer (Hrsg.)
Kommunikation kleiner und mittlerer Unternehmen –
Jahrbuch der KMU-Forschung und -Praxis 2013
Lohmar – Köln 2013 • 428 S. • € 67,- (D) • ISBN 978-3-8441-0251-2

Martin Dyk
Leitlinien einer zielführenden Finanzsektorregulierung am Beispiel von Kreditverbriefungen
Lohmar – Köln 2013 • 296 S. • € 59,- (D) • ISBN 978-3-8441-0264-2

Wolfgang Chr. Fischer
Private Households and Money Supply
Lohmar – Köln 2013 • 184 S. • € 48,- (D) • ISBN 978-3-8441-0265-9

Michael Dietrich
Reverse Mortgage – Chancen und Einführungshemmnisse für Kreditinstitute in Deutschland
Lohmar – Köln 2013 • 88 S. • € 37,- (D) • ISBN 978-3-8441-0269-7

Florian Englmaier
Managementansätze zur Überwindung von Informations-asymmetrien am japanischen Private-Equity-Markt
Lohmar – Köln 2013 • 276 S. • € 58,- (D) • ISBN 978-3-8441-0278-9

Thomas Bernhardt
The European Alternative Investment Fund Managers Directive (AIFMD) – An Appropriate Approach to the Global Financial Crisis?
Lohmar – Köln 2013 • 228 S. • € 55,- (D) • ISBN 978-3-8441-0285-7

JOSEF EUL VERLAG